DATE DUE

JL 2 '03			
AP 2 6 '05			
MY 1 7 '06			
JE 7 '06			
MY 2 1 '07			

RETAILING TRIUMPHS
AND BLUNDERS

RETAILING TRIUMPHS AND BLUNDERS

Victims of Competition in the New Age of Marketing Management

Ronald D. Michman
Alan J. Greco

QUORUM BOOKS
Westport, Connecticut • London

R

Library of Congress Cataloging-in-Publication Data

Michman, Ronald D.
   Retailing triumphs and blunders : Victims of competition in the new
age of marketing management / Ronald D. Michman, Alan J. Greco.
      p.   cm.
   Includes bibliographical references and index.
   ISBN 0–89930–869–4 (alk. paper)
   1. Retail trade—Management.   2. Retail trade—Decision making.
I. Greco, Alan James.   II. Title.
HF5429.M483   1995
658.8'7—dc20   95–19469

British Library Cataloguing in Publication Data is available.

Library of Congress Catalog Card Number: 95–19469
ISBN: 0–89930–869–4

First published in 1995

Quorum Books, 88 Post Road West, Westport, CT 06881
An imprint of Greenwood Publishing Group, Inc.

Printed in the United States of America

The paper used in this book complies with the
Permanent Paper Standard issued by the National
Information Standards Organization (Z39.48–1984).

10 9 8 7 6 5 4 3 2 1

For Ruth, who willed this book
For Laura and Carol, who understood
For Marc Ross and Andy Robert, our future

Contents

Preface

Success comes when managers act on their organization's specific capabilities and advantages. Today's merchants need to look beyond financial statements to ensure profitability. To proclaim a strategy and then not to execute it is worse than not to have one. Essentially, the role of retail management is to manage present and especially future changes that will affect their organizations. In order to achieve these objectives, retail organizations need to understand the past to manage present and future operations successfully. Retailers must determine what they can do either differently or better than the competition. Five key areas have been identified for ensuring the success of a retail organization. These key ingredients among retail organizations appear to determine the degree for either success or failure: innovation, target market segmentation, image, physical environmental resources, and human resources.

This volume has been divided into 11 chapters. Selected aspects of store-based institutions and service strategies are presented and provide a comprehensive overview of retail strategies. Each chapter depicts a profile of a selected institutional format in the American retail distribution structure. The concept of competition frequently blurs the strategic and operating differences among retail types as each format reacts to the successes of others. Each chapter has been analyzed according to intertype and intratype environmental competition that challenges the well-being of the specific type of retail institution. Chapters focus on the following retail institutions: department stores, mass merchants (J. C. Penney; Sears, Roebuck; and Montgomery Ward), variety stores, supermarkets, discounters, specialty clothing stores, home improvement centers, franchised hamburger chains, hotels, credit cards, and in-home shopping institutions. A chapter on credit cards has been included since it is a service that all retailers employ and because it has influenced the strategies of many different types of retail institutions. Another chapter has been included on nonstore retailers who use strategies beyond the traditional retail formats. Some retailers, such as

Penney, Brooks Brothers, and Neiman-Marcus, use both in-store and non-store formats to service their customers. Efforts have been made to analyze specific retailers according to their strategic positioning strategies. The continued development of services retailing, such as hotels, is of major economic and managerial consequences since these institutions appear to be adapting to familiar retail marketing techniques.

The point is this: Retailers live in a world of galloping change. Adjustment to the world of change, and this anticipation of change, is vital for retail operations to progress smoothly. Retailers like The Limited have successfully coped with changes. Retailers like Wal-Mart and Home Depot have successfully anticipated change. Other retailers such as W. T. Grant and E. J. Korvette have become relics of past retailing history.

Many of the accounts of retail failures have focused on the shortsightedness of management executives. This work offers a much broader perspective by isolating five factors—innovation, target market segmentation, image, physical environmental resources, and human resources—that have contributed to retailing failures when not used correctly. It is hoped that managers and students, by focusing in particular on these variables, will now be equipped with a more powerful tool for duplicating success and avoiding failure. The gap between successful, failing, and merely surviving retail organizations is widening each day.

This work provides a starting point for executives, researchers, and students to obtain more appropriate insights in order to understand the complexities and interrelationships in retail management. Hopefully, these insights will foster a more proactive approach, rather than a reactive approach, to market opportunities.

Acknowledgments

Every book owes its knowledge, personality, and features not just to the authors but to a team of hard-working individuals behind the scenes. A great debt is owed to our research assistants, James Illo, Lisa Noll, Kim Grove, and Beth Dunkin, who helped pull together information from numerous sources. Thanks are extended to Dean James Pope, who encouraged the continued progress of this book while the senior author assumed emeritus status, and to Sue Harvey for her management skills. Special recognition is extended to Joyce D. Yocum, who not only typed all of the chapters but helped with many organizational aspects of this project. The senior author's family has been a mainstay through some difficult periods while researching and writing this book. All that was accomplished could not have been without that special patience and understanding of Laura Michman Dessel and Carol Michman. The second author acknowledges the support and encouragement of Dean Quiester Craig and Dr. Melvin N. Johnson in the School of Business and Economics at North Carolina A&T State University. Naturally, even though a team effort is cited, any errors of omission or commission are our responsibility.

CHAPTER 1

Department Stores: Dinosaurs and Champions

Successful Department Store Strategies

- Store positioning
- Locate in shopping malls
- Cluster stores for promotional purposes
- Emphasize services not offered by competitors
- Store environment must reflect excitement or showmanship
- Upgrade sales personnel
- Emphasize fashion leadership for specific target market
- Limit sales promotion activities
- Effective use of new technology

Unsuccessful Department Store Strategies

- Passive promotion of store brands
- Price competition
- Reliance on past patronage loyalties
- Continuation of successful strategies with changing environmental conditions
- Downgrading services to reduce prices
- Ignoring population shifts within the city
- Continuing use of old technology that worked in the past

The department store scenario includes such illustrious names as R. H. Macy, Gimbels, Dayton Hudson, Neiman-Marcus, Bullock's, Rich's, Marshall Field, Lazarus, Filene's, Sears, Montgomery Ward, Bloomingdale's, J. C. Penney, and Saks Fifth Avenue, among others. Failures have taken their toll with such pillars of retail trade as Ohrbach's, B. Altman, Garfinckel, and R. H. White. Carter Hawley Hale Stores with such department stores as The Broadway, Emporium, Thalhimers, and Weinstocks filed for Chapter 11, protecting the chain from bankruptcy. The parent company of Bloomingdale's, Burdines, and Rich's also filed for protection. Meanwhile, another pillar of department store trade—R. H. Macy—is struggling for survival. On the other hand, J. C. Penney, Nordstrom, Dillard's, and Dayton Hudson have emerged with success stories. Clearly, the department store scenarios are ones of dinosaurs and champions.

Many department stores have reduced services and eliminated departments to compete with discount stores. Durable goods such as refrigerators and washing machines are not offered for sale anymore, and neither is a wide assortment of electronics. Instead, many department stores are providing more breadth and depth in offering such merchandise items as dishes, linens, housewares, and kitchen gadgets. A high-profit department is apparel, and department stores like Kaufmanns' in Pittsburgh and Famous-Barr in St. Louis have increased store space for its sale and eliminated the offering of many appliances.

In considering the successes and failures of department stores, mistakes have been made, but these organizations have survived by making constant adjustments of such variables as innovation, target market and image, physical environmental resources, and human resources. These department store retailers did not necessarily earn high grades using all variables, but some of the variables were implemented in an exceedingly capable manner. Historically, a one-price policy introduced by A. T. Stewart, the forerunner of

Wanamaker, constituted an innovation. Branch store operations were pioneered by Filene's, and the renowned Automatic Bargain Basement was also an innovation. Today, Nordstrom has innovated with its service policies and commission plan, and J. C. Penney has advertised its private-label store brands in *Business Week* and *Fortune*, thereby giving these store brands national stature with competitive manufacturers' brands.

J. C. Penney has successfully done more than any other department store to change its target market and image. Once known as a "Main Street merchant," the seller of jeans and work clothes targeting blue-collar workers, Penney has developed a fashion leadership image in cultivating a new target market. The women's and men's apparel departments have more than doubled in square feet, and major appliance and home electronics equipment and other hard goods departments have been discontinued. J. C. Penney had identified the three major segments it desires to serve: young juniors, who are highly fashion conscious; contemporaries, who spend more money than any other segment on quality clothing; and conservatives, who want comfort and value. Thus, J. C. Penney has emerged as one of the new department store champions.

Physical environmental resources have played an important part in the success of Dillard's. Dillard's state-of-the-art information system has helped achieve some of the highest sales volume and profits in the department store sector. Penney's new contemporary decor has created an ambience of fashion. Neiman-Marcus has established stores in major metropolitan centers such as Atlanta, Miami, Washington, D.C., St. Louis, Chicago, and other cities. This location strategy has helped Neiman-Marcus achieve a national image and reputation for serving upper-income consumers.

Filene's was a pioneer in making important advances in employee relations and training programs. An employee suggestion system was put into effect as early as 1899. Filene's was one of the first to establish a minimum wage for female employees, to develop employee training techniques, and to encourage an association in 1898 as a means for reconciling employee grievances. Today, Nordstrom has motivated its employees to provide exceptional customer service. Nordstrom's salespeople earn more than double the national average in retailing. Salespeople are trained to write thank-you notes to customers and to help provide total customer satisfaction.

Some department stores have failed because many have provided a stale and unexciting physical environment to customers. Another reason has been that some department stores have been unable to implement effective inventory management systems, thereby lowering costs to either match or at least approach the prices offered by discounters. Department stores were also slow to locate branches in shopping malls and in the suburbs following population movement. Rather than a single reason for department store failures, there have been a number of reasons.

DEPARTMENT STORES: YESTERDAY

It is not clear who founded the first department store in the United States. The majority of authorities claim that it was R. H. Macy in about 1860; others would claim Ernst Lehmann, founder of The Fair, Chicago, in 1874, or John Wanamaker, in Philadelphia in 1876. Shortly before World War I, Macy of New York, Dayton Hudson of Detroit, and Marshall Field of Chicago each claimed to be the "largest department store in the United States."

The early department store established a one-price policy that at once became popular with customers since it was a departure from personal price negotiation. Because of its large assortments, the department store was noted for one-stop shopping. The department store of yesterday featured a central location and a multitude of services such as the return of unsatisfactory merchandise for exchange or refund and merchandise delivery. The merchandise return policy was especially well received since many specialty stores did not offer this service. Moreover, nonselling functions were centralized, which not only increased efficiency but earned the approval of customers.

When department stores were thriving before World War II, they were considered minicities. Today, that image is reserved for the megashopping malls. Lazarus in Cincinnati, Ohio, provided an auditorium, and Hess's, based in Allentown, Pennsylvania, offered a children's barbershop and a free art school for customers. Many department stores offered such amenities as a nursery, beauty parlor, free decorators' consultation, travel agents, and fashion shows. While some of these services may have been retained by some department stores, most have been withdrawn. Department stores continue to offer more personal services than discounters such as gift wrapping, theatrical display windows, in-store restaurants, and luxurious restrooms, particularly in their flagship stores. At one time, salespeople were plentiful, but today salespeople are scattered and can be hard to find in some department stores. Customers shopped primarily in department stores yesterday, but today warehouses, superstores, and discount department stores have replaced department stores in popularity.

MACY'S: NEW YORK

R. H. Macy developed four strategies that were instrumental for a successful operation. A one-price policy was offered, which was a departure from the norm of bargaining between store and customer. That policy is now taken for granted in most retail transactions, but at that time, it served as a welcome relief for many customers. Macy's was not the originator of the one-price strategy, but it was one of the first retailers to make it successful.

The second strategy was to sell for less. Thus, the origin of the slogan "Nobody but nobody undersells Macy's." Prevailing strategy was to offer to match the price of any item that was purchased in the store and found by the customer to be sold for less elsewhere. Although this strategy operated well historically, it was to cause difficulties when confronted with intertype competitors such as Kmart.

The third strategy was to buy and sell for cash. Since Macy's paid cash for its merchandise, below-market prices were obtained. This had the net effect of increasing merchandise turnover. Moreover, since Macy's sold only for cash, errors made in the extension of credit were avoided.

The fourth strategy was to advertise continuously and vigorously. Macy's during this period invested 3 percent of sales in promotion at a time when competitors like Lord & Taylor and Arnold Constable were spending only 1 percent. Rowland Macy had a flair for promotion. Advertising was directed to the female customer.

Rowland Macy added department after department to the store. Luxurious soaps, costume jewelry, pocketbooks, tea sets, and toys were added during the Civil War period. Other departments such as books, gourmet groceries, and stationary were all added before Rowland Macy's death in 1877. The marketing environment in the United States was shifting from an agrarian to an industrial society. Customers came to urban cities to enjoy a family shopping trip. The first department store lunchroom was opened in 1878, and great emphasis was placed on making shopping convenient for the customer. Macy responded to customer desires to shop quickly by adding numerous departments that facilitated time-saving, one-stop shopping. Rowland Macy was a much earlier counterpart of Wal-Mart's Sam Walton. Macy knew the first names of some 300 employees and knew how to motivate employees to render superior customer service.

MARSHALL FIELD'S: CHICAGO

Marshall Field and Company brought a charm and dignity to Chicago that was unmatched in any other city. Even the store's doormen earned a special place in the hearts of Chicagoans and visitors. Field's became a tourist attraction with its clocks, its largest-selling basement aisle, its boast of providing the largest indoor Christmas tree in the world, and more display windows than any other store.

Marshall Field and Company was a retail innovator that revolved its strategies around the axiom "Give the lady what she wants." Field's was the first retail department store to offer a personal shopping service and was among the first to exchange merchandise and offer a delivery service. Field's opened a tearoom to provide lunch for shoppers so that they would not go home or elsewhere for lunch. In the decade of the 1890s, as many as 1,500 people were served in the tearoom each day. Field's cultivated an atmosphere of refinement and gentility. Field's adamantly believed that low prices alone would not promote customer patronage and that honest dealings also had to be extended to build customer loyalty.

Field's, because of natural disasters such as fire and other reasons, changed its location to respond to a shifting urban population. Historically, Field's relocated to other sites a few times and in each instance constructed an even larger store with more services and more departments. Effective public relations was a continuing promotional strategy. The store was the headquarters of the Red Cross and Liberty Loan drives during World War I.

By 1954, Field's claimed the largest department store restaurant, the largest retail shoe operation, the largest china department, the largest toy operation, and the largest book department and was the largest importer of linen and ladies' fashions. The store retained its elegance through the years. Everything about Field's was developed for customer convenience and "to give the lady what she wants." Service was paramount.

NEIMAN-MARCUS: DALLAS

Neiman-Marcus was founded in 1907 as a specialty department store catering to women's ready-to-wear needs and later added men's wear. The store was the most elegantly equipped department store in the South. By 1910, fashions from Paris were sold, and the store added accessories, infants' wear, and girls' apparel. Strategies emphasized luxury and spectacular showmanship and well-known brand names in the fashion world.

Until the Great Depression of the 1930s, the store targeted the wealthy market segment. As more and more oil fields were discovered in Texas, the store prospered. Public relations was an effective strategy as Neiman-Marcus helped launch Southern Methodist University and founded the Southwestern Medical Center. The store helped bring grand opera to Dallas. Weekly fashion shows were held in Dallas, and fashion shows were also given in other cities. Neiman-Marcus was carefully building a national reputation for fashion.

The store's reputation was enhanced by selling glitter merchandise such as Dior gowns for thousands of dollars and ladies' jeweled pipes. Camels and even midget submarines were sold through their catalog. Eventually, in 1938, Neiman-Marcus presented fashion "Oscars" for distinguished service in the field of fashion. Awards were extended to such notables as Hattie Carnegie, Christian Dior, Lilly Dache, Jacques Fath, and others. Over the years, sculpture and art were imported. Neiman-Marcus had brought culture to Dallas, with a European flavor emanating from Paris and Rome. Eventually, Neiman-Marcus stores were established in St. Louis, Detroit, and other cities and served not wealthy but upper-income segments.

FILENE'S: BOSTON

Filene's department store was founded in Boston in 1881 and through the years made numerous contributions to the development of retail trade. Filene's contributions to retailing included important advances in employee relations and training. Junior executives were hired, systematically trained, and evaluated before these human resource methods were known in the industry. Noted authorities in industrial training, including Frank B. Gilbreth, were hired to develop and implement employee training techniques. An employee suggestion system was put into effect as early as 1899. In contrast, many business organizations did not use employee suggestion systems until World War II. Filene's encouraged formation of the Filene Cooperative Association in 1898 as a means for reconciling employee grievances. A few years later, a Board of Arbitration was formed. Filene's was one of the first to establish a minimum wage for female employees. Saturday store closings during the summer months were inaugurated in 1913, and winter vacations were scheduled in addition to summer vacations in 1925. Before World War I, an employee credit union was also established.

Many of Filene's merchandising strategies made an indelible mark on retail trade. Branch store operation was pioneered. College and high school fashion advisory boards were formed. Cycle billing, which led to an orderly procedure for end-of-month accounting, was instituted. The Charga-Plate, a method of customer identification and credit, was first used by Filene's. Finally, the world renowned Automatic Bargain Basement was started in 1909. Basement merchandise was automatically reduced 25 percent after 12 selling days, a further 25 percent reduction was made after 18 selling days, and another 25 percent reduction was made after 24 selling days. If after 30 days the merchandise was still not sold, it was then donated to Boston charities. Many competitors unsuccessfully attempted to emulate Filene's Automatic Bargain Basement concept. Filene's earned a place in department store retailing history as an innovator and as a great retail trade statesman.

MODERN-DAY SUCCESS STORIES: STRATEGIES

Department stores have been confronted with keen competition from discount stores, specialty stores, and superstores such as Herman's in sporting goods and Toys "R" Us in the toy field. In order to compete effectively, promotional strategies have placed emphasis on full service, quality brands, and fashion leadership. Some department stores have either eliminated or reduced their offerings of major appliances. Instead, the stores offer a comprehensive selection of fashion merchandise featuring both national and store brands. Saks Fifth Avenue and other department stores have successfully sold their private labels. Closeouts, discontinued lines, or seconds are not offered. However, Neiman-Marcus, whose clearance centers are named Last Call, sends merchandise to the clearance center that represents a buyer's mistake that has not sold in its stores. Prices are usually below discount store prices.

New department store branches are located in more expensive rental locations in either shopping centers or districts directed to a higher level of pedestrian traffic. This strategy tends to somewhat offset competition from the discount store but not the specialty store, since many specialty stores are located in the same shopping mall as the department store. Department stores emphasize more elaborate fixtures, luxurious carpeted floors and dressing rooms, and many interior and exterior displays. Again, this strategy counters the discount stores but not the specialty stores.

Department stores endeavor to provide extensive sales force assistance, but this strategy has not always been implemented very well. The selection and training of a high-quality sales force have presented many problems since salary scales in retailing are not always competitive with other industries. Traditionally, department stores have not been able to offer salespeople high commissions in departments other than furniture, appliances, carpeting, or suits, dresses, and coats. Understandably, high employee turnover has been a problem.

Department stores have tried to offer extensive services in order to combat competition. These services have included mail and telephone ordering on a sometimes 24-hour basis, widely available credit, and free alterations. Mail and telephone services have gained in popularity, and many stores located in urban centers derive as much as from 10 to 15 percent of their revenue from such services.

NORDSTROM: THE GOAL OF CONSUMER SATISFACTION

Nordstrom, a Seattle-based department store chain, has become legendary for its exceptional customer service. Moreover, the Nordstrom culture that worshipped the customer has been portrayed as a benchmark for retail department stores. Despite labor problems, Nordstrom has been the department store success story of the 1980s and is envisioned as a remarkable retailer that will achieve a national reputation for excellence in the 1990s.

Nordstrom plans to become a formidable retail department store chain with more than 80 stores that will span 13 states. Such cities as Chicago, Minneapolis, Denver, Boston, and Paramus, New Jersey, are included for store openings. Already, the chain has about 15 units in California. The Nordstrom mystic is a mix of solicitous service, valet parking, and soothing piano music.

New market development has been facilitated by legendary service. Salespeople commonly write thank-you notes to customers or even make home deliveries. In conjunction with superior service, Nordstrom carries the broadest assortment of styles and sizes of any major department store in the United States. Styles and colors are presented in a depth not seen in other department stores. Focus is placed on employee training programs, goal setting, and communications. Salespeople have been known to accompany customers from department to department in helping with the total shopping task.

Nordstrom's salespeople earn more than double the national average in retailing. Management has reported that employees made an average income in excess of $23,000 a year, compared with the national average of $12,000. A few Nordstrom salespeople earned over $100,000 in 1990. The Nordstrom culture is far different than other department stores. Salespeople's duties and responsibilities are much different in Nordstrom's than in traditional department stores. Many of these activities involve unpaid work. Consequently, some former employees have charged illegal employment practices and have sued the company for millions of dollars in back pay. Nevertheless, Nordstrom employees voted two to one against union representation.

In Paramus, New Jersey, a Nordstrom unit opened in 1990 and offered employees an hourly wage up to $9.50 an hour plus commission—well above the industry standard of $6 to $7. Still, employee turnover remains high because of the intense work environment and the high standards. Eventually, Nordstrom eliminated the base salary, and salespeople work strictly on a commission basis. A number of other department stores have attempted, in various degrees, to emulate the Nordstrom commission plan. These stores include Burdines, a Florida-based chain, Bloomingdale's, and The Broadway, a California-based chain. The Carter Hawley Hales Stores have implemented the Nordstrom plan in more than 100 units. However, if implementation is poorly handled, high employee turnover is the result.

DILLARD'S: COST-EFFECTIVENESS

Dillard Department Stores is based in Little Rock, Arkansas, and excels at using state-of-the-art information systems and at acquiring other chains and using information systems to make them efficient. To illustrate, the J. B. Ivey & Co. chain, with 23 stores in the Carolinas and Florida, was transformed into a technology-equipped modern operation with point-of-sale registers that are hooked into computers at the headquarters with bar-coded labels on merchandise capturing customer information at the register. This technology implementation allows for improved analysis of customer demand patterns and increased cost-effectiveness and merchandising efficiencies.

Dillard's tends to be first or second in market share in second-tier cities, such as Memphis and Tulsa. Known brands are carried such as Liz Claiborne in women's clothes and Hickey Freeman in men's. Fewer sales are offered than at competitors since Dillard's favors an everyday pricing strategy that promotes customer loyalty. Carrying well-known brands has worked well for Dillard's. If a known brand does not sell, generally only a 15 percent markdown will move it off the selling floor, in contrast to a store or private-label brand frequently worked down from 30 to 40 percent.

Dillard's computer network operates automatically from the company warehouse when sales figures warrant it. In turn, the computer network reorders automatically from suppliers. Consequently, Dillard's is less likely than their competitors either to experience stock-outs or to be loaded up with unfashionable items that require markdowns. However, if a mistake is made, Dillard's maintains a half-dozen clearance centers and unloads some merchandise for less than wholesale. Computers cannot predict consumer tastes. The clearance centers sell merchandise that has not sold in Dillard stores around the country at prices less than discounters can offer.

Dillard's has experienced profit margins greater than competitors', partly because they are devoted to market research, and focus-group and one-on-one interviews, which are expensive methods of research, are conducted on a continuous basis. Computer-aided design software is also used to assess consumer demand patterns. Moreover, Dillard's acquires or builds other department store units utilizing a cluster store strategy in particular locations for economies of scale in promotion.

As time-pressed consumers modify their shopping habits, Dillard's has followed a traditional strategy in terms of store format but has implemented inventory controls and new computerized technology, which have resulted in bigger profit margins. Although not known for its glitter, Dillard's is generating operating ratios way above department store averages. Dillard's may not be spectacular, but it has achieved higher sales volume and profits than Nordstrom's in the department store sector. Dillard's unlike many department store chains, operates only four downtown stores and locates most of its stores in shopping malls. The merchandise assortment emphasizes brand names like Evan Picone, Christian Dior, and Liz Claiborne. Upscale merchandise is targeted to an upscale customer. Dillard's avoids frequent sales in favor of an everyday pricing strategy, which counters many department store practices. Moreover, unlike many retailers, Dillard's centralizes not only accounting and legal functions but advertising and purchasing. Merchandise may vary from store to store, but not much individuality is tolerated. Stores that bear the Dillard name feature the same decor of wood floors, peach and gray marble, and brass details. This approach assures uniform quality and maintains low operating costs.

J. C. PENNEY: A NEW CHAMPION

J. C. Penney has successfully repositioned itself as a department store. In 1983, Penney eliminated major appliances and hardware departments, and in 1988, home electronics, photography, and sports equipment were eliminated. Meanwhile, Penney has focused on fashion leadership in cultivating its target market segment. The women's apparel section has almost doubled in square-feet selling space, and the men's department has more than doubled. Penney has also redesigned and redecorated its stores.

Penney now uses more boutiquelike appearances for items like lingerie. Sleek wooden shelves and more contemporary displays have replaced clearance bins and crowded circular racks. The Penney image has changed to reflect an ambience, value, and taste that are decidedly fashionable and upper-status. Penney has attempted to convince higher-grade national brand manufacturers that it has discarded its second-string image and to sell their merchandise to Penney. Penney's advertising strategy has reinforced this new image by promoting its men's apparel brands in such publications as *Fortune* and *Business Week*.

Supplier relationships have changed. Computer-to-computer hookups account for more than three quarters of the firm's merchandise. The electronic data interchange emphasizes a system that automatically replenishes merchandise. Moreover, the Penney organization pays its bills on time. This has not always been the situation with other department store chains; suppliers appreciate a climate of financial stability.

Repositioning to emphasize fashion and style necessitated upgrading the store atmosphere and changing locations. Many Penney outlets were located in downtown districts, and at one time, the store was referred to as "a Main Street merchant." Therefore, Penney opened new stores in shopping malls in order to reach its new target market of working women, who are important purchasers of women's apparel. The mall locations made Penney more competitive with regional department store chains such as Rich's of Atlanta. The new stores' contemporary decors developed an ambience of fashion. A number of existing Penney stores were closed, and others were extensively remodeled to reflect the new fashion orientation. Because of this change in fashion image, Halston—an important manufacturer—and other manufacturers decided to distribute their brands through Penney and were no longer fearful that it would tarnish their fashion image.

Penney has taken a leadership role in interactive home video shopping through cable television services currently available in homes in suburban Chicago. To bring the buying organization and top management closer to field operations, Penney relocated its headquarters from New York to Dallas. A satellite communication network was established between headquarters and stores. Penney also sells its private-label men's clothing in Japan and Singapore and maintains licensed catalog operations in Bermuda, Brazil, Aruba, Moscow, and Iceland.

DAYTON HUDSON: A MODEL OF DIVERSIFICATION

The Dayton Hudson Corporation oversees a number of retail formats. The department store division consists of over 60 stores under the name of Hudson's, situated primarily in Michigan, Indiana, and Ohio; Dayton's, situated primarily in Minnesota, North Dakota, South Dakota, and Wisconsin; and Marshall Field's acquired in 1990 and situated in Illinois, Ohio, Texas, and Wisconsin. A second division, known as Target, includes over 550 stores in 32 states and is an upscale discount store with a broad assortment of high-quality fashion and basic hard-line and soft goods that delivers more than 60 percent of the company's overall sales and profit.

Mervyn's is the third division and is a moderate-priced discount department store chain carrying nationally branded and private-label goods. The Mervyn division operates over 275 stores situated in 15 states. Dayton Hudson plans to reposition Mervyn's to more effectively compete against such chains as Sears. The stores will carry a wider selection of merchandise that would attract budget-minded women who desire to shop quickly. Shopping carts and checkout counters at exits will be provided, instead of situating them in various departments. New merchandise will be added for plus and petite-size women, body and bath products, children's books, luggage, and licensed sports apparel. Mervyn's hopefully will gain the image of a notch above a discount store but below its current position as a low-end department store. Although it may be speculative, their strategy is not viewed positively since Mervyn's may blur its image.

The goods and services mix in the Dayton Hudson department store organization division has evolved on the basis of dominance, quality, and fashion. Dominance is interpreted differently for various merchandise lines, but essentially it means that customers will have a choice within the best selection of items that they desire. Broad merchandise selection provides leadership over competition. Quality is emphasized by its merchandise, services, facilities, and communications. Dayton Hudson's communications strategy uses advertising and displays to support and reinforce the goods and services mix. Fashion is interpreted as fashion leadership for each store in the organization in its respective price range.

Each operating company develops long-range goals, five-year financial plans, and estimates of return on investment. The strategic plans are the basis for capital allocation from the headquarters. Performance reviews focus on goals achievement and are carried out by the headquarters.

With the Marshall Field acquisition in 1990, Dayton Hudson has become an important part of department store trade. Dayton Hudson should now be able to obtain volume discounts—in such merchandise lines as tableware—that were not possible before the acquisition. A stronger merchandise assortment is now possible since Marshall Field's has a known reputation in home furnishings, a weakness of Dayton Hudson, and Dayton Hudson is strong in children's clothing, which was not one of Marshall Field's strengths.

The Target and Mervyn divisions contribute more than 75 percent of operating profit to the Dayton Hudson organization. Consequently, Dayton Hudson was considered an important factor in the discount department store field competing with Wal-Mart and Kmart. The acquisition of Marshall Field has brought a strong, widely recognized name to the department store division. Many operations have been integrated to provide greater operating efficiencies. The department store division is in the process of remodeling and upgrading operations that should make it a strong competitor in the department store trade.

REASONS FOR DEPARTMENT STORE DECLINE

Many customers find shopping in traditional department stores stale and unexciting. In an effort to increase profits, many department stores have stressed operating efficiencies by decreasing the number of sales personnel, and have scaled back effective merchandise displays and store decor. These department stores have decreased prices and have tried to compete directly with the discount department stores such as Kmart and Wal-Mart. Department store customers who like the enjoyment of browsing have accordingly found fewer reasons to browse and fewer reasons to make purchases in department stores. Such department stores were unable to decrease costs sufficiently to profitably match discount department store prices.

Changing environmental factors have made price strategies more important to consumers. Price-conscious consumers have in the past decade become more attracted to discounters and factory manufacturers' outlets. Enclosed shopping malls that are air-conditioned and protect against inclement weather conditions have grown in popularity. Department stores were once viewed as the leading one-stop shopping institutions. But, in recent years, shopping malls, composed of countless specialty stores with great depth and breadth of product assortment, have been perceived as comprehensive one-stop shopping centers replacing the traditional department store. The idea of mass markets once served by department stores has been replaced by market segmentation strategies. Retail organizations are narrowing their focus and targeting specific consumer segments.

Population shifts to the suburbs have also caused decline in traditional department store patronage. Many chain department stores have experienced a blurring of their image in branch and suburban stores that serve different consumer segments. Part of this problem has been caused by a deterioration in customer services. Even credit card services have changed as the bank Visa and Master Card have become more acceptable. Meanwhile, the department stores still have the high costs of administering their own credit cards.

It is significant to note that department stores have been involved in relocation shifts historically, even though population shifts to suburban communities may appear as a recent development to those who cannot remember the relocation problems of only a generation ago. For instance,

Lord & Taylor of New York City opened a store at 47 Catherine Street, at the lower end of the Bowery, in 1825. In 1860, the population shift and business development warranted a move to the northwest corner of Grand Street and Broadway. After the Civil War, New York City expanded northward. By 1872, Lord & Taylor occupied a building at the corner of Broadway and Twentieth Street as the old shopping area became deserted and a new one prospered. The move to its present location on the Thirty-ninth Street corner of Fifth Avenue took place in 1914 as the shopping district again shifted.

Location is of paramount importance to the success of the department store. More than one store has fallen victim to the shift in shopping districts and relocations of the city population. For example, John Wanamaker established a new store only a few blocks from the downtown schools of New York University in 1907 and in the affluent community of Washington Square. At this time, many stores were already moving uptown from lower Manhattan. When this residential area decayed, in 1954 Wanamaker was finally forced to close. R. H. White in Boston, established for 104 years, met with a similar experience.

The downtown area of the metropolitan city has found its development arrested. Many of the properties in the vicinity of the main shopping area have deteriorated, and traffic arteries to the main shopping district have become congested. There has also been a movement of the residential population to the city outskirts. The city shifts like rings within a target, each move proceeding outward from the center. The department store has existed within this framework of urban development and must constantly adapt to these environmental changes. Department stores unable to adapt to urban development, changing traffic patterns, and population shifts will become casualties in the future, as they have been in the past.

The lack of effective retailing mix strategies constitutes another reason for department store decline. The passive promotion of private labels or store brands placed department stores at a disadvantage when competing with the discounters selling national brands. J. C. Penney was one of the few department stores to establish the quality of its store brands. Moreover, department stores have been slow to compete with direct marketers. It is only recently that such department stores as Saks Fifth Avenue, Macy's, and Nordstrom have undertaken promoting their merchandise assortment on a television channel. Both Sears and Montgomery Ward found that consumers have not responded that well to general merchandise direct-mail marketing. Sears has discontinued its general merchandise catalog. Specialty catalogs have satisfied consumers' purchasing patterns, and Montgomery Ward has reentered the market, endeavoring to satisfy this market segment.

Department stores have been at a loss to develop effective strategies to counter the development of superstores or category killers such as Toys

"R" Us and Herman's in sporting goods. The superstore's depth and breadth of merchandise assortment and its appeal of one-stop category shopping have taken significant market share away from department stores. Inroads into the market share of department stores have also been made by drugstores and supermarkets with the effective strategy of scrambled merchandising.

Successful apparel-based specialty stores such as The Limited and The Gap have also taken market share away from department stores. Because department stores did not develop their own private labels, they were unable to display merchandise that differentiated themselves from their competition. More and more specialty stores and off-price retailers such as Marshalls, Loehmann's, and Dress Barn seized significant market share.

MARKETING MISTAKES: MACY'S

In 1857, Rowland Macy opened a small dry goods store on Fourteenth Street in New York City. Through a series of additions, Macy's became a full-fledged department store in 1877. In 1902, the Herald Square store at Thirty-fourth Street opened and has remained there ever since. The first Thanksgiving Day parade marched through Manhattan in 1924, and Macy's boasted that the Herald Square store was the largest in the world.

Retailing operations, by 1970, were organized into six geographical divisions: Macy's (New York); Lasalle's (Ohio); Davison's (Georgia); Bamberger's (New Jersey); Macy's (Missouri-Kansas); and Macy's (California). The Macy's chain comprised more than 70 department stores.

Several emerging trends contributed to the difficulties of the Herald Square store after World War II. Many middle-class customers completely abandoned the Thirty-fourth Street store as the population relocated to the suburbs. Moreover, by the 1970s, while the immediate area was still in good condition, the peripheral area began to decay as adult book shops, massage parlors, adult cinemas, and other services predominated. The number of paying passengers using the Herald Square subway station fell by almost one half.

For several decades, there had been pronounced population shifts uptown. Such fashionable stores as Lord & Taylor, Saks Fifth Avenue, and Bergdorf Goodman were located a considerable distance away from Herald Square. Other stores began to locate around Fifty-eighth Street, and even Gimbel's opened a branch on East Eighty-sixth Street as the population shifted within the city of New York.

Competitive forces have also been detrimental to Macy's continued success. Specialty chains such as The Gap and The Limited have seized a sizable portion of department store sales. The Macy image as a store for everyone ignored present strategies of market and lifestyle segmentation. Competitors selected niches and served these markets much better than

Macy's. Competition from Kmart and other discounters was especially destructive for Macy's since the slogan "Nobody but nobody undersells Macy's" was deeply embedded in the shoppers' minds. Macy's could not match the cost efficiencies of the discounters. Moreover, the enclosed shopping malls with specialty stores diminished the one-stop shopping strategy of Macy's since these specialty merchants carried a greater depth and breadth of fashion goods.

Organizational complications were another force contributing to Macy's difficulties. Macy's acquired I. Magnin & Company and Bullock's in 1988 from Federated Department Stores and had difficulty paying a $400 million note. Macy's posted a $1.25 billion loss for 1992—the worst in company history. Major problems were concentrated in California, but the New York store still reflected difficulties that have beset many metropolitan department stores. I. Magnin, the upscale specialty retailer owned by Macy's, continues to lose money. Management appears divided on whether difficulties are expense and profit oriented or sales oriented. Recently, the situation has exacerbated itself, and Macy's was acquired by Federated Department Stores in December 1994. Federated plans to operate its department store chain with Bloomingdale's at the upper-price tier; Macy's, Bullock's, Burdines, Rich's, Lazarus, and Bon Marche at the midprice tier; and Stern's at the low-price segment.

The discount revolution without question has not been taken seriously by Macy's management. Macy's, like Sears, Roebuck, has underestimated the impact of the discounters and changes in consumer purchasing habits. Consumers in a thrifty buying mood have opted for quality store brands and for even purchasing fashion goods from discounters. Macy's has been unable to control inventory handling expenses and to implement a computerized inventory control system as effective as Dillard's. In addition, the decay of the metropolitan area near the store and a crime-ridden subway system have driven a great many customers to suburban shopping centers and enclosed shopping malls. Another detrimental trend not always noted was the ineffective selling performance by the sales force. Nordstrom initiated the change from fixed salaries to commission selling, but Macy's, with its highly unionized sales force, has found that such change can encounter great resistance. Unfortunately, a lethargic sales force on the main floor of a department store can give customers an erroneous impression of the rest of the store even if salesclerks are doing their jobs in departments on other floors.

RETAILING FAILURES: UNSUCCESSFUL STRATEGIES

The heart of department store trade was in New York City. Department store failures in New York City were spectacular since many of these stores—Gimbels, Ohrbach's, S. Klein, Gertz, and B. Altman's—in the

1980s had established regional, if not national, reputations. But these failures were to parallel other department store failures such as Goldblatt's and Wieboldt's in Chicago; Miller and Rhodes in Richmond, Virginia; G. Fox in Hartford, Connecticut; and Garfinckel's in Washington, D.C.

These department stores were unable to position themselves to serve either upscale shoppers or lower-income shoppers. Upscale consumers were served by Neiman-Marcus, Lord & Taylor, and Saks Fifth Avenue. Middle-income shoppers were served by very competitive specialty stores such as The Gap and The Limited and warehouse clubs. Discounters such as Kmart and Wal-Mart served both middle-income white-collar and blue-collar workers as well as lower-income consumers. Hess's Department Stores, almost 100 years in existence, in 1994 agreed to sell 20 of its stores to Bon-Ton Stores of York, Pennsylvania, and the other 10 stores to May Department Stores of St. Louis and go out of business by the end of the year. This causality represents another loss to the competitive discounters.

The Gimbel's chain, consisting of 36 stores spread out from New York to Philadelphia to Pittsburgh to Milwaukee, was the most notable failure. In 1989, B. Altman's, a 124-year-old department store, failed. For those with long memories, it was the end of the carriage trade. The specialty stores, the discounters, the off-price retailers, and the enclosed shopping malls were the victors. Only the upscale department stores survived the 1980s.

In 1988, the Campeau Corporation acquired Federated Department Stores. This was the largest department store acquisition in the history of retail trade. Department stores included in the takeover were Abraham & Strauss, Bloomingdale's, Bullock's, Burdines, Filene's, Foley's, Goldsmith's, Lazarus, I. Magnin, and Rich's. Prior to the purchase of Federated Department Stores, the Campeau organization acquired Allied Stores, the sixth largest department store chain. Department stores such as the Bon Marche, Jordan Marsh, Maas Brothers, and Stern's were included in this purchase.

However, the Campeau organization had overextended itself. Budget cuts at Bloomingdale's and Jordan Marsh tarnished their image for customer service. Inventory levels went out of control throughout the chain. In 1990, bankruptcy was declared. Environmental forces such as the downturn in the economy also contributed to the poor performance of the Campeau Corporation. Thus, organizational buyouts were another factor contributing to the decline of the department store.

LESSONS LEARNED FROM SUCCESS AND FAILURE

Although Nordstrom was successful with its sales commission plan that motivated talented salespeople and weeded out deadwood, other department store chains have not been successful in implementing such a plan.

Dayton Hudson's difficulties, for example, emanated from its sales force, many of whom did not desire to give up a straight salary-plus-commission plan. In response, the United Auto Workers tried to organize salespeople at Hudson's stores in Michigan. Dayton Hudson was forced to reduce the number of workers who would be covered by the new plan. Furthermore, research suggested that customers mistrusted salespeople who were paid entirely on a commission basis.

Ineffective selling by sales personnel has downgraded the service image of department stores. Department store management must decide if they wish to become discounters or provide effective services not offered by discounters. Since these services are costly, management cannot expect to match the low operating costs or the low selling prices of the discounters. If the high road is taken, sales personnel should be upgraded, and coordinated services of delivery, alterations, gift wrapping, and other customer services must also be upgraded.

Store positioning is of paramount importance to a successful marketing strategy. Department stores cannot continue to be all things to all people. A distinctive niche must be selected. Upscale department stores such as Neiman-Marcus have been successful. Competing directly with discounters, either Kmart or Wal-Mart, off-price retailers, or warehouse stores has not worked. Low prices cannot be matched unless accompanied by low operating costs.

Location is exceedingly important for department stores. Department stores located in shopping malls, all factors equal, seem to be much more successful than downtown stores. Urban decay, parking, and an assortment of other problems have challenged downtown department stores. Department store chains that have clustered their stores geographically for advertising purposes seem to do well.

MANAGEMENT VISION

Management vision should extend to retail strategies and the adaptation of strategies to competitive environmental conditions. Department stores, for example, cannot hope to match the low prices of discounters and therefore would find it advisable to limit the number of merchandise sales during the year. Department stores need to cultivate a merchandise image that reflects value for the price and price consistency.

A sense of showmanship that lends itself to an exciting shopping environment will be needed in the future. Store decor and atmospherics must reflect a dramatic shopping experience. A generation raised on television and computerized games will demand a new shopping excitement. Fashion leadership for a particular market segment will lend itself to this shopping excitement.

Alliances between department stores and specialty stores might well achieve these new objectives of creating shopping stimulation for a new generation. Alliances between department stores and specialty stores would provide more depth and breadth in merchandise assortments for a specific target market or a specific market niche. These strategic alliances might be particularly useful in acquiring and operating home television channels. Some department stores such as Neiman-Marcus have achieved national store name recognition, while others, such as Jordan Marsh with department stores in New England, have gained regional recognition. Strategic alliances with specialty stores could further strengthen store recognition of both institutional types in specific geographical locations.

Strategic alliances might also be well received by consumers when shopping by mail-order catalogs. Shared costs by different institutions would be a positive strategy. Merchandise assortments would present more depth and breadth. A possible expansion of the target market might also be possible. Such strategic alliances, especially between upper-status institutions, could be rewarding since upper-status target markets increasingly demand value and may comparison shop to achieve this objective.

Dillard Department Stores and Wal-Mart have formed a venture with Cifra SA, Mexico's largest retailer, to open Dillard stores south of the border. This alliance operates more than 40 warehouse clubs, discount superstores, and groceries and apparel stores in Mexico. This new alliance hopes to capitalize on the expertise of each partner to operate department stores.

MANAGING CHANGE

Many technological advances will have a profound impact on department store operations in the future. Already Dillard's has implemented a computerized control system in inventory management that establishes a differential advantage. Computer-to-computer linkages with suppliers have reduced ordering time and improved inventory flow. Thus, Dillard's has been able to balance its merchandise assortments more rapidly and improve its operational ratios.

A video-ordering system should enable retailers to efficiently present information, receive orders, and process transactions with customers. A video-ordering system may be oriented toward in-store and/or in-home shopping. Basic formats extend to television programming, interactive computer programming, and merchandise catalogs. The Home Shopping Network is the largest retailer in this category. Saks Fifth Avenue has been one of the department stores to establish leadership in television programming. In an interactive system, an in-home consumer uses a personal computer to view graphic or pictorial representations. Sears has invested heavily in this type of system.

Some of the benefits of this new technology are that there is less need for new, expensive store locations; inventory requirements are diminished; geographical coverage can be expanded; orders can be placed 24 hours per day, seven days a week; and fewer human resources are needed. On the other hand, expensive, complex items do not readily lend themselves to video shopping. A number of customers would prefer to shop in stores because they believe that shopping is fun. Moreover, store image, which is so important to department stores, is harder to portray via graphic or pictorial representations. Nonstore retailing is a distinct trend of the future, and department stores must adapt to this environmental change.

Strategic alliances can be carried one step further from merchandise catalogs or television programming between department stores and specialty stores. Department stores are in a position to lease space to specialty stores. Already, Montgomery Ward has assumed a leadership role in this area by leasing space to Toys "R" Us.

The discount revolution has limited the size of the middle market. Department stores such as Garfinckel's in Washington, D.C., and B. Altman's in New York have felt the impact of this market trend. The upper market is served by stores like Neiman-Marcus and Bloomingdale's. Penney's has positioned itself to serve the upper-middle market, and Kmart and Wal-Mart are effectively serving remaining markets. Double-income families and the emergence of women who seek either careers or jobs have changed retailer market segmentation guidelines.

Positioning market segment strategies will become more important in the future. Bloomingdale's will provide fashion leadership. Kmart and Wal-Mart provide price leadership. Nordstrom is providing extraordinary service. Toys "R" Us and Herman's in sporting goods provide depth of merchandise assortment. Department stores must learn how to compete with these superstores, and some form of strategic alliance may be helpful to both department stores and superstores.

There are two retail models of evolution that have had an impact on the growth, development, and changing patterns of department stores. The first has been referred to as the *wheel of retailing* and the second as the *dialectical process*. According to the wheel-of-retailing model, retail innovators emerge as low-price institutions emphasizing a low cost structure and low profit margin requirements. As time progresses, these innovators upgrade customer services, locate in more convenient locations, and offer a broader assortment of merchandise; gradually, costs and consequently prices increase. The impact on department stores has been the price sensitivity of consumers and their willingness to forego department store services for the low prices of the discounters. Moreover, price-sensitive shoppers are not store loyal. In contrast, prestige-sensitive shoppers like to shop at stores with high-end retailing strategies—thus, the success of stores like Lord & Taylor and Saks Fifth Avenue. Historically, new institutions have been better able to implement a low expense and low price structure, and traditional stores have found it very difficult to compete. Dayton Hudson operates Mervyn's, a discount chain, and department stores in an effort to control the trading-up process so that its market focus remains distinct and prevents cannibalizing each other's sales.

The dialectical process views retailing as an evolutionary system in which different retail institutions adapt to each other, which results in new retail strategies. The central premise of the dialectical process is that when challenged by a differential advantage both department stores and discounters will try to negate the strengths of each other. This will result in department stores and discounters becoming more like one another and creating a competitive position of their own. Kmart has evolved in this manner by locating in suburban locations, by extending limited service, and by maintaining average margins and merchandise turnover.

CONTROVERSIAL RETAIL MANAGEMENT DECISIONS

The most controversial retail management decision in the department store trade has centered around how to combat the competition of the discounters. More recently, competition from specialty stores located in shopping malls and the superstores has posed significant threats to department store effectiveness. These developments meant that the department store had to change its traditional mode of operation.

Successful department store organizations are close to their customers, concentrate on satisfying customer needs, and stress customer satisfaction. Four department stores—Dillard's, Nordstrom, Penney, and Dayton Hudson—emerge victorious in combating environmental competition. Dillard's focused on an expense control system that resulted in customer satisfaction through superb inventory management. Nordstrom took the high road and offered splendid service that discounters could not hope to match. Penney changed its target market and even its merchandise assortments by satisfying the fashion desires of more multiincome families. Dayton Hudson diversified by controlling both Mervyn's and Target in order to present clear images of its department stores and discount stores. Aware that a blurred image has been responsible for many store failures in the past, efforts were made to target distinct consumer market targets with correct merchandise assortments, services, and prices. Each of these organizations was an innovator in adopting strategies that were a great departure from the past. Each organization had adapted to environmental change by developing strategies under uncertain conditions.

CHAPTER 2

Mass Retailers: Gone Are the Days

Strategies in a Changing Market
- Anticipate changing market segments
- Locate new stores in new shopping centers
- Locate new stores in new markets
- Strong development of store brands
- Modernize stores
- Develop strong store images
- Clearly defined objectives
- Target-precise market segments
- Promoting innovation

Mass Retailer Mistakes
- Departure from basic fundamentals
- Allowing store image to tarnish
- Lack of continued innovation
- All things to all people
- Inability to shift strategies
- Disregard of competitive forces

Montgomery Ward, J. C. Penney, and Sears, Roebuck were all mass retailers. Their target market was Mr. and Mrs. America. Suddenly, times changed. The portrait of the American family—situated in central cities and shopping on Main Street, U.S.A., with the husband as the breadwinner and the wife as the household manager, with two or more children—was no longer the norm. By the 1990s, this family situation represented no more than 10 percent of the population. This traditional family, as depicted in the 1950s television programs *Father Knows Best* and *Leave It to Beaver*, had changed and with it so had the shopping habits of Mr. and Mrs. America.

Montgomery Ward, J. C. Penney, and Sears, Roebuck responded to environmental changes in different ways. The patterns of these responses underscore some managerial lessons that demonstrate the importance of maintaining a consistent store image and of understanding that past success does not guarantee continued success. Moreover, these managerial lessons show the need for changes in strategies as social and environmental influences change and emphasize that research studies are a guide—but not a substitute—for decision making.

Management decisions are complex and frequently based upon many interacting variables rather than a single one. The controversial retail management decisions that led to both successes and failures are examined with the objectives of trying to learn which basic fundamentals are characteristic of successful and unsuccessful management decisions. Can we learn from a study of past successes and failures? Montgomery Ward, J. C. Penney, and Sears, Roebuck were all mass retailers, and each made different types of decisions to satisfy the change in shopping habits of Americans. The tasks of identifying and serving evolving buyer needs have never been more challenging. Since many retail organizations such as W. T. Grant, Korvette, and Robert Hall have been forced out of business and current events present ominous signs that other inflexible or poorly managed retailers will follow, the opportunity to grow has never been greater for creative, inno-vation-minded, and environmentally aware retail organizations.

In considering the successes and failures of the mass merchants—Sears, Penney, and Ward's—mistakes have been made, but these organizations have survived by making constant adjustments with such variables as in-novation, target marketing, image, physical environmental resources, and human resources. These mass retailers did not necessarily obtain high grades using all variables, but some of the variables were used and imple-mented in an exceedingly capable manner. Innovation took place when Montgomery Ward developed its specialty store-within-a-store strategy and when J. C. Penney made the decision to emphasize family apparel mer-chandise and to discontinue its in-store hard goods lines such as home electives, sporting goods, and photography equipment.

Target market and image variables were addressed by Penney by devel-oping its own private-label brands, which have been especially successful in its Stafford and Gentry collections. Sears has confused its image by shift-ing from strategy to strategy, hoping to avoid declining sales.

Physical environmental resources were used by Penney in upgrading its decor and thereby its image. Montgomery Ward also had to change its image by changing physical store characteristics to reflect its specialty store-within-a-store strategy.

The human resource variable does reflect a weakness. Sears and Mont-gomery Ward do not have an outstanding executive like Leslie Wexner of The Limited, or Bernard Marcus of Home Depot. Penney has been able to motivate employees with clear and precise objectives. These objectives have changed the image of Penney and enabled Penney to position its fashion image by using a total organizational effort. Although Sears has streamlined itself and closed marginal stores, there is still a host of problems that have not been surmounted.

The day of the mass retailer is over. Today, retailers struggle to stay ahead of intense competition in an oversaturated store environment and endeavor to develop an appropriate market niche. Once-proud names, B. Altman, Bonwit Teller, and Garfinckel's have closed most of their stores. Macy's is experiencing difficulties, and Sears is still trying to determine what it wants to be. The future holds promise for those mass retailers who address their problems in the long term rather than using short-term tactical strategies.

MASS RETAILERS: YESTERDAY

The historical significance of these three mass retailers—Montgomery Ward, J. C. Penney, and Sears, Roebuck—develops the perspective that the triumphs and disasters of the past have a real meaning for retailers today. Why, despite the promise of these institutions, were changes in their retailing operations a necessity? Was there a fatal flaw or a combination of variables that caused one institution to succeed and another to flounder? The historical significance of these three retailers is found in the evolution of their cultures, philosophies, and industry positionings.

MONTGOMERY WARD

Montgomery Ward opened in Chicago in 1872 as the first large mail-order business organization. Ward, as a traveling salesman, had worked among the farmers and understood their dissatisfaction with the general stores and Yankee peddlers at that time. During this period, farmers formed an organization known as the Grange, which promoted cooperative purchasing and reduced prices to the farmers by eliminating the middleman. Ward became the official supply house of the Grange, which helped in penetrating rural markets. Ward understood that the old general store and peddlers did not guarantee their goods and that shoddy goods were sometimes sold. Therefore, deeply rooted in the philosophy and culture of the Ward organization was the policy that merchandise could be returned to the company without transportation charges both ways if the customer was dissatisfied. Growth was phenomenal. The Ward catalog grew from 8 pages in 1874 to 240 pages by 1884.

Ward had established agencies similar to present-day catalog order offices by 1926, but merchandise had to be purchased by mail and not in the agencies. The thinking at this time was that direct retail selling might take away business from the mail-order operation. Finally, because of increasing customer demand and as archrival Sears was opening retail stores, Ward entered the retail business. Ward opened up stores in towns with populations between 4,000 and 75,000, while Sears favored larger locations. Before the onset of the Great Depression, Ward had opened 500 stores and Sears 324 by 1929. Although Montgomery Ward was the initial market leader in mail-order retailing, Ward eventually became a follower of Sears.

Montgomery Ward adopted a no-growth policy after World War II. This philosophy was founded on the mistaken belief that a severe depression would occur. Management maintained that it would be more prudent to expand when costs were lower during the depression. As a result, Montgomery Ward contracted, and other competitors, such as Sears, expanded and grew.

During the period from 1945 to 1952, Ward did not open any new stores. Affluent consumers were moving to the suburbs during this period. Shopping centers were developed and successfully competed with the downtown business district for customers. Consumer shopping patterns were changing, but Ward resisted expansion.

There were other facets of the Ward business organization that were affected by its conservative posture. Montgomery Ward had a 41.7 percent market share of the mail-order industry in 1945, while Sears had 50.7 percent. These figures had changed significantly by 1951. Sears' market share had increased to 66.1 percent, and Ward's share had declined to 28.3 percent. Sears allocated about $300 million for some 300 new or modernized stores, while Ward spent practically nothing during this period. Consequently, by 1952 Sears attained a sales volume of two and a half times the Ward sales volume and realized almost twice the net profits. Whereas, before World War II, Sears was only slightly ahead of Ward in sales volume and profits, this situation had changed considerably.

It was not until new management came in 1955 that Montgomery Ward began to recover from its no-growth strategies. Ward was unwilling to change strategies even when it became evident that mistakes had been made. The anticipated economic downfall that management had forecasted had not taken place.

When Sewell Avery, former chief executive officer who insisted that economic conditions after World War II would be similar to the Great Depression of the 1930s, was ousted in 1955, many expressed the opinion that Ward's future was indeed promising. Montgomery Ward was the third largest nonfood merchandiser after Sears and Penney, and it was expected that a revitalization program would be implemented.

These promising expectations were shattered with the announcement that earnings had declined in 1960. The problem was not so much the new stores but the old stores. Most of the older stores were badly located in nongrowth areas of the Midwest in downtown areas that lacked adequate parking space and encountered intense suburban shopping center competition. Moreover, the older stores were of smaller size with a rigid cost structure. Many of these older stores needed to be closed.

Gradually, the emphasis on small-town locations was changed, and new or renovated stores were opened in heavily populated urban areas. Most of these stores were opened in shopping centers, but a few were freestanding. Clusters of stores were opened in these urban areas, which accounted for more than 70 percent of sales and pretax profits. However, many of these changes were too late, and Ward's was purchased by the Mobil Corporation in 1974.

A period of experimentation continued, but it was not until Ward's changed its target market and aimed for younger, more affluent families in the early 1980s and later restructured its organization that its fortunes began to improve and the turning point at long last was reached.

SEARS

Richard Sears in 1886 founded the R. W. Sears Watch Company in Minneapolis, Minnesota, and the following year moved his business to Chicago. Aloah C. Roebuck was hired as a watchmaker, and by 1893, the corporate name of the firm became Sears, Roebuck and Company. Soon jewelry and diamonds were added to the merchandise mix, and a small catalog was printed. The initial policy of providing a warranty on some of the watch parts for six years and a money-back guarantee if the customer was dissatisfied was a significant departure from traditional selling practices of the times. During this period in American history, the selling practice was caveat emptor—let the buyer beware. Relatively few merchants were willing to return the customers' money if they were dissatisfied with the merchandise.

Sears offered farmers a viable alternative to the high-priced rural stores. Through volume purchasing, merchandise was offered at reasonable prices. The marketing environment was also conducive to Sears' success. The large-scale development of railroad and postal services offered prompt delivery and provided the infrastructure for mass retailing.

Since its beginning, Sears was an adaptive and flexible organization. In the automotive age, the farm population came into the cities to see the merchandise before buying, and mail-order sales began to decline. Moreover, American cities began to expand, while rural populations dwindled. Thus, Sears wisely embarked on a plan to establish retail stores during the 1920s. Moreover, stores were established in Florida, Texas, and California, where population growth was envisioned. The decision to sell insurance from their retail stores in 1931 was a genuine innovation and resulted in the Allstate operation.

Sears and Ward's were arch competitors in the 1920s and 1930s. Actually, Ward's expanded more aggressively in the late 1930s, but after World War II, Ward's sales were only about two thirds of Sears'.

Sears, in the 1920s, decided to centralize all purchasing and promotional operations in Chicago and to control store operations from territorial headquarters, which was a unique management structure at that time and proved to be highly effective. Furthermore, Sears had merchandise made to its own specifications, thus controlling decisions concerning cost and quality of merchandise. This management structure was to contribute to the many visionary and innovative decisions that were made throughout Sears' history.

The early Sears, Roebuck was dominated by Richard Sears, who was a showman and gave merchandising a perspective of excitement and drama. It was Roebuck who caused Sears to exercise caution and financial restraint.

After World War II, Sears expanded aggressively. Sears preempted prize locations as the population relocated to the suburbs and moved from the East to the West. Sears pioneered the concept of the outlying store serving the entire family long before the advent of the shopping centers. Sears made a decision in the mid-1950s to expand its soft goods lines and to become a rival of the department store. This repositioning involved a change of store image from one selling hardware, tools, and fishing tackle. A few years later, Sears began to emphasize fashion and style. The Sears automotive center has been another retail innovation. Motorists are able to obtain all their automotive needs, including gasoline, at these centers. The building of Sears, Roebuck has been a story of business decisions based on social and economic trends and the willingness to innovate in selling and distribution methods.

Sears was one of the first national retailers. This was accomplished by investing in supplier corporations and developing its own brands. Vertical marketing systems develop when a single firm owns two or more aspects of the production-distribution process. For example, the Sherwin-Williams Company not only manufactures paint but owns or franchises retail stores. Sears has either complete ownership in manufacturing companies or has assumed partial ownership—partial vertical integration. Such firms as Whirlpool, Kenmore, and Coldspot appliances, Globe-Union with auto batteries, and Universal-Rundle with plumbing fixtures are either owned or partially owned by Sears. Sears, by developing those vertical marketing systems, realized a high degree of control over the cost and quality of functions that were performed. Allocation of functions, a smooth operation of the system, and control were achieved because Sears was in a position to manage the entire system and to thereby reduce costs and eliminate duplication.

Based upon "The Headquarters Merchandising Plan, 1979–1989" for Sears, major changes in objectives and strategies were forthcoming. Sears considered its target market to be the home-owning, middle-class market and that its strategy should reflect the habits, needs, tastes, and social behaviors of this group. In the planning document, Sears believed that it was not a fashion store, not a store for the affluent, not a store seeking fads and novelties, not a discounter, not a store for the avant-garde, not an exciting store, and not a store that anticipates the markets' desires and needs. Some of the organizational changes included the deletion of the women's apparel budget department in some stores and reduction of the amount of space for it in other units, and expansion of service for the automotive department, appliances, and the home entertainment business. Moreover, the promotional focus should result in customers considering Sears to offer high value of the dollar—which meant that Sears would increase its price lines.

This five-year plan neglected to consider changes in the lifestyles of Mr. and Mrs. America. The plan did not cite new consumer characteristics such as double-income families and the increasing number of women seeking not only jobs but careers. Sears in the past was a customer-driven store, but Sears either had miscalculated or had neglected some important fundamentals. Moreover, Sears' subsequent move to an everyday low-price policy in 1989 without an accompanying low-cost structure created financial problems for the merchant.

J. C. PENNEY

James Cash Penney opened what was to be called the "Golden Rule" store in Kemmerer, Wyoming, in 1902. Penney's was immediately in a competitive struggle with the "company store." The Penney credo was to treat each customer fairly and to render full value, quality, and satisfaction. At the time, this philosophy offered the customer a welcome relief from the company store and its "let the buyer beware" policies.

The success of this customer-oriented philosophy helped Penney to expand the number of its dry goods stores in other communities with a Main Street location mainly in small towns in the Midwest. Later, Penney began to locate in medium-sized cities. Merchandise was offered in a frugal store environment. Penney continued to serve thrifty customers with the best possible product for the price charged.

James Cash Penney, himself, possessed the thrifty puritanical values of the time. As the story goes, Penney measured the life cycle of a broom, and if the broom did not wear out according to the cycle, then Penney knew that his store manager did not maintain a clean store. James Cash Penney insisted upon neatness and cleanliness.

The Penney organization had almost 1,500 stores by 1933, which was only 30 years after the opening of its first store. The same strategy was used in all stores: a cash-only policy, customers could return merchandise if not satisfied (this was originally a new policy at this time), low prices, and honest merchandise values. Penney stores were opened in small towns, and managers were well-known and-respected members of the community. The organization moved away from a decentralized organization to a uniform operation with budgeting systems, uniform store layout arrangements, and promotions. Centralized buyers assumed authority over pricing policies. Store managers were evaluated against other store managers' performance. Emphasis was on uniformity and efficiency.

Sears, Roebuck was the model for efficient, progressive, large-scale general merchandise stores. J. C. Penney and Montgomery Ward were found lacking by comparison. Although Penney's was doing well, the organization remained only a dry goods and clothing operation until the 1960s. Penney's did not carry appliances, sporting goods, furniture, or auto supplies. These merchandise categories were stocked by Sears and Wards and by other department stores. Moreover, the extension of credit to customers increased significantly from 1940 to 1970, but Penney's retained its original policy that customers should make purchases on a cash-and-carry basis. This philosophy was embodied in the puritanical credo that individuals should purchase only what they could pay for immediately. The philosophy of "buy now, pay later" was in opposition to the puritanical credo. Finally, most of the units of the Penney chain were in smaller communities west of the Mississippi. Growing metropolitan areas and the affluent East were ignored.

The Penney organization was very successful with its strategies up to World War II. The number of stores had doubled since the 1920s to 1940 from about 750 to some 1,500. The Penney organization both financed and created managerial resources. Each store manager could purchase a one-third partnership in a new store, provided he had trained an employee to effectively manage a new store. Thus, managers received effective training, and profits were reinvested to establish new stores.

It was not until after World War II that operations became more centralized. But emerging problems of credit extension to customers, merchandise diversification, and targeting urban markets still remained.

In 1957, J. C. Penney maintained a cash-and-carry philosophy and carried only dry goods and clothing. Penney stores were predominately situated in sparsely populated communities west of the Mississippi. At that time, an executive of the J. C. Penney organization wrote a memorandum to the corporation's board of directors. This memorandum, which had a profound impact on the future growth of J. C. Penney, recommended (1) that Penney's merchandising position be compared with that of its major competitors, (2) that new marketing opportunities be examined, with particular attention being given to predicted changes in population, shopping habits, leisure time, and work trends, and (3) that the organization should construct future stores in the suburbs of major metropolitan areas where population was growing and that future stores should be larger in order to increase profitability.

Although the J. C. Penney Company was apparently a profitable organization, there was a growing awareness that Penney's was not responding to a changing environment. The Penney organization concentrated on selling staple merchandise to customers who were now better educated with higher taste levels and had both the income and desire to upgrade their purchasing. Moreover, Penney's was unable to focus on such fast-growing merchandise categories as fashion and hard goods since present policy restricted merchandise offerings to staple soft goods.

The first dramatic policy change was the introduction of customer credit in 1958. By 1963, moderately priced fashion apparel created by designers such as Mary Quant of London and Victorie and Ariel of Paris was introduced. New merchandise lines had been added, including appliances, household electronics, furniture, automobile tires and accessories, and sporting goods. The first J. C. Penney Company catalog also appeared in 1963 in an effort to expand merchandise lines and improve customer service.

In 1969, Penney acquired the Thrift Drug Company of Pennsylvania in an attempt to broaden their customer market since their catalog-selling operation could also be based in these drugstores. In the 1970s, Penney operated both the Treasure Island Discount Stores and some supermarkets. However, both ventures proved unprofitable and were terminated.

The J. C. Penney Company's entry in the 1970s into the full-line department store mode was with a merchandise assortment offering very much like that of Sears. Penney's was much more hard-lines oriented than the regional department stores located in the shopping malls. Research studies were conducted that concluded that customers in shopping malls desired fashion-oriented merchandise of high quality, that specialty stores in malls were not the appropriate environment for selling major appliances and hardware.

MASS RETAILING: TODAY

The mass retailers—Sears, Montgomery Ward, and J. C. Penney—offer a great assortment of general merchandise, are frequently located as the anchor store in a shopping center or district, have strong credit card penetration, and are national retailers in scope. All at one time or another have maintained a strong catalog or mail-order system. These mass merchants compete with one another on the basis of their product, place, price, and promotion strategies. However, retail competition is more complex than these mass retailers competing against each other. Another type of competition pits retail stores of essentially different operating types against one another. For example, discount stores and specialty clothing retailers sell many of the items offered in the merchandise assortment mix of the mass retailers. Another dimension is vertical system competition. Sears, for example, controls manufacturing firms and performs many wholesaling functions. Manufacturers such as Sherwin-Williams (paint) and Goodyear (automotive supplies and tires) with their retail stores and others also compete with these mass merchants. Since these mass merchants own interests in other firms and maintain their own distribution centers and credit services, competition is much broader as one system competes with another.

The mass merchants become willing to change strategies when changes in consumer behavior, shifts in population, new technology, and new lifestyles are either reflected or anticipated in changes in purchasing behavior patterns, but not all of these changes were made before significant market share was lost to competitors. Whether the activity is merchandising, promotion, or physical distribution, change dominates the atmosphere. Change is a driving force that pervades the dynamics of retail management decisions. The turning point must be reflected in a change in the culture, philosophy, and actions of the mass merchant.

For some reason, the mass merchant has lost touch with its customer. Other retailers either of the same type or of more focused types are better serving the customer. The mass merchant must then find some sustainable differential advantage over the competition that might be reflected in carrying merchandise of better quality, serving the customer differently or better, reducing costs, or targeting specific consumer groups.

Market segmentation, accordion, and Porter theories and strategies are helpful in understanding the development and present-day strategies of mass retailers.

Sears continued to try to serve Mr. and Mrs. America and to be all things to this target market. Specialty stores like The Limited and The Gap began targeting demographic and psychographic market segments in narrowly defined product classifications. These specialty stores fragmented the broad market of Sears by using a differentiated focus strategy and eventually captured larger shares of this market. Sears also continued to stress its private label in a world of nationally televised national brands. Sears, with its increasing cost structure, was unable to compete with discounters. To further complicate matters, Sears believed that its opportunities were in such areas as financial services and neglected its core merchandising business.

Market segmentation is the process of breaking the mass market for consumer or industrial goods up into smaller, more homogeneous submarkets based on relevant distinguishing characteristics. These market attributes would include the size of the market, the geographic location, and the demographic, lifestyle, and shopping behavior of purchasers or potential buyers. Each submarket is evaluated on size, accessibility, behavioral differences, and degree of current need fulfillment. Through market segmentation, the firm can select the best target market, given the company's resources and the competitive environment, and cater to its needs and wants. Market segmentation or differentiated marketing can, however, be quite costly, especially if more than one target market is identified and each one must be reached using substantially different marketing programs. The firm must balance the increased costs and the projected revenues from multiple target markets and varying techniques used to reach these markets.

Mass marketing is a strategy that is less commonly used in the United States. An average customer profile is developed within a product market. Mass marketing does not segment markets, and therefore some authorities refer to this strategy as *undifferentiated marketing*. The original Model T developed by Henry Ford had no options and came only in black. The model was sold at a reasonable price to a broad consumer market through the use of only one basic marketing plan. However, economic growth, growing familiarity with the automobile, and technological change altered the sustainability of Ford's cost leadership strategy and created the opportunity for General Motors to successfully employ a differentiation strategy. For some years, Sears, Roebuck appears to have used mass marketing or undifferentiated marketing as far as some lines of merchandise are concerned, thus creating the potential for competitors to utilize cost leadership, differentiated, or focused strategies.

Retailers use a counterapproach to mass merchandising that is referred to as *positioned* or *focused retailing*. Retail organizations concentrate their efforts on a specific segment or segments and not on the mass market, such as Sears. Positioned or focused retailing creates a high level of consumer loyalty and counters more conventional competitors. Montgomery Ward has converted its existing stores so that positioned retailing can be used effectively. For example, Ward's includes an Electric Avenue appliance and consumer electronics shop, a Home Ideas home-furnishing shop, and other specialty formats.

J. C. Penney repositioned itself to emphasize fashion and style, which necessitated upgrading store atmosphere. New stores reflected a contemporary look, establishing an ambience that customers associate with fashion-oriented stores. To reflect this new image, existing stores were either closed or extensively remodeled. New stores are situated in shopping malls instead of at the downtown locations of many of Penney's old stores. Consistent with this new image, Penney signed a design and licensing agreement with Halston Enterprises, a well-known designer of women's clothing and cosmetics, in 1982.

THE ACCORDION THEORY

The retail accordion theory maintains that retail store development and evolution can be explained by monitoring changes in the merchandise mix. According to this theory, the merchandise mix expands and contracts much like an accordion in different time periods. Historically, the old general store led to the development of the department store, which led to the specialty store and now to the superstore. The most recent contraction of the retail accordion is the result of the tendency for specialty stores to become more specialized in the 1970s and the 1980s by following a focus strategy. These retail formats such as Herman's in sporting goods and Toys "R" Us in toys have afforded consumers very deep selections in stores carrying a limited number of merchandise categories.

The impact of this theory can be illustrated by demonstrating the movement of Sears after World War II. Sears was retailing leader in establishing stores in suburban malls. But some malls permitted numerous specialty stores to fragment the Mr. and Mrs. America target market of Sears. Moreover, Sears lost market share to large discounters like Kmart and Wal-Mart, which Sears allowed to grow without competitive retaliation.

THE PORTER THEORY

According to Michael Porter, three planning concepts can be used to attain a competitive advantage. First, a differentiated offer in the form of a product or service can be directed to consumers. Second, the organization may become a low-cost producer among a group of competitors. Third, the organization can operate in a protected market segment. The Porter model identifies three generic strategies: cost leadership, differentiation, and focus. A cost leadership strategy appeals to a wide market and offers goods or services in large quantities. Retailers are able to minimize per-unit costs and extend low prices through economies of scale. On the other hand, with a differentiation strategy, the retailer aims at a large market by offering goods or services viewed as distinctive. Some view these offerings as unique by virtue of design, features, or reliability—price is not an important variable. Finally, a focus strategy aims at a narrow target segment through low prices or a unique offering. Costs are controlled by establishing a specialized reputation, concentrating efforts on a few key merchandise lines, or serving a market that may be unsatisfied by competitors. For Porter, above-average performance in an industry is related to a firm's ability to select a strategy that is sustainable relative to competitors.

To illustrate this theory, Kmart and other discounters entered the market with cost leadership strategies against Sears, Penney's, and Ward's. Kmart maintained a low overhead and sold nationally branded merchandise. As time has marched on, Kmart now is confronted with competition from more differentiated discounters, such as Wal-Mart, who sell fashion-oriented merchandise. Moreover, focused discounters have entered the market, such as Herman's sporting goods, Barnes & Noble in books, and catalog showrooms in appliances and jewelry. These focused discounters not only have compromised Kmart's competitive advantage but have challenged the positions of the mass retailers—Sears, Penney's, and Ward's.

MANAGING CHANGE

Predicting change with any degree of accuracy is a complex task. The number of factors that must be considered and the volatility of these factors are staggering. In retailing, three areas of environmental uncertainty are especially important: changing consumer characteristics, resource changes, and competitive actions. Consumer demographic patterns, attitudes, activities, interests, opinions, and lifestyles define the retailing opportunity for merchants. Since retailers have direct contact with consumers, these changes in consumer characteristics are especially important. For example, the movement of consumers from urban to suburban areas in the 1950s and 1960s had a profound impact on retailers. Resource changes could include escalating energy costs, product shortages, and fluctuating interest rates. Moreover, competitive actions also make environmental analysis a difficult process.

HOW J. C. PENNEY MANAGED CHANGE

The J. C. Penney Company successfully repositioned itself in the 1970s. Unlike other national mass retailers, who relied on existing and outdated success formulas, the Penney organization changed its operational mix, locational, and merchandising strategies during this decade. The competitive environment varied depending upon location. Those stores situated in communities remote from metropolitan areas tended to compete with discount operations, such as small Kmarts, Wal-Marts, and regional stores. In this competitive environment, Penney provided the most service, the best ambience, the most fashionable merchandise, and an attractive price/value opportunity. However, many Penney stores were located in communities near metropolitan areas and were located in large shopping malls. The competition was not only Sears and Montgomery Ward but Bullocks, Foley's, Jordan Marsh, and Lord & Taylor, as well as stores like Bloomingdale's and Marshall Field.

In the early 1980s, the J. C. Penney Company developed an ambitious program of repositioning its stores through a new brand development policy. The approach was to offer private-label or store brands that would be as fashionable as national brands. The Penney Stafford line of men's suits was developed to compete with Botany, Palm Beach, and Cricketeer. Their Gentry line has a trimmer fit and includes suits, sport coats, dress shirts, and all-weather coats. A design/licensing contract was signed with Halston Enterprises to distribute fragrances and cosmetics to Penney stores. Household linens and bedding were added under the brand names of Halston III, Lee Wright, and Kathy Hardwick. The Wyndham line was developed for the contemporary career woman. Their store brand known as The Fox was rated in a research study in knit shirts as a close third behind Izod and Arrow in prestige. Moreover, such national brands as Nike, Adidas, and Levi Strauss were offered. Penney's decided to eliminate selling major appliances, paint and hardware, and lawn and garden supplies and also closed down all of its shopping mall automotive centers in order to gain floor space for the expansion of fashion and leisure departments.

Penney's had introduced a modernization program in all of its approximately 550 department stores by 1986 and now operates more than 1300 department stores. Moreover, several hundred stores were refurbished in smaller markets. Emphasis was placed on a contemporary look that would add an element of excitement to the shopping experience. The merchandise offering was aimed at providing a balanced mix of private-label, national brands, and designer labels. Assortment planning allowed individual stores to tailor their merchandise offerings to customer needs, reflecting variations in climate, lifestyle, and personal preference. Efforts were made to offer prices on Penney private-label merchandise that were 10 to 20 percent below department and specialty store competition. However, if Penney products were clearly superior, then premium prices were charged.

J. C. Penney seems to be basing its new strategies on a combination of factors rather than a single outstanding factor. Penney's is targeting to the double-income family and especially the female in the workforce. There is also recognition that men do much more shopping than formerly. Moreover, the belief is held that its customers are more interested in merchandise assortment and product attributes than price and that attractive, uncrowded displays draw customers. The new strategy seems also to consider that many other department stores have also cut back on appliances and that competitors have gotten complacent.

There are a number of potential challenges that confronted Penney when implementation of its new strategies was made. First, customers may not accept Penney as a retailer of fashion merchandise. Second, new types of competition include boutiques as well as middle-range department stores. Third, some manufacturers who have traditionally sold their brands to such retailers as Neiman-Marcus and Bloomingdale's may not want to sell to Penney since they may fear a loss of prestige or status. Finally, expansion and change may be too rapid. In the past, some retailers have expanded too quickly and have suffered losses because their organizations could not control costs and because executives were poorly prepared for the changes.

HOW SEARS MANAGED CHANGE

Sears in the 1980s adopted a new philosophy to sell national brand names, which was a departure from the development and selling of its own store brands. For example, national brands such as Cheryl Tiegs and Diane Von Furstenburg were added in merchandising the fashion line since this area constituted a weakness for Sears. National brands were also added in appliances, in order to present a more balanced merchandise presentation and to increase market share. Sears sells its general merchandise lines through a nationwide variety of selling locations. Retail stores are designated full-line department stores, or "A" stores, medium-size department stores, or "B" stores, hard-line merchandise stores, or "C" stores, and surplus stores. Most of the B stores have 50,000 to 70,000 square feet of sales area and in the 1980s sold the firm's strongest merchandise lines, which consisted of tools, appliances, and automotive supplies. Sears has opened 200 small stores in rural or small towns to take the place of its closed mail-order sales offices. These locations have traditionally been a stronghold for Sears. However, Sears is still trying to determine what it wants to be, and this will mean added strains in the oncoming years.

In the early 1980s, Sears diversified into financial services. Coldwell Banker, the largest independent commercial and residential real estate brokerage, was acquired. At that time, Coldwell Banker operated 249 residential real estate offices, 54 commercial real estate offices, 24 mortgage banking offices, and 32 real estate management offices.

Dean Witter Reynolds, an international financial services company involved in securities and commodities brokerage, investment banking, and insurance, was also acquired. Dean Witter maintained about 330 offices in the United States, Canada, the Far East, and Europe and serviced more than 740,000 individual and corporate accounts. Dean Witter Reynolds was the fourth largest registered brokerage firm in the United States.

In 1986, Sears launched Discover, the first new general-purpose credit card since the 1960s. The Sears financial network now included Dean Witter Reynolds, Coldwell Banker, Allstate Insurance, and the Greenwood Trust, which is a bank. Sears' initial plan was to charge no fee for its Discover card and to rebate up to 1 percent of users' charge volume in cash.

A number of reasons would seem to be responsible for the development of the Sears financial network. Sears forecasted that there would be an increase in consumer savings and an increase in various financial services. It had not envisioned a change in legislation that occurred in 1986 that would make the establishment of IRAs (individual retirement accounts) more restrictive. Sears believed that small savers and investors would be more comfortable dealing with its financial network than with brokers or bankers. Moreover, Sears had already established the concept of selling financial services through the Allstate Insurance firm and by offering H & R Block tax services in its stores. Another important reason for envisioning success in the selling of financial services was the large list of customers that had Sears charge accounts. The demographic analysis of these charge customers indicated that many had already established brokerage accounts.

The financial services area has been a bright spot in the $56 billion (in 1991 sales) Sears megalith. If profits from Allstate Insurance and the Sears credit card are included along with Dean Witter and the Discover card, nearly all of Sears' earnings from 1985 to 1991 have come from financial services. The Sears merchandise group, in contrast, has lost 22 percent of its market to its four largest competitors from 1971 to 1991. The retailer's heavily promoted 1989 strategy of "everyday low prices," for example, failed. Sears chairman Edward A. Brennan continues to struggle with a retail operation that seems increasingly out of control.

Plagued with cash problems, a $38 billion debt load, and under pressure from disgruntled shareholders, the Sears board of directors, in September 1992, voted unanimously to break up the "Great American Company." The company spun off Dean Witter and the Discover card. Sears sold 20 percent of Allstate Insurance Companies, which it purchased in 1934. Additionally, the company sold Coldwell Banker in December 1993, the nation's largest real estate broker.

The spinoff cut Sears' debt load in half, but without earnings from the other businesses flowing into it, the retailer will be under even greater pressure to perform well. But, to date, the merchandising operation, saddled with a crippling cost structure and outdated stores in marginal neighborhoods, has been unable to pull out of its earnings slump.

HOW MONTGOMERY WARD MANAGED CHANGE

Montgomery Ward in the 1980s made the decision that if "you can't beat the discounters, then join them." Ward, now a subsidiary of the Mobil Corporation, made the decision to convert 100 of its eastern and midwestern stores to the Jefferson-Ward format, which is a discount posture and would represent more than a third of store units. Mobil had purchased Ward's in 1974, and it had become a downright embarrassment. Although this strategy was found to be poorly researched and executed, certain aspects were salvaged, and Ward's embarked on what was to be called *hybrid discounting*. Ward's replaced its big-ticket items with smaller-ticket items and self-service merchandise lines such as health and beauty aids. Ward's also decided to stock branded goods and to deemphasize its private-label products. This was an attempt for Montgomery Ward to position itself in a different direction than Sears and to no longer be considered a poor clone of Sears. Already J. C. Penney had focused on selling higher-priced fashions. Now all three of the mass, national retailers had shifted in different directions.

Ward tried valiantly to close the gap with its competitors and granted generous credit terms to customers. However, skyrocketing interest rates transformed its credit operation to an albatross. Consequently, an accelerated expansion strategy emphasized the Jefferson-Ward discounting format. The expansion of Jefferson-Ward was unprecedented. Discounting was unfamiliar territory for Ward's management. Sales data were late, causing inventory problems, and stores either received more or fewer goods than ordered. Decision making was centralized, and managers now had to adjust to less freedom. Expansion had been too rapid, and bottlenecks quickly arose in many facets of the operation.

Ward ceased operation of its 113-year-old catalog business in 1985. The environment had changed, and a general merchandise catalog was no longer in great demand. Instead, specialty catalogs utilizing a differentiated focus strategy had made inroads and were now the growth area.

Montgomery Ward began to change from a general merchandise retailer to a specialty retailer. But past strategies still haunt Ward's progress. Location strategy was the worst of the three national mass retailers. Ward had not invested heavily since the 1950s to become the anchor store in important regional malls where many upscale customers shop. Ward has also been a late starter in selling national brands.

Montgomery Ward has made progress as a specialty retailer emphasizing its "store-within-a-store concept." It is still too early to forecast either the success or failure of this strategy.

MANAGEMENT VISION

A study of the mass retailers—Montgomery Ward, Sears, Roebuck, and J. C. Penney—directs itself to how well these mass merchants have responded to change through the years. Revolutionary changes developed during the 1980s that emanated from the 1960s. Social, economic, and retail institutional change in the United States has occurred at an unprecedented pace. These developments, with roots in post–World War II America, have revolutionized retailing operations and strategies. The subsequent changes have contributed to the retail revolution.

- *Demographics.* The traditional family consisting of the husband in the workforce, the wife as a full-time household manager, and two children is disappearing. Less than ten percent of total households now fit the typical American family of past decades. Couples marry at a later age, there are fewer children, the divorce rate is soaring, there are more single parent households, more wives are in the work force and the singles market has grown appreciably. Moreover, the teen population is shrinking and the elderly population is rapidly increasing. Double-income families and a new wave of immigration have altered the market opportunities of many markets. These new demographic trends have led to greater emphasis on market segmentation among retailers.

- *Economic conditions.* Economic change is an uncertainty. There has been an internationalization of resource markets. Double-income families have changed consumer expenditure patterns. The economy has changed from a manufacturing orientation to a service-based network. Roller-coaster interest rates have made managerial decisions more subject to higher degrees of risk. The new information age has placed more emphasis on data analysis and dissemination to decision makers through marketing decision support systems. Strong price competition has intensified as more educated consumers demand value.

- *Competition.* The emergence of off-price retailing, off-price shopping malls, unprecedented acquisitions, the expansion of home improvement centers, the oversaturation of stores, and relentless promotion have all contributed to the decline in market share of the mass retailers. Cost leadership and focus strategies adopted by competitors have caught the mass retailers in the middle. There has also been a development of boutiques, scrambled merchandising (the selling of goods not related to the primary mission of the retailer), and varied retailing styles that have also contributed to the decline in market share of the mass merchants. The growth of all-weather shopping malls, furthermore, has intensified retail competition.

• *Technology.* New electronic technologies of retailing have emerged, and home shopping via cable television is only in its infancy. Computer technology has placed a much greater emphasis on cost control and inventory management, which the mass retailers had been slow to adopt. The need to integrate financial planning with merchandising programs has changed the way business was previously done, and the mass retailers have lost opportunities because they did not sufficiently realize the long-term benefits of effective financial analysis, planning, and control.

• *Services retailing.* Sears has envisioned the long range of benefits of stock brokering, consumer banking, travel services, and insurance planning but because of limited financial resources was forced to spin off these businesses, which required additional investment to continue to grow. J. C. Penney has added insurance to its format. Montgomery Ward lags far behind in this area. The growth of service retailing has had an impact on these mass retailers. For example, specialty catalog retailing from organizations like L. L. Bean, Bonwit Teller, Lane Bryant, the Horchow Collection, and in-flight shopping catalogs of major airline companies are among the new forms of competition. The growth of direct marketing by manufacturers, in-home selling, and electronic retailing such as cable TV has also had an impact on Sears, Penney, and Ward's.

Sears, Penney, and Ward's envision how they should respond to retail competition in different ways. Sears envisions struggles on two fronts, one against discounters like Kmart and Wal-Mart and the other against specialty retailers who have adopted superstore formats. Sears has formulated a two-pronged strategy of countermoves by building larger general merchandise stores with a greater emphasis on apparel and by expanding its specialty operations. Competition comes from stores like Wal-Mart, Home Depot, Kmart, and The Gap. The merchandise group is divided into seven areas: home appliances and electronics, automotive suppliers, home improvement products, home furnishings, and men's, ladies', and children's apparel. This organizational structure allows Sears to measure how profitable each category is in contrast to specialty competitors. Sears has closed its McKids stores—a joint venture started with McDonald's—but has developed Kids & More departments within existing Sears stores. Sears leases suit departments to Hartmarx, which operates them under the Kuppenheimer brand name. Sears also realizes that brands such as General Electric and Amana are not the enemy, and these brands and other national brands are sold alongside of the Kenmore private-label brand. Although its overhead has declined recently, Sears is still far behind competitors in cost control, distribution capabilities, and merchandising techniques. Sears' costs are higher than Wal-Mart's and Kmart's, and the grouping of national brands with Sears brands has not increased sales significantly.

J. C. Penney has sold its headquarters building in Manhattan and has moved to Texas in an effort to better position itself in the Sunbelt. Emphasis is on family apparel merchandise and expansion of women's fashion apparel assortment with the contraction of hard goods lines such as home electronics, sporting goods, and photography equipment. However, Penney has failed to acquire such important clothing and cosmetic brands as Liz Claiborne, Evan Picone, and Estée Lauder, which are preferred by many female shoppers. Private labels need to be ordered months in advance, which reduces flexibility, and their catalog business, which was so successful in the 1980s, is facing intense competition.

Montgomery Ward, no longer under Mobil's control, seems to be successful with its specialty store-within-a-store strategy. This consists of large departments in such important areas as appliances, home furnishings, apparel, and auto parts. A new target market has been selected composed of younger, more affluent customers, and a remodeling program was implemented. Costs have been reduced by selling its credit card operation. Ward's store culture and atmosphere are now much more exciting than in its earlier days. Older stores are being remodeled to reflect the store-within-a-store format. Expanded departments are each given their own names, such as Electronic Avenue, Home Ideas, Auto Express, and Gold 'N Gems in the Apparel Store. Ward is also developing more efficient distribution centers and placing new point-of-sales terminals in all its store units. Even though Ward is progressing in the right direction, it still has a long way to go to become competitive in such areas as cost control, distribution capabilities, and merchandising skills.

LESSONS LEARNED FROM SUCCESS AND FAILURE

The findings from an analysis of these mass retailers reveal that if they had adhered to the basic fundamentals of their founders, their operations would have been much more successful. Departure from the basics was coupled with the loss of market share as competitors emerged to close vital prevailing gaps to satisfy consumer wants and needs.

History reveals that Sears was a showman. He added excitement to merchandising. Roebuck was very cost conscious. These two qualities propelled Sears, Roebuck to become at one time a top major retailer. Today, this organization suffers from a stodgy image. Merchandising is dull. Sears is also a high-cost merchant with a cumbersome bureaucracy. Operating costs are about 28 percent of sales, compared with Wal-Mart's 16 percent and Kmart's 20 percent.

Sears has continued with its merchandising policy directed toward innovation. Sears developed a prototype of "the store of the future." Innovation has historically been part of the culture and philosophy of Sears. Sears has changed its organizational structure, demonstrating a flexibility for change. However, cost containment, the early responsibility of Roebuck, was allowed to get out of control.

The Sears organization has demonstrated continuous scanning and monitoring of the environment. With the aid of strategic planning concepts, Sears embarked on financial services retailing. The recognition of a continuing trend of women entering the labor force and pursuing careers and the emergence of new lifestyle trends has increased the importance of family financial planning. Sears' move into financial services reflected future-oriented social and economic trends. However, financial problems ultimately caused Sears to divest its profitable financial services, insurance, and real estate brokerage businesses.

Whereas Sears had made inroads into financial planning for its customers, a closeness to the retail store needs of its customers was not demonstrated. The move into financial planning services was spectacularly successful. However, Sears had not listened, intently and regularly, to the retailing needs of its customers whose lifestyles were changing. The Sears private-label apparel brands had an image of lower quality when compared to many national brands. Consumers seemed to believe that Kmart and Wal-Mart sold merchandise of better value for the price than Sears. The store atmosphere of Penney's was more exciting and interesting than Sears'. Further evidence of Sears' apparent indifference to consumers appeared in the form of charges by attorneys nationwide in 1992 that its auto centers cheated customers by recommending unnecessary repairs.

Although Sears had achieved a differential advantage in location strategy by obtaining preferential locations in suburban shopping malls some years ago, in the early 1990s, Sears has many outmoded stores in left-behind neighborhoods. In addition, the retailer's differential advantage in other merchandising strategies was no longer present. The store's image was blurred, atmospherics were dull, and a weakness in apparel merchandising was glaring.

The fundamental message that can be derived from the Montgomery Ward situation is that a firm cannot stand still. A moderate growth policy is necessary for the firm to survive. Market opportunities and threats are ever present in the environment, and adaptable behavior should be the basis for strategy development. A continual reassessment of the environment, including industry structure, is needed, and this may result in corresponding shifts in strategies.

Montgomery Ward has suffered from strong intra-and intertype competition. Either poor positioning or foggy target marketing or both gave Ward's an image of a "me too" store that did not do things as well as Sears, Penney, Wal-Mart, or Kmart. The lack of genuine innovation in merchandising strategies gave Ward's an image of a nonprogressive store and a relic of the past. Corporate takeovers caused experimentation, but it was without purpose and direction. Finally, in an attempt to meet the competition of specialty retailing, Ward's implemented the "store-within-a-store" strategy that did demonstrate a direction different than its competitors—Sears and Penney's. Ward's left the general merchandise mail-order catalog business only to return to it later with a specialty merchandise catalog. This change in strategy has solidified and strengthened Ward and helped to differentiate its image away from Sears. Ward has now been able to compete with Penney's, Kmart, and the general merchandise department stores.

Montgomery Ward still has problems. Private brands have reemerged as an important patronage strategy, and the Ward brand does need strengthening. Moreover, markets have become more fragmented, and specialty retailers such as Loehmann's, The Limited, and The Gap pose serious competition. Off-price chains, home electronics retailers, and home improvement stores have developed newer formats. Ward, on the other hand, has high consumer recognition but still has to establish a new image. The new Ward's still must establish a distinctive image in merchandise assortment offerings, fashionability, shopping pleasure, locational convenience, and promotional emphasis. The implementation of information technology that will help speed inventory turnover and offer improved cost control is still necessary to remain competitive in the price struggle to satisfy customers.

J. C. Penney has developed a clearly defined objective to gain consumer acceptance as a fashion merchandiser. New types of competition exist from specialty retailers as well as middle-range department stores. Not all of Penney's experimentation has been successful. Its frontal attack on The Limited with its Mixit brand targeted to junior sportswear customers was a failure. But Penney is gaining strength, as learning takes place from even unsuccessful strategies. However, Penney's has promoted strong customer acceptance for its store brands and has managed to sell desired national brands as well. The buying function has been reorganized, as a satellite-based, televised communications system allows buyers to show items to stores for immediate orders. This innovation has increased inventory turnover. Penney still lacks the trendy image of Bloomingdale's or the exclusive image of Neiman-Marcus, but Penney has made considerable inroads in the competitive world of fashion retailing. Penney has not hesitated to change its merchandising mix by eliminating unprofitable merchandise lines such as home electronics, sporting goods, and photography. This flexibility in changing merchandise lines and updating behind-the-scenes store handling and receiving procedures has moved Penney forward in the retailing competition environment, but ominous signs are present that expansion and change may be too rapid.

Penney has demonstrated a willingness to act and to abandon familiar modes of operation. Through research, Penney has been able to detect changing consumer preferences. Research alone is not a guarantee of success even if it is interpreted correctly. Research is an aid for decision making and not a panacea. Promoting change and fostering an environment of fresh, original thinking have constituted a strength of the Penney organization.

The mass retailers—Sears, Ward's, and Penney—demonstrated striking and yet dissimilar characteristics as each organization evolved. Each organization began with a clear philosophy and a culture that affected its respective retailing strategies. Historically, each organization was close to its customers and emphasized extending fair merchandise value for the price in conjunction with service quality. In the beginning, each organization closely monitored costs. These factors were basic fundamentals and were the basis for many sound retail management decisions. The lessons learned from these three national retailers is that organizations cannot stray far from their points of origin without a blurring of store image. Certainly organizations must practice responsive retailing in accord with the changing environmental needs and wants of their customers, but these organizations must first identify very closely how their customers have changed through the years and whether a present customer segment is still large enough to be profitable. Should it be discerned that the customer segment has contracted for any reason, a broader or another customer segment must be cultivated.

Penney's has achieved rapid growth without a loss of operational effectiveness through the use of decentralized management. Other retailers might look to Penney's model of decentralization. Upgrading a store image is a challenge that has confronted Ward's, Penney's, and Sears and is not easily accomplished and takes years of costly effort. Heavy investments must be made in advertising, refurbishing, inventories, and markdowns. A change in store image also means that new human resources will be needed to provide the required expertise and that old customers might be lost in efforts to attract new customer segments.

CONTROVERSIAL DECISIONS

Penney, Sears, and Montgomery Ward have all been involved in the controversial decision arena. Many of the early decisions of Sears were indeed controversial. These decisions involved the departure from mail order to the establishment of retail stores in the 1920s. The decision to sell insurance from its retail stores in 1931 was a genuine innovation and resulted in the Allstate operation. After World War II, Sears expanded aggressively. Sears preempted prize locations as the population relocated to the suburbs, and moved from the East to the West. Sears pioneered the idea of the outlying store serving the entire family long before the advent of shopping centers. The Sears automotive center was another retail innovation. The building of Sears, Roebuck in the past has been a story of sound business decisions based on social and economic trends and the willingness to innovate in selling and distribution methods.

Sears announced in 1981 another bold and daring plan to become the leading purveyor of consumer financial services by seeking positions in stock brokerage, real estate, and money market funds. Proposed takeovers were formulated with Dean Witter Reynolds, the fifth-largest stock brokerage organization, and Coldwell Banker and Company, the largest real estate broker. Sears has also developed the Discover Credit Card Corporation, competes with finance companies, banks, and thrifts.

The Sears organization had successfully moved into—and because of financial difficulties, moved out of—the area of financial services. The remaining retail organization has been floundering for the past ten years. The decision to carry brand-name appliances and compete with discounters backfired. Since Sears' costs are higher than either Wal-Mart's or Kmart's, profit margins diminished sharply. Many of the Sears stores are old and badly in need of renovation which is occurring in the mid-1990s. The imagination, creativity, and proactive approach of former Sears strategies seem lacking in the new Sears. Sears has opened 200 stores in rural or small communities after closing its sales catalog offices in 1993 but are still trying to determine what image to reflect. As of 1995, Sears is placing more emphasis on its apparel business by allocating about 7 percent more square feet each year for clothing for the next several years. Still, policymaking guidelines are still unsettled, and Sears is still in the process of adjusting to old and new competitive challenges.

The Penney organization has successfully modified its target market through the years. The old target market of people who work with their hands has been changed to an upscale consumer interested in fashion. Penney is appealing to the double-income family interested in social mobility. In earlier days, J. C. Penney was a dry goods chain, located on Main Street, throughout the United States, specializing in selling practical clothing for the family, work clothes, piece goods, and a small amount of housewares. Population shifts from the central city to the suburbs diminished the importance of Main Street locations. Cultural patterns changed, and now there is increasing emphasis on consumption and easy credit terms.

J. C. Penney recognized the strategic importance of changing lifestyles, values, and the demographic distribution of purchases. The Penney approach was not to react to change but to anticipate change. Long before strategic planning became popular, Penney was utilizing a proactive approach to decision making.

Montgomery Ward decided not to follow the J. C. Penney example to target the upscale consumer but instead evolved into a hybrid discounter called Jefferson-Ward. The mass merchant approach was abandoned, and emphasis was placed on high-turnover, low-margin basics and centralized management. Ward's added self-service lines and more branded products to offset the image of offering primarily private-label products. This approach of operational evolution failed because Ward's had not clearly developed a competitive differential. Moreover, Ward's was following a reactive strategy to the competitive environment rather than a proactive approach.

Strategies that are hastily formulated in a time of crisis are not always successful. Ward's has since developed "a store-within-a-store strategy" that seems to be working. This strategy positions Ward's against boutiques rather than discounters. Still, the latter was a strategy developed from a reaction to the changing marketing environment rather than a strategy that anticipates a changing marketing environment.

J. C. Penney, among the three mass merchants, would appear to be capitalizing on a proactive approach and, as of this writing, would seem to be the most successful.

CHAPTER 3

The Old Five-and-Dime: An Endangered Species

Environmental Considerations
- Rate of target market deterioration
- Target market potential
- Strength of merchandise assortment
- Fixed and variable costs
- Location shifts

Strategies in the Decline Stage
- Image maintenance
- Eliminate marginal items
- Maintain profit margins
- Psychological appeals to loyal customer base
- Use a cost-focus strategy
- Emphasize location strategies: small towns, strip centers, and older neighborhoods

New Target Market Considerations
- Upscale appeals
- Broaden merchandise assortment
- Upgrade decor
- Add higher-price lines
- Enhance shopping comfort
- Redesign store layouts to facilitate customer movement
- Use brighter and more colorful visual displays

F. W. Woolworth and McCrory, both with more than 1,000 store outlets, dominated variety or five-and-dime store sales in 1990. The old five-and-dime is in the decline stage of the retail life cycle and virtually obsolete as originally structured. Variety stores have demonstrated the weakest performance of any retail store category over the past 15 years. Merchandise assortments generally include notions and needlework, school supplies, stationery, toys and games, housewares, and health and beauty aids.

S. S. Kresge, once a leading five-and-dime chain, reorganized its operating format from which Kmart evolved in the 1960s. Dollar General sells similar kinds of merchandise as traditional variety stores, once known as the "five-and-ten," but sells merchandise in plainer surroundings and at much lower prices. There are other chain organizations that are spinoffs such as All for $1, Everything's A $, and The Dollar Tree. These organizations do not offer merchandise priced higher than $1. Although Woolworth's is well diversified, its variety store division is in financial difficulties, and McCrory is operating under the protection of the bankruptcy act. Therefore, it is proper to refer to the old five-and-dime or variety stores as an endangered species.

A store's strategy should appropriately balance the variety and assortment of its merchandise. The balance should focus on the store's format, target market, and marketing strategy. Variety stores, or the five-and-dime, have developed competitive advantage by offering a wide variety of goods to facilitate one-stop shopping. Customers expect to be able to purchase a wide range of product lines at variety stores. In contrast, specialty stores stress assortment over variety. Each specialty store, such as paint, apparel, or electronics, concentrates on only a few product categories. Specialty stores develop competitive advantage by the breadth of choice offered within each category. Variety stores such as Woolworth and McCrory offer a wide selection of product lines but limit their assortments within each product line. Customers like the wide variety of products and the convenience of one-stop shopping. Since there is relatively weak customer loyalty for the brands offered in these merchandise categories, there is a limited danger in losing potential customers. However, managers of variety stores are confronted with the dilemma that by reducing assortment or eliminating a department in favor of adding a new department could decrease the loyal customer base.

The strategic challenge for the old five-and-ten or variety store organization is that supermarkets, drugstores, and discount stores are selling more and more variety store–type merchandise. Traditional trade distinctions are rapidly evaporating in a changing, if not turbulent, market. After the bankruptcy of W. T. Grant in 1976, new retailing patterns were to change competitive strategies of variety store organizations.

Four key ingredients seem to be important for either success or failure among variety store retailers: innovation, target market segmentation and image, physical environmental resources, and human resources. Originally, Woolworth, W. T. Grant, and other variety store chains entered the marketplace as innovators offering low-price competition. However, in later years variety stores lost this innovating edge. Stores such as The Dollar Tree that targeted prices at a dollar or less entered the market and became the new innovators.

The target market size diminished, and the old five-and-dime image became blurred. Woolworth, W. T. Grant, Murphy's, and Neisner's focused on a more upscale market, thereby blurring their images and also changing their target markets. Dollar General Stores entered the market and seized market share of the remaining variety store market that had diminished considerably.

Woolworth has retained a very valuable asset, a collection of favorable leases on its variety store locations. Ben Franklin has developed favorable sites in secondary locations and has assumed the role of a dominant supplier of merchandise to these localities.

In later years, it is only the Dollar General Store with its continued focus on serving the remaining part of the variety store market that has earned high grades. However, there is not one individual who has emerged in either the successful Dollar General or Ben Franklin chains who can be cited along with Sam Walton of Wal-Mart or Bernard Marcus of Home Depot as a people motivator.

The failure of variety stores has been a lack of continued innovation and the inability to adjust to a changing target market, thereby blurring their images. Physical environmental store sites have been a strength but not used wisely. Human resource management was carelessly used by W. T. Grant and not used well by other variety store chains.

Variety store chains needed feedback to monitor results and to determine if objectives were accomplished. Since adequate performance evaluation was not present, a worsening situation was not identified until corrective action was too late. As variety store chains became larger, the need for better controls increased. Unless these controls are in place, overwhelming problems can develop. Although measures of customer satisfaction or dissatisfaction were available, these resources were not adequately utilized by variety store chains.

THE OLD FIVE-AND-DIME OF YESTERDAY

The oldest variety store chain, F. W. Woolworth, opened its first store in Lancaster, Pennsylvania, in 1879 to sell items priced 5 cents or less. Fifty years later, in 1929, Woolworth had approximately 2,100 stores and annual sales over $273 million. J. G. McCrory started a 5 cents to $1 chain in 1882 and by 1929 had more than 220 stores with over $40 million in sales. S. S. Kresge separated from the McCrory organization in 1899 and by 1929 had more than 500 stores with more than $145 million in sales.

Frank W. Woolworth was one of the first mass merchandisers to make purchases straight from the manufacturer in an attempt to eliminate the middlemen. Merchandise was displayed on counters, where customers could see and touch the goods. Although Woolworth was founded on innovation in merchandising, the company was slow to grasp the significance of many post–World War II trends. For example, Woolworth followed its competition into the suburbs. Merchandise lines were slowly upgraded and new ones added. Moreover, the organization was slow in converting to self-service and modernizing its stores.

In 1973, sales climbed 19 percent to $3.7 billion. This was more than twice the company's volume of 1963. The Woolworth organization numbered 2,058 variety stores, 283 Woolco Discount Stores, 1,481 Kinney Shoe Stores, and 266 Richman Clothing Stores. International operations were situated in Great Britain, Canada, Germany, Mexico, and Spain.

The F. W. Woolworth Company entered the discount department store market in 1962. This new division was named Woolco and was originally to be operated on an autonomous basis. Other Woolworth operations such as Kinney Shoe and Richman Brothers were acquired in 1963 and 1969, respectively, and operated independently. In 1971, however, it became apparent that the autonomous arrangement between Woolworth and Woolco had limitations. It was hoped that this new union would strengthen the mass-purchasing power of the Woolworth organization. Since both organizations complemented each other, it was believed that certain economies in promotion and distribution would be possible.

Woolworth opened 31 new variety stores and 31 new discount stores in 1971. Discount stores were previously constructed in new shopping centers and malls. Variety stores were concentrated in large cities and neighborhood shopping areas where, historically, Woolworth derived its greatest

strength. Since 51 percent of its sales were derived from variety store operations, management believed that this operation was successful and
should be continued.

S. S. Kresge, in contrast, had decreased the number of its variety stores
from 750 to 487, and Kmarts had been increased from 53 to 580 from
1962 to 1972. Kmart discount outlets were comparable to Woolco operations. Most of the Kmart stores had been opened in suburban locations.
Using a cost leadership strategy, Kmart generated almost 90 percent of
Kresge's sales. In 1970, S. S. Kresge surpassed the Woolworth Company
in total sales. Profits of the Woolworth Company by 1972 were only half
as much as in 1962.

Following World War II, and during the 1950s, a changing environment
confronted Woolworth, Kresge, and others in the variety store industry.
The expansion of drugstore and supermarket chains into general merchandise diminished the market share of variety stores in many of the limited
lines of merchandise that had formerly contributed substantially to profit
margins of the old five-and-tens. The suburban shopping center boom adversely affected the Woolworth and Kresge variety store chains that were
primarily situated in main street locations. The severest challenge, however,
emanated from aggressive expansion by discount store operators who sold
many merchandise lines carried by variety stores but at sharply reduced
prices.

The threatening external environmental conditions confronting variety
store operations in the early 1960s was met with managerial indecisiveness
at Woolworth. The company proceeded cautiously in enlarging and upgrading its variety stores and slowly organizing its autonomous Woolco
discount operations in 1962. Essentially, the Woolworth organization did
not commit its resources to either variety or discount store retailing. Woolworth in 1973 was composed of about 2,000 variety stores, which generated slightly more than half its sales, and close to 300 discount stores,
which accounted for about 40 percent. This ambivalent approach contributed to performance difficulties. Neither Woolworth variety stores nor
Woolco discount stores possessed distinct identities in the minds of consumers. For example, Woolco's prices were often equivalent to Woolworth's prices on the same product. Procrastination in the centralization of
buying and distribution for both its variety and discount operations was
another important reason for low profitability.

IMPACT OF COMPETITIVE FORCES ON THE OLD FIVE-AND-DIME

The old five-and-dime followed the wheel-of-retailing hypothesis. This
institution entered the market as low status, low margin and then gradually
acquired more elaborate facilities. Increased overhead and higher operating
costs were incurred. Variety stores left a profitable market segment un-

served and became more vulnerable to new types of institutions that stressed lower costs and prices. The variety store was first challenged by supermarkets pursuing a strategy of scrambled merchandising. Variety stores were challenged again by discount stores. The market segment left unserved by the old five-and-dime was to be served by such chains as the Dollar General Store and organizations selling items for no more than $1 such as Everything's A $ and The Dollar Tree. These organizations have successfully targeted a lower socioeconomic market segment overlooked by many organizations such as Kmart, which changed its target market and decided to target a more mainstream market. Thus, the variety stores lost market share to discount stores and to organizations serving a distinct lower socioeconomic target market.

Strong variety store expansion by Woolworth and others was not universally accepted in the past. Displaced competitors reacted emotionally. Wal-Mart has encountered such opposition in Massachusetts and other eastern states. The old five-and-ten seemed to threaten small merchants' existence. Rallies and protests were held in many cities at the turn of the century.

Standardization of Woolworth's and other variety store organizations provided for consumer purchasing expectations. Familiar store fronts greatly improved store recognition and simplified choice decisions for geographically mobile customers. Socializing among customers was encouraged by Woolworth since this organization was probably the nation's largest restauranteur, and many customers gathered at the coffee shop for morning coffee and met there also for lunch and afternoon breaks.

Competitive pressures such as the rise of the discount store and the growth of shopping malls and suburban shopping centers weakened the variety store's position. Woolworth, Murphy's, Neisner's, and later McCrory became more upscale. Wal-Mart and Kmart did a better job in maintaining low costs and implementing computerized inventory systems. The variety stores had lost their low-price appeal to the more cost-efficient discounters.

The role of the variety store as a social gathering spot was also challenged by suburban shopping centers and later by enclosed shopping malls. The old coffee shop and soda fountain, where many congregated, was replaced by shopping malls containing a variety of restaurants and even health spas, libraries, motion picture theaters, game arcades, and other recreational facilities.

The standardization process of the malls with department stores as anchors and, depending on the size of the malls, outlets serving different market segments enhanced their one-stop shopping appeal. A variety of restaurants ranging from fast-food chains, ethnic food, and upscale full-service eateries with fine silverware and linen tablecloths and napkins replaced the counter-service restaurants of the old five-and-ten. Consequently, the old five-and-ten was unable to successfully compete with newer forms of competition.

NATURAL SELECTION

Adaptive behavior was a necessary strategy for the old five-and-dime to survive in the long term. As an economic institution, retailers compete with one another to serve precise consumer market segments. There is a wide range of conditions that might require adaptive behavior. The dynamic environment of retail trade includes changes in the social, cultural, political, legal, technological, economical, and competitive structure of the marketplace. Required adaptations by variety stores would include modifications in the product assortment, price offerings, or promotional mix to targeted customers. Locational shifts might also be necessary due to changes in shopping behavior.

Throughout retailing history, the relative importance of retailing institutions has shifted. For example, the hardware and infants' wear stores declined in importance as discount stores gained prominence. The Ma and Pop grocery store declined in importance as the supermarket became more dominant. Specific products had reshaped retail outlets. Drugstores, for example, sold about 75 percent of ice cream, and now food stores are the dominant seller. Variety stores were once a very important distribution outlet for toys. Food stores, discount stores, drugstores, and toy warehouses have become more important outlets for toys in the past 30 years. During the process of change and survival of the fittest, some institutions prosper; others fail to make it.

Population shifts also account for the natural selection process in distribution channels. When population shifted from the central cities to the suburbs, gigantic shopping centers were constructed to accommodate the needs and wants of new homeowners. Consequently, many downtown stores in the central cities lost customers. Some stores were unable to survive because of these population shifts and the competition from stores in the suburban shopping centers. Stern's and Sak's Thirty-fourth Street in New York City, R. H. White in Boston, and Rosenbaum's in Pittsburgh were department stores that were in business more than 50 years, yet had to close their doors in downtown locations. Many of the variety store chains such as Woolworth, Kresge, and W. T. Grant were also situated in downtown areas and experienced difficulties. The theory of natural selection explains the changes in institutions that result in modification or destruction of a particular channel of distribution, type of firm, or specific firms.

The product life cycle is another contributing factor to the survival of the firm. For example, manufacturers are constantly endeavoring to determine if their products can be introduced and sold in new types of retail institutions. Superstores such as Toys "R" Us and Herman's in sporting goods have taken market share away from variety stores. The relatively new interest in patronizing flea markets has also taken away market share from the old five-and-ten. Manufacturers have learned that demand for many types of products can be increased significantly by finding new distribution outlets. Since many products are lost in the decline stage of the retail life cycle, manufacturers have come to realize that the decline stage in the product life cycle need not occur simultaneously with the decline in the retail life cycle. New distribution outlets and new products are constantly introduced into the marketplace. As the old products and distribution outlets decline in popularity, producers search for new distribution outlets that will be better able to serve the needs of customers.

Much of the decline in variety store institutions can be traced to the failure of management to both recognize and respond to changing needs of customers. Many people vacated apartments in the central cities in order to purchase homes in the suburbs. As new homeowners, this segment of the population had many new needs. This consumer group wanted appliances, garden equipment, new forms of recreational equipment, and different types of clothing. Since the old five-and-dime did not identify and respond to these changed needs, survival became precarious.

FACTORS THAT INHIBIT CHANGE

- *Costs.* The addition of new merchandise lines complicates inventory problems for retail management. Many store units might not have adequate display space or are unable to implement new inventory control procedures. Naturally, the major consideration is whether costs will increase faster than revenue. As each new product is added to the merchandise assortment, handling costs are increased.

- *No-growth motives.* Some managers desire the security of offering a merchandise assortment that is familiar. Risk-averse managers would prefer not to diversify, since there is a fear of the unknown. Expansion would bring many problems with which these managers are not prepared to cope and would require adjustments in the day-to-day operations of their businesses.

- *Market conditions.* Although the manufacturer and retailer are dependent on each other, this dependence is not equal. For instance, in the marketing channels where the retailer is dominant and many manufacturers compete for available space, the retailer needs only to make a minimum selling effort. Large supermarket chains, for example, are able to exercise undue leverage in negotiations with suppliers. Variety store management used this strategy poorly with suppliers.

At one time, variety stores such as Woolworth and W. T. Grant were innovative distributive institutions but became content with maintaining the status quo. The discount store and the strategy of scrambled merchandising were the aggressors in the natural selection process. Over time, new types of institutions and strategies emerge, and existing institutions need to respond quickly or face destruction.

COMPETITIVE RESPONSES

The elements of competitive responses are found in a strategic plan. The retailer often begins with a general plan that becomes more specific as different options and payoffs become clearer. The retail plan should help in establishing goals, identifying and satisfying target market segments, and developing competitive advantage dimensions. By using proactive planning, a retailer can make strategic moves ahead of competitors.

Market opportunity is closely related to the innovative process. *Market opportunity* refers to potential demand. Consequently, market opportunity encourages innovation. Marketing opportunity interacts with the development of retail strategy since it will determine the strategies of the merchandise assortment, the price lines, and the communication of the store's image. The retailer will restructure or modify existing strategies if (1) present customers are sufficiently dissatisfied, (2) the present organization strategies resist the wants and needs of a sufficient number of users, (3) alternative competitors can be readily substituted, and (4) new types of retailers are taking away present customers. The discount department store is a good example of an innovative type of institution that has appeared in the past. Traditional retailers have recognized this new market opportunity, and such firms as Woolworth with Woolco and Kresge with Kmart have attempted to serve this new market. It was believed by both organizations that corporate resources would permit entry into this new type of innovative institution.

WOOLWORTH: A STRATEGY OF DIVERSIFICATION

Woolworth grew through diversification. This strategy was used so that Woolworth would not be overly dependent on one merchandise line or type of business. New business formats were aimed at new markets. Distribution and promotion orientations were both accordingly different from those usually followed. Successful diversification requires great human and financial resources and entails considerable risk.

Woolworth viewed its variety store operation as a cash cow. A *cash cow* in this framework is a high–market share business format in a relatively low-growth industry. Woolworth had an established customer loyalty base that was difficult for competitors to penetrate. Sales were steady without high retailing costs, thereby generating more cash flow than required to maintain its market share. Surplus cash was used to support other business formats. This strategy as used by Woolworth was oriented to loyal customers, periodic price discounts, and reminder advertisements to encourage repurchases. This strategy did not operate that well in the decade of the 1980s as the discount stores and scrambled merchandising eroded Woolworth's loyal customer base.

The Woolworth Corporation has diversified in location, store formats, and life cycle stages. Woolworth diversified in location with nearly 9,000 stores, approximately one third located in Europe, Mexico, and Australia, generating over 40 percent of total revenues. The company has more than 40 different store formats that sell such varied merchandise as footwear, apparel, athletic equipment, costume jewelry, watches, household goods, candy, health and beauty aids, and appliances. Under the Kinney Shoe Corporation division, the Foot Locker, World Foot Locker, Lady Foot Locker, Champs Sports, Little Folks Shop, and Kids Mart chains are operated. The F. W. Woolworth division operates the variety stores, the Rx Place chain of deep-discount stores, Afterthoughts, Carimar, The San Francisco Music Box Company, and The Best of Times specialty chains. The Richman Brothers Company and Susie's division were closed. Store units were closed in approximately 15 percent of the Kids Mart and Little Folks stores and 25 percent of the Kinney Shoe Stores. Approximately 10 percent of the Woolworth and Woolworth Express stores were also closed. Woolworth operates The Bargain Shops, Northern Reflections, and Foot Locker stores in Canada.

As part of its ongoing effort to distance itself from its declining general merchandise business, Woolworth, in 1994, sold 120 of its 142 Woolco discount departments in its Canadian subsidiary to Wal-Mart. The remaining 22 stores were either converted to other formats, sold, or closed. The Woolco store group in the United States was closed in 1983. Lacking a sustainable competitive advantage in large-scale discount store operation, Woolworth has chosen to develop its relatively more profitable specialty retailing business.

An important strength of the Woolworth Corporation is the maintenance of different store formats in various stages of their life cycle development. In the introductory stage, and therefore candidates for explosive growth, are Northern Reflections, a dressier, less-casual clothing outlet; Kids Foot Locker; The San Francisco Music Box chain; and The Best of Times chain, with a variety of clocks. In the accelerated development stage are the Champs Sports, Lady Foot Locker, and Afterthoughts boutiques stores. The Kinney Shoe Stores are in the late accelerated development stage of the retail life cycle. The Woolworth variety stores are in the decline stage. Accelerated development and decline store formats can generate cash flow to finance growth in new and developing store formats.

THE OLD FIVE-AND-DIME AT WOOLWORTH STAGGERS

The old five-and-dimes at Woolworth must compete with the likes of Kmart and Wal-Mart but do not have the economies of scale to offer the lowest prices. A short-range, reactive strategy was to more firmly develop Woolworth Express, smaller streamlined variety stores that offer much higher-volume merchandise such as health and beauty aids. Woolworth Express was intended to be a growth vehicle in important mall locations. Woolworth Express features a main aisle down the center of the store, front to rear, called the Express Lane, that is used to display promotional merchandise. Theoretically, this strategy would double the sales per square foot of the five-and-dimes.

Even in Great Britain the old concept of offering lots of merchandise items at cheap prices is dead. Present competitive forces have made the marketing of variety items in five-and-tens extremely difficult. The Woolworth variety stores in Great Britain now emphasize specialty retailing by establishing six departments: entertainment, home and garden, kitchen products, fashion accessories, candy, and children's toys and clothing. Groceries and adult clothing merchandise items that once accounted for 25 percent of revenues have been discontinued.

Even in Canada, Woolco stores have not fared well. Although failure has come later than in the United States, Woolco finally announced that it will phase out its operations. Competition had intensified in Canada, and Woolco lacked a distinct image and target market. Physical resources such as an inventory control system as excellent as Wal-Mart's was also lacking. Woolworth stores are in great difficulty, suffering from a blurred image, and would seem to be staggering.

Woolworth announced in fall 1993 the closing of its old-fashioned five-and-dime stores in the United States. Once its core business, these stores will soon become a memory and a part of business history. Approximately 450 stores will be closed, and while another 450 variety stores will remain open, it is anticipated that these, too, will fade into the annals of retail history. Situated on Main Street locations, subject to consumer disinterest in downtown shopping and the relentless competition of suburban malls, these stores were devastated by lack of store traffic. Long-term, low-cost leases played an important role in supporting profit margins, but that probably masked the five-and-tens' drop in revenue stemming from a declining customer base. The impact of Toys "R" Us, Bed Bath & Beyond, Kmart, Wal-Mart, Dollar General, and others was too much to withstand. Woolworths has been plowing its resources into specialty retail stores that have generated twice the operating profits of the dime stores. Moreover, suburban mall locations are typically viewed by shoppers as safer and more accessible retailing environments.

Although Woolworth variety stores are staggering, the remaining stores are still viable. Favorable locations have enabled the remaining stores to survive. Competition is intense, but the discounters are situated some miles away. Remaining five-and-dimes are situated in inner-city and densely populated suburban locations. These stores carry such basic merchandise as housewares, hardware, cosmetics, and toys in the front of the store while stocking few low-margin items like videocassettes and video games. Apparently, consumers do little comparison shopping in discounters for the basic items carried by the remaining Woolworth stores.

McCRORY: A CONTRARIAN STRATEGY

The hollow shells of five-and-dimes remain in downtown areas like fossils of the past. McCrory has acquired many of the old five-and-dime chains such as J. J. Newberry, McLellan, T. G. & Y., S. H. Kress, H. L. Green, and G. C. Murphy. The McCrory organization has also included Silver, Elmore, Britts, and Kittinger stores, names that have long since vanished from Main Street, U.S.A. One of the major factors operating against McCrory was the high cost of rent. Five-and-tens are considered convenience stores and therefore need to be located in densely populated areas or in malls. Both locations have become relatively expensive. Many long-term leases have been terminated, and landlords are specifying rent increases of tenfold or more for renewal.

McCrory's target market is characterized by a limited budget and is composed of a high percentage of minorities. Fifty-five percent are families with income levels below $20,000 a year. Heavy-user customers constitute only 13 percent of the total target market but make 45 percent of the purchases. Approximately 46 percent are black or Hispanic with family incomes under $20,000. Since more than half of all U.S. households have incomes under $25,000, this segment represented a vast potential market.

Generally, price points are kept below $10. About 20 percent of the merchandise assortment is especially aimed to the demographics of the neighborhood. Buyers are employed who specialize in the purchase of merchandise for ethnic groups and even reflect diversity in satisfying Cuban-American and Mexican-American needs. McCrory targeted predominately urban areas.

The McCrory organization announced in January 1992 that nearly one quarter of its 1,100 stores would be closed. The following month, operating under the names of McCrory, G. C. Murphy, J. J. Newberry, S. H. Kress, and T. G. & Y., bankruptcy was announced. The 109-year-old retailer had operated under a dying retail formula. The five-and-dime store concept was unable to compete with operations such as Toys "R" Us, warehouse clubs, and the discount chains.

BEN FRANKLIN: A MARKET SEGMENTATION STRATEGY

Butler Brothers was a part of City Products Corporation in 1974 and administered about 2,400 franchised Ben Franklin Variety Stores. Butler Brothers charged an annual franchise fee based on sales volume. For example, a store in the sales volume range of $180,000 to $199,999 in 1974 paid a fee of $1,425, which represented 0.75 to 0.71 percent of sales. Generally, the franchise agreement provided for some type of restriction on the location of the franchise so that it served a definite trading area. Although it is difficult to compute averages, about 90 percent of a unit store's merchandise requirements were purchased from Butler Brothers.

All Ben Franklin Stores were offered assistance in site selection studies, store layout, and leasing arrangements. Unit stores benefit from both local and national advertising. Butler Brothers provided extensive training of prospective franchisees in all aspects of retail operation. A zone manager generally supervised from 10 to 20 stores and devoted considerable time to reviewing inventories of unit stores and other types of merchandising assistance. A basic control system consisted of stock checklists, and seasonal records were provided by Butler Brothers to unit stores. Butler Brothers subleased properties and then in turn subleased to franchisees. Some private-label brands were developed by the parent organization. According to the Butler Brothers organization, average sales were approximately $85,000 per store, and net income was 11.62 percent of sales in 1974.

Ben Franklin, based in Des Plaines, Illinois, is a variety store chain of more than 1,300 franchised stores today. Each owner is a part of the community. While McCrory targeted urban areas, Ben Franklin targeted secondary locations in small towns and assumed the role of a dominant supplier of general merchandise to these populations.

Ben Franklin has recently converted about 200 of its general merchandise stores into specialty craft outlets. The merchandise assortment includes T-shirts with do-it-yourself foils and points as well as traditional knitting, quilting, and decorating supplies. All of the 200 crafts shops are in metropolitan areas. Therefore, Ben Franklin has elected not to compete directly with Toys "R" Us and discounters such as Kmart and Wal-Mart.

More than half of the Ben Franklin variety stores are situated in towns of 50,000 people or less. Since stores are franchised, owners are active participants in the community and are known to their customers. The craft outlet stores are given much credit for the surprising comeback of the franchised chain. According to market research, the Ben Franklin name is favorably received among consumers. Much of the Ben Franklin target market, like McCrory's, is composed of minority groups.

W. T. GRANT: A STORE FAILURE

A milestone in retailing history was made in 1976 when the W. T. Grant chain became the largest retail chain ever to file for bankruptcy. The company was started in 1906 and established an impressive record for selling low-priced, basic merchandise such as soft goods, draperies, and small wares. In 1972, W. T. Grant had more than 1,200 stores and was a prominent pillar along with Woolworth among variety stores.

There is usually not a single factor attributable for the demise of a large organization; rather, a combination of factors and events build upon each other. In the mid-1960s, W. T. Grant, like many other retail organizations, expanded. However, Grant's expansion exceeded the efforts of Woolworth, Sears, Roebuck, and a great many other retailers. W. T. Grant opened over 400 large stores of over 50,000 square feet each. There was an attempt to change an image of carrying limited-price items in small wares, wearing apparel, and soft goods. Merchandise lines such as furniture and appliances were added. As a result, the store's image and its market positioning became blurred from the customers' standpoint. Some units remained variety stores, others were perceived as junior department stores, and others were perceived as discount. W. T. Grant tried strongly to veer away from the variety store image. The transition period caused a dilemma because customers became confused. Customers who had perceived Grant as a variety store offering low-priced convenience goods were not eager to spend money on more costly items. Appliances and furniture did not sell well. The merchandise assortment was not geared to customer expectations. Compounded by the general downturn of the economy, Grant's situation became grave.

One supplier and creditor of W. T. Grant maintained that some of the major mistakes were that merchandise lines were not distinctive enough to compete with competition and that there was overexpansion into large stores. Furthermore, installment credit was indiscriminately extended to customers just at a time when consumers were being placed in precarious circumstances due to inflation and recession.

About a year before its liquidation, W. T. Grant had over 1,000 stores in 42 states and employed over 70,000 people. In an attempt to avert bankruptcy, a number of changes were made. More than half the W. T. Grant stores were closed because they were deemed to be unprofitable. The payroll was sliced almost in half. Merchandise lines, such as furniture and appliances, were discontinued. This action helped to reduce the extension of credit to customers. Departments were rearranged; women's and children's wear were placed near the front entrance and men's wear was removed from this location. Sales per square foot of floor space were about $30, half of what was expected, and efforts were made to increase this figure. The varying sizes of store units also added to Grant's difficulties.

Store units ranged from 54,000 square feet to 180,000, with different interiors and exteriors.

The pursuit of growth at any cost had weakened W. T. Grant in numerous ways. First, a merchant needs to develop a distinctive image in order to be successful. But because of ill-conceived expansion, Grant's image became blurred. Second, growth needs to be carefully planned and controlled. The organization needs an effective time period to train managers and personnel to operate new units. New units were opened by W. T. Grant before personnel were adequately trained. Location research and analysis are also a necessity. Third, prudent merchandising policies and financial arrangements are also an important part of the planning process that was lacking in Grant's retailing strategy.

DOLLAR GENERAL STORES: A FOCUSED, DOWNSCALE STRATEGY

Dollar General operated more than 2,150 general merchandise stores in 1994. Originally a wholesaling firm started in 1939, Dollar General changed to a retail format in 1954. Stores are situated predominantly in lower-income neighborhoods in rural towns of less than 25,000 population in 24 midwestern and southeastern states. Family income of its average customers is under $25,000 a year. Many customers are in the 25 to 45 age range, and a significant segment are retired. Usually, the merchandise is not priced over $25, with simple price points of $1, $5, and $10 or in multiples such as 2 for $5. Efforts are made to conform prices to the currency denominations carried in pocketbooks and wallets.

The merchandise assortment is generally 60 percent soft goods and 40 percent hard goods but has recently shifted more to hard goods. Cleaning products account for a significant percentage of inventory. Toasters and other minor appliances are also carried. Although most of its merchandise sells for a few dollars, Dollar General has offered Adidas and L. A. Gear athletic shoes for $20 a pair. Therefore, customers are surprised occasionally when they find such bargains as a new pair of Nikes for about half what they cost in sporting goods stores or an inexpensive Gitano or a pair of Levi jeans.

Dollar General attempts to convey the image of a convenience bargain store. While such discounters as Wal-Mart have broadened their appeal to reach middle-income consumers through a differentiated discounting strategy, Dollar General has continued to grow by serving an overlooked and neglected market as part of a focused strategy. Promotion is unconventional in that word-of-mouth referrals are heavily depended upon. Radio and circular advertising is used to reinforce word of mouth. Advertising constitutes about 1.5 percent of sales.

Until recently, inventory management was impeded by imprecise data from outdated electric cash registers. For example, when Wal-Mart sells a toaster, its merchandise scanner automatically orders a replacement, but if Dollar General sold a toaster, its register informs management only that a $10 houseware item was sold. Costs are held to a minimum. Shipments are dispatched to stores on a 14-day cycle, with a few higher-volume stores getting weekly delivery. Deep inventories are maintained of sweatshirts, underwear, and jeans. Buyers are geared to make value purchases such as factory seconds, items with tiny flaws, or merchandise that manufacturers could not sell for some reason to their regular customers. Warehouse operations were converted to automation and were consolidated in 1989. This action represented a substantial savings, but the firm has been slow to take advantage of new technology, including merchandise scanners. The delayed adoption of scanning technology is a part of a penny-pinching policy that appears to work but that could possibly be detrimental in the future.

DOWNSCALE COMPETITORS: A NEW RETAILING STRATEGY

Stores that price each item for $1 are springing up across the United States. Most of the dollar retailers operate with the same purchasing strategy: odd lots, closeout items, and factory overruns of miscellaneous merchandise. The merchandise is neither damaged nor defective. It may be discontinued because of changes in the packaging, container size, color, or logo.

Chains such as All for $1, Everything's A $, The Dollar Tree, Dollar Bill$, Uncle Buck's, and Lots for Less are growing by leaps and bounds. Such chains are becoming one of the largest categories of new retail tenants in regional malls and neighborhood strip shopping areas. Most dollar retailers rely on word-of-mouth communication and do not use newspaper advertising. These chains usually have a well-lighted plainness, with bright paint on the walls and linoleum on the floor. Stores are crowded with racks and racks of goods. Dollar stores must be managed carefully, since it can be difficult to obtain merchandise of good quality that can be offered for a dollar, and because prices are rising continuously due to inflation. Already, All for $1, Inc. has filed for bankruptcy protection.

The recession has not necessarily been an explanation for the dollar store's growth. Customers are just as likely to be executives as low-income consumers. These stores are a response to the consumer's continuing search for value. As such, the dollar stores serve a market niche that has been overlooked in the frenzy of retailers to serve an upscale market.

LESSONS LEARNED FROM SUCCESS AND FAILURE

Dollar General nearly destroyed itself by purchasing and offering customers pricier merchandise. Management had forgotten that many present customers were low-income people who were willing to shop in a store with sparse surroundings in return for low prices. Although Woolworth and W. T. Grant both offered a broader merchandise assortment with higher-price lines, it is possible to speculate that if they had continued to serve their existing markets, both chains might have remained profitable. The lesson learned here is that while an existing market segment might diminish in size, a large share of a smaller market might still be profitable. Many retailers have raced to serve an upscale market, but Dollar General and other chains such as Everything's A $ have profitably followed a focused strategy by continuing to serve a smaller, viable downscale market.

The Kresge organization recognized that the old five-and-dime was vulnerable and made a major commitment to develop a new format—the Kmart discount store. Kresge was one of the innovating five-and dime-chains. Kresge entered the market as a low-status, low-price competitor. Gross margins were substantially below competitors'. Minimal customer services were offered. The old five-and-dime offered a modest shopping environment in terms of exterior and interior facilities, which were standardized. At the time, many five-and-tens occupied low-rent locations in the downtown or neighborhood shopping centers. The product assortment offered was quite limited. Kresge fell into the trap of entering the trading-up phase of the wheel-of-retailing model. Realizing that it was entering a vulnerability phase, a new discount store format was developed, and the old five-and-tens were gradually phased out.

Kmart has conformed to the wheel-of-retailing pattern. Originally based on a cost leadership strategy, Kmart has since added more expensive merchandise to its low-price lines and recruited a number of celebrities to sell a more differentiated merchandise mix. Such celebrities as Jaclyn Smith (dressier women's apparel), author Martha Stewart (household goods), and racing car driver Mario Andretti have been enlisted to promote Kmart's private labels. To appeal to a more upscale market, Kmart has enlarged and refurbished many of its stores to include wider aisles, taller and deeper shelves, and more eye-catching displays. W. T. Grant's demise reminds retailers that growth should not be more rapid than the organization can support with respect to training of personnel, location research, prudent merchandising, and financial planning and control. Moreover, the store's blurred image reflected a disregard of traditional retailing fundamentals. Consumers became confused as to whether W. T. Grant was a junior department store, a variety store, or a convenience discounter. W. T. Grant competed with Sears and J. C. Penney but could not match their established brands or merchandising techniques.

Variety stores entering the decline stage of the retail life cycle generally experience market share losses, marginal profitability, and an inability to compete successfully with new competitors. The variety store can still survive by serving small, marginal, unserved markets in small towns, older locations, and decaying neighborhoods. However, profit performance, under these conditions, is usually weak.

ILL-FATED MANAGEMENT VISION

Dollar General in the mid-1980s nearly conformed to the wheel-of-retailing model by adding more upscale merchandise to its offerings. Soon closeout and irregular merchandise constituted only 10 percent of sales, approximately half of what the company considered ideal. Dollar General also used debt financing to acquire two smaller but similar chains located in Florida, the Midwest, and the South. Debt soared from $13 million in 1982 to $71 million in 1985. Earnings declined from $21 million in 1984 to $4.3 million in 1986. In response, Dollar General reversed itself and returned to its original format. Dollar General had avoided the fate of Korvette and so many other retailers who had adhered to the wheel of retailing and were crushed.

W. T. Grant viewed sales maximization as its ultimate objective. Even though W. T. Grant maintained a very high sales level, it still plunged into bankruptcy. Profitable sales, and not just sales volume, are a much broader organizational goal that escaped management at W. T. Grant. Emphasis should have been on total business management of merchandise assortments, costs, target markets, and even volume goals in delineated categories.

The economic environment is of critical importance to retailers because economic periods of prosperity, recession, and recovery and other economic factors as inflation, disinflation, or the value of the dollar relative to the currency of foreign competitors have a tremendous impact on prices. Economic changes require substantial marketplace adaptation within the same organization over time. Kresge made this adaptation with the birth of Kmart. Woolworth spawned Woolco but blurred its image with consumers by offering similar price lines and merchandise in both Woolworth and Woolco stores. A price focus strategy was needed for the Woolco division, while Woolworth stores needed to remain on the same track. In addition, Woolco received stepchild treatment from the parent company. Insufficient resources were allocated for the development of the new Woolco division.

McCrory committed all of its resources to sustaining the five-and-ten concept. Kress, Murphy's, Neisner's, and other variety store chains were acquired and operated within the five-and-dime framework. But McCrory did not shift to a cost/price focus strategy, as did Dollar General and those stores selling merchandise for only $1. McCrory failed to realize that competitive forces had changed. Kmart and Wal-Mart, Dollar General, and the $1 stores all seized a part of the variety store market share. Through scrambled merchandising, supermarkets sold school supplies and other paper products, discounters sold toys and apparel, and even drugstores sold health and beauty aids, low-priced toys, and school supplies. McCrory had not adapted to the changed competitive environment.

CONTROVERSIAL DECISIONS

Basically, there are five growth strategies for retailers to consider:

1. Increase the number of store outlets in presently served markets.
2. Add to the merchandise assortment new product lines for presently served markets.
3. Enter new markets with the existing store format.
4. Diversify with new store formats or store acquisitions.
5. Any combination of the above strategies.

The first three strategies involve challenges to retail management that direct themselves to either the existing merchandise assortment, existing markets, or both. Top echelon management typically make decisions to diversify. The least heralded and probably the hardest retail management decision to pursue is to remain in the core business.

Dollar General is a very visible core retailer. Overall, after a brief unsuccessful departure from the old five-and-dime concept, Dollar General returned to its core business. Its strategic positioning has remained steady and on course. Dollar General, although serving a diminishing market, has been remarkably successful. One of its keys to success has been a higher degree of commitment to this focused strategy than its competitors.

The Kresge organization gradually phased out its five-and-ten stores and, with Kmart, developed a new store format. With an eye to the future, management realized that the five-and-ten concept had reached its maturity and that a new retail organizational format was vital to satisfy emerging customer needs. Retail history has demonstrated that there is a retail life cycle where mature retail formats eventually decline.

The Ben Franklin stores remained for the most part in the core five-and-ten business. Emphasis on location in small towns in strategic sites helped to avoid direct competition with the discounters. Location segmentation also helped to retain a loyal customer following. An analogy can be made to the A & P organization, which, while doing poorly in urban and suburban markets, managed to retain its profitability in small towns. Location strategies stressing site segmentation in communities is paramount in retail decision making.

The McCrory organization, by acquiring other five-and-tens such as J. J. Newberry and Kress, broadened its merchandise assortment. However, its location strategy was flawed. McCrory stores were situated in many decayed urban areas that had fire, theft, and insurance problems. McCrory did not grasp not only that the retail life cycle of growth, accelerated development, and decline was operating but that the loyal customer base of the five-and-ten concept in urban areas had gradually vanished. Retail management was misled by bottom-line results supported by low rental leases. But when these low-cost leases expired, higher rentals and higher fire, theft, and insurance costs took their toll in lower profits.

The Woolworth organization chose diversification as its basic strategy. Retail business formats such as the Foot Locker and Kinney Shoe have been profitable. Woolworth tried to develop Woolco, a discount format similar to Kmart, but blurred its image by carrying similar merchandise offered by the Woolworth five-and-tens. Woolworth lacked commitment to innovate with its five-and-tens and also found its loyal customer base diminished in urban areas where many of its stores were situated. Woolworth was unwilling to stay the course with its target market.

W. T. Grant endeavored to serve an upscale market. Once again, a management team had blurred its stores' image and precipitated the organization's downfall. Decisions to radically modify its merchandise assortment with major appliances and other merchandise lines were inconsistent with the store's original positioning. A management obsession with growth overshadowed prudent merchandising and location strategies and led to disastrous results.

Strategic retail planning begins with the firm monitoring its environment. The retailer's environment is in a perpetual state of change with new opportunities and threats developing. Shifts in the retailing environment have caused—and will continue to cause—many shocks and surprises for merchants. The old five-and-tens were forced to decide if they should redefine their target market by limiting store outlets to their best markets served, adjust their product offerings in varying degrees, or leave a shrinking market entirely. Controversial decisions involve not only a future orientation but a commitment to the implementation and control of strategic decisions.

CHAPTER 4

Supermarkets: Competitive Victims

Strategies in a Mature Market
- Cost focus
- Use of modern technology
- New business formats: superstores, warehouse, no-frills stores
- Financial productivity
- Consumer affairs orientation
- Price competition
- Shift to nonprice variables
- Total customer satisfaction
- Core geographical market segmentation

Supermarket Mistakes
- Overreliance on price competition
- Lack of store modernization
- Lack of strong consumer-oriented images
- Status quo mentality
- Weak store positioning

A supermarket is a comprehensive departmentalized food store featuring a narrow breadth and width of assortment of not only food products but nonfood products as well. The basic strategy of the supermarket has been to offer items purchased on the basis of impulse buying, low prices, and self-service. Supermarkets offer such nonfood items as small appliances, housewares, auto accessories, and even prescription drugs and flowers. In recent years, supermarkets have expanded their offerings of generic products. Supermarket chains account for approximately 60 percent of food volume sales. Supermarkets generally offer few services, but a little more than convenience stores, and make heavy use of promotional media.

A conventional supermarket consists of approximately 20,000 square feet, offers about 10,000 items, and has sales around $1 million or more a year. Competition in the food industry is causing supermarket organizations to adopt new strategies. One challenge to the supermarket industry is that it is oversaturated with competitors such as Safeway, A & P, Kroger, American Stores, Winn-Dixie, Giant Food, and Weis. Another challenge is that various types of institutions (hypermarkets, deep-discount drugstores, supercenters, warehouse stores, gourmet shops, health food stores, and convenience stores) are taking away market share. Some supermarket organizations have reduced costs and emphasized low prices by offering more store brands, generic products, bulk packs of nonperishables, and fewer customer services. Other supermarket organizations have expanded their store size and product assortments by offering more nonfood merchandise lines, by targeting ethnic groups with special food lines, and by offering service departments such as pharmacies and banking services.

The supermarket was the first large-scale retail institution to sell merchandise by using such strategies as impulse buying, the promotion of national brands, and customer self-service. The supermarket structure has served as a model for retailers in such specialty lines as Toys "R" Us in toys, Levitz in furniture, and Herman's in sporting goods. Eventually, the supermarket was able to develop its own private-label brands in competition with national, regional, and local manufacturer brands. Private-label brands were once regarded as somewhat inferior in quality to national brands, but they have made extraordinary inroads in market share in the 1980s and early 1990s.

In considering supermarket failures, even the most successful organization has made mistakes but can and does survive as long as factors such as innovation, target market and image, physical environmental resources, and human resources contribute more frequently to success and only infrequently result in failure. Innovation in the supermarket industry occurred years ago when Piggly Wiggly introduced self-service, and King Kullen scrambled merchandising. The introduction of new business formats such as superstores, warehouse stores, box stores as developed by Jewel T and Aldi, and convenience stores as developed by 7-Eleven have served as viable innovations.

Factors such as target market and image have been sharply developed by Food Lion, Weis, and Giant Food. Food Lion has developed a cost-focus approach and is perceived as a discounter by its target market. Weis serves midsize cities and carefully selects locations where it can dominate the trading area. Giant Food was the first large chain to offer unit pricing, open dating, and fish labeling and is perceived as a very consumer-oriented affairs chain by its target market.

In the early days of supermarkets, both A & P and Kroger used vertical integration to strengthen physical environmental resources. Even though A & P has stumbled, its physical integration, which manifested itself with the development of store-label brands, has sustained this organization. The use of new technology has helped American Stores especially with their Jewel and Lucky Store divisions to maintain a competitive advantage.

Safeway, in an effort to regain lost market share, has hired executives outside the supermarket industry to give a fresh perspective and approach to a stagnating organization. Safeway's investment in physical resources such as superstore formats has sustained it, and its investment in human resources has advanced the organization. Safeway broke the tradition of the supermarket industry of promotion from within by hiring executives of pharmacies, delicatessens, health food departments, liquor stores, and the nongrocery enterprises to develop and operate these departments.

Supermarkets are competitive victims inasmuch as the market is oversaturated. Low margins, the high cost of new technology, and higher labor rates have contributed to supermarket problems. But more than anything else, the competition from discount stores, convenience stores, new business formats, and supermarkets themselves has caused contraction in the industry. As competition has intensified, the struggle for mere survival has become a challenge. In response to this challenge, Winn-Dixie has introduced home delivery in selected areas. Moreover, the fastest growth in on-line debit cards continues to be in the supermarket industry.

SUPERMARKET RETAILING: YESTERDAY

A & P was founded in 1859 as the Great American Tea Company by George Gilmer and George Huntington Hartford and originally had been a tea wholesaler. By 1869, the name was changed to the Great Atlantic and Pacific Tea Company, and a line of groceries was added to be sold to the public. In 1912, small stores were opened that were primarily one-person operations with modest fixtures and situated in low-rent locations. Dry groceries were the only merchandise line—meat, produce, and dairy products were not offered.

The Grand Union Company, under the name of Jones Brothers Tea Company, was founded in 1872, and the Kroger Company followed in 1882. Safeway was founded in 1915 as a proprietorship and became incorporated in 1926.

The term *supermarket* was first used in the 1930s. The emergence of the supermarket in food distribution was contingent on low prices, high volume, and the development of technologies such as the cash register, mass communications, packaging and refrigeration, and the automobile. Self-service retailing in food retailing was introduced by Clarence Saunders in Memphis, Tennessee, in 1912 in his Piggly Wiggly stores. Michael Cullen implemented the self-service concept in supermarkets in the beginning of the 1930s.

The large chains were slow to develop supermarkets. The A & P in 1936 had only 20 supermarkets. Net profits were higher for the supermarket than for the small-chain grocery store. The chains were able to realize cost savings by closing three or four small grocery stores in a community and opening a supermarket, usually located in a low-rent area, but with ample parking facilities. Since only one store manager was needed, salary expenses were also reduced.

Prior to the development of the supermarket concept in the early 1930s, consumers made daily trips to the neighborhood grocery store to purchase small quantities of groceries and to replenish such items as milk and bread. Purchases were made through a salesclerk who suggested specific items and obtained the merchandise from the shelves for the customer. Small stores might offer credit and home delivery. In sharp contrast, the supermarket eliminated such services and offered lower prices.

Present-day supermarkets are planned for maximum efficiency. The sales and profitability of each item are analyzed from checkout scanners, and floor space is allocated accordingly. Supermarkets have continued to evolve, and new forms of supermarkets are now present.

Since 1859, the Great Atlantic and Pacific Tea Company, more commonly known as the A & P, has been to food retailing what Sears, Roebuck was to catalogs and what Woolworth used to be to variety store retailing. It was not until the 1960s that many problems began to plague A & P. Originally A & P entered the marketplace as a discounter of tea, coffee, and spices. It was not until 1869 that retail branches were established. The original stores were gaudy beyond belief, with a facade done in Chinese vermilion and gold leaf. In 1878, the chain adopted a more conservative decor, and more than 100 stores were located in such metropolitan areas as New York, Philadelphia, Baltimore, St. Louis, and St. Paul. By 1900, A & P had about 200 stores situated around the country and established a series of wagon routes to cover the rural areas. A & P at this time offered customers S & H green stamps, free deliveries, charge accounts, and premiums.

In response to an upsurge in the cost of living, A & P in 1912 returned to its discount structure. Services such as home delivery and charge accounts and promotional giveaways such as trading stamps and premiums were eliminated. These new A & Ps became known as *economy stores* and were located in extremely accessible locations. This expansion continued until 1936 when the emerging supermarket format became a serious threat to A & P.

B. H. Kroger had only a few years' experience as a grocery clerk when, at the age of 22, he decided to open a grocery store in 1882. His Great Western Tea Company made a profit in its first year of operation. In pre-supermarket times, chain stores and independents alike were small neighborhood corner grocery stores that offered credit and delivery service. These stores carried a limited selection of dry grocery items. Meat, produce, and dairy departments were not offered. In contrast to the independents, the chains offered improved management skills and expertise, which stimulated growth. The Great Western Tea Company's rate of expansion was slow initially, but by 1902, there were 36 stores and its name was changed to the Kroger Grocery and Baking Company. By 1930, Kroger had approximately 5,200 stores and was second only in size to A & P, which had about 15,700 stores. Like A & P, Kroger was vertically integrated with its own bakery, coffee-roasting, meat-packing, milk, and warehousing facilities.

The American Stores Company's development was based on mergers and acquisitions. Before the supermarket prototype emerged in the 1930s, H. C. Bohack (1887) of Brooklyn, New York, Gristede Brothers (1891) of New York, National Tea (1899) of Chicago, Ralph's Grocery Company (1873) of Los Angeles, J. Weingarten (1901) of Houston, and First National Stores of New England (1926) were added to the chain. American Stores, however, was slow to change over to the supermarket format. Even by 1941, American Stores was not a serious competitive threat in the supermarket field. Significant acquisitions added Jewels Companies in 1984 and Lucky Stores in 1988. Today, American Stores is primarily a holding company that operates units in 35 states under various names.

Frank V. Skiff in 1899 with a horse, wagon, and $700 established a coffee route. Spices, tea, and other staple groceries were also carried. In 1901, the Jewel Tea Company was officially established. Jewel developed its chain store organization by acquiring 77 Loblaw Stores in Chicago and 4 in the Midwest in 1932. By 1936, Jewel had about 100 stores in operation. Jewel was built on the policy of trusting a customer with an "advanced premium," which set the company apart from competitors and contributed substantially to its early success. To illustrate, the housewife was offered part of a china set on the condition that purchasing would continue. Premium coupons were given and used to purchase the complete set. Although the retail stores were a substantial source of Jewel's future sales volume, the chain was developed through home service by operating a number of routes with horse and wagon.

The forerunner of the supermarket was the Piggly Wiggly chain founded by Clarence Saunders in 1916. These stores were small self-service groceries with open merchandise displays in which customers carried over-the-arm baskets that they received as they entered the single U-shaped aisle that led to the checkout register. This arrangement facilitated self-service, but these stores were probably too small for efficient use of the self-service concept. Many chains such as Kroger and Safeway opened Piggly Wiggly franchises. Numerous imitators such as Handy Andy and Jitney Jungle also entered the market. Although Clarence Saunders came upon hard financial times and lost control of the organization, Piggly Wiggly is still a supermarket operation and still franchises its units.

Interestingly, until 1930, Michael Cullen had worked for Kroger. Cullen offered the president of Kroger a proposal outlining the concept and operation of a new kind of food store (the supermarket) with a focus on low prices, larger square footage, cash sales, no delivery service, and low-rent locations with ample parking. In his proposal, Cullen maintained that he could achieve nearly ten times the volume and profits of an average A&P. Kroger's management rejected Cullen's proposal, and Cullen subsequently resigned.

Michael Cullen is generally credited with introducing the supermarket concept into food retailing in the 1930s. The supermarket concept advanced the fundamentals of low prices supported by high volume, self-service, large product assortments, and free and ample parking. However, this concept was easily imitated, and by the end of the decade, the chains made a successful transition to the supermarket structure and the King Kullen stores had lost their competitive advantage.

The King Kullen stores were situated in abandoned factories and warehouses, in low-rent locations on the borders of populated areas. Facilities were simple. Service was minimal. Shopping carts were used, and national

over 50 percent are from ages 25 to 54, over 20 percent shop between 11 P.M. and 7 A.M., over 80 percent live or work less than one mile from the store, and about one third of purchases are made on weekends. The number of convenience stores has just about doubled since 1975. 7-Eleven has shared in this growth, and the potential for future growth is still present.

PLANNING A RETAIL STRATEGY

Competitive structure theories are helpful in understanding the development and evolution of supermarkets and planning a future retail strategy. Among these theories are the wheel of retailing and the dialectic process.

The wheel explanation states that new types of retailers enter the market as low-status and low-margin institutions. These institutions are located in less convenient locations (saving on land purchases or leases), offer few services, and are inexpensively furnished. As these institutions mature, they gradually develop into institutions offering many services, acquire more elaborate facilities, feature higher prices, and carry merchandise lines that convey higher status. Discount houses and supermarkets are examples of these kinds of institutions. Vending machines, home video ordering systems, the growth of branch department stores, and the rise of suburban shopping centers are exceptions to the wheel hypothesis.

The Great Atlantic and Pacific Tea Company emerged as a discount seller of tea in 1859 and developed according to the wheel hypothesis. By 1900, A & P offered many customer services and had become much like its traditional competitors. The cost of living accelerated greatly, and in 1912, A & P turned into a traditional retailer until the 1930s when the supermarket developed. A & P reentered the market as a low-price institution.

As retail institutions develop, additional product lines are carried and more distribution outlets are added to provide greater access to the goods and services. When combined with the theory of competition for differential advantage, the wheel explanation appears to offer an understanding of the evolution of food chains and some other forms of retailing.

The dialectic process is a "melting pot" theory of retail institutional change in which two substantially different forms of retailing merge into a new institution of retailing. To illustrate the dialectic process, the supermarket would represent the established institutional form (referred to as the *thesis*). The box and warehouse stores would represent the innovative institutional form (known as the *antithesis*), and the superstore would represent the new form, which is a composite of the original two forms (or the *synthesis*).

The dialectic theory is offered as an alternative to the wheel-of-retailing theory. Dialectic theory applied to retailing is a development of Hegel's philosophy, the law of logical development, which stated that any idea by the very nature of things negates itself. Soon the original idea is combined with its negatism and called the antithesis. Eventually, the original idea and its negated form become indistinguishable and form a synthesis, which is then vulnerable to repeating the process. The dialectic process was tested and has been offered as an explanation of the retail evolution of department stores, service stations, supermarkets, and drive-in restaurants. These authors further maintain that the dialectic process is a comprehensive strategic tool applicable to the development of newer institutions in retailing since it focuses on mutual adaptations in terms of offerings, services, and prices that occur at all levels of the structure. The wheel-of-retailing theory would better explain past formations in retailing, but the dialectic process appears more useful in explaining recent developments in retailing relating to changes in supermarket structure.

One characteristic of retail supermarket competition is its local-market orientation. Whether or not the supermarket is a member of a large chain, it must attract customers from local-market areas. Supermarkets are in competition with national, regional, and local outlets situated in the same markets. Consequently, supermarket management needs to be more concerned about local competition in individual markets than competition at national levels.

Retail sales are generally more concentrated at local levels than at national levels. Usually, two or three supermarkets command a large share of the total food sales in an area. Many of these two or three organizations have many store units in the same market area to achieve market penetration. Their size gives these large firms many competitive advantages over smaller competitors situated in the same location. The level of competition among these large organizations is very intense. Price reductions or promotions such as double couponing are quickly responded to by the other competitors.

Local-market competition reduces the value of analyzing national supermarket competition. Each market must be examined separately since market share could vary significantly from locality to locality. In developing strategies, supermarket management must analyze and respond to local competition.

Discount department and drugstores have used scrambled merchandising to their advantage by selling more packaged foods. Many fast-food restaurants continue to offer a larger variety of prepared foods for takeout. Wholesale clubs have been effective at competing with conventional supermarkets.

Competitive dimensions related to merchandise offerings concern the freshness and quality of meats and produce and the availability of branded grocery items. There are a number of other types of food stores that have eroded the market share of supermarkets. These other food store forms include various kinds of superstores. The superstore would appear to be a viable innovation in the distribution structure for food, specialty foods,

STRATEGIES TO COUNTER COMPETITION: SELECTED SUPERMARKET ORGANIZATIONS

The supermarket organization that adheres only to traditional competitive strategies will find itself in trouble as food retailing grows more complex. Scrambled merchandising, with restaurants selling take-out food, drugstores selling packaged foods, and discount organizations selling more items that are sold in supermarkets, presents ominous threats. Wholesale clubs and membership stores will also take some share of the market away from supermarkets. Supermarkets have added prepared foods to their merchandise assortment to reduce the threat posed by fast-food restaurants. Moreover, numerous services have been added, including dry cleaning, banking, dental, and legal services, in order to attract more customers. Nonfood items such as prescription drugs, flowers, greeting cards, and housewares have successfully increased sales and profits. Even A & P has come out of its doldrums and lethargy by acquiring a number of regional chains, including Super Fresh, Kohl's Food Stores, Family Mart, Shopwell, and Waldbaums. Nearly 500 stores were closed between 1980 and 1983. New superstores and warehouse stores were opened, and existing stores were remodeled to feature delis, on-premise bakeries, and large meat and fish departments.

FOOD LION: A COST-FOCUS STRATEGY

Food Lion is the fastest-growing supermarket chain in the United States and also the most profitable. The strategy at Food Lion is to compete on a cost leadership basis with no-frills stores and low prices. After a precarious beginning in 1957, Food Lion decided to become a discount-oriented supermarket.

Food Lion, with headquarters in Salisbury, North Carolina, is primarily based in eight southeastern states but expanding rapidly into Pennsylvania and Texas. The company sells basic groceries at low prices and many items at cost such as baby food, cat food, dog food, and detergents. Food Lion has become to the supermarket industry what Wal-Mart has become to discount organizations.

The continued development of Food Lion distribution centers serves as the basis for expansion. Four new centers were completed at the end of 1987. By 1992, the number of distribution centers grew to ten, and the number of stores to over 1,000. Food Lion stores range from 25,000 to 29,000 square feet and are slightly smaller than the average supermarket. Conventional supermarkets stock 20,000 items as opposed to approximately 15,000 for Food Lion.

The Food Lion philosophy is to keep operational tactics simple. Every job is clearly defined, from bagger and cashier to produce and store manager. Distribution, buying, and pricing are centralized. The stores are decorated simply, and the prices are lower than competitors'. New stores are added to an existing market area, which Food Lion calls the *ink blot* formula. This has the impact of complete saturation of a market. Food Lion would rather build its own stores according to its own specifications than purchase existing stores. In keeping with its philosophy of keeping things simple, Food Lion has used banana boxes for storage purposes rather than expensive plastic bins and also repairs old grocery carts instead of purchasing new ones.

Food Lion in 1986 received the Martin Luther King, Jr., Award in recognition of its humanitarian efforts. Food Lion received the award for contributing trucks to aid southeastern farmers during a prolonged drought. Food Lion has also been recognized for providing equal opportunity employment and establishing express lanes for handicapped consumers. However, in 1991, the United Food & Commercial Workers International Union and 182 current and former Food Lion employees filed a complaint with the Labor Department, charging the company with wage and hour violations involving employees working off the clock without overtime compensation. Union-free Food Lion denies the charges, which to date are unresolved.

More recently, in November 1992, the ABC News *PrimeTime Live* television show alleged the improper handling of food at Food Lion stores. Initially, Food Lion's president and chief executive officer (CEO) Tom E. Smith accused ABC of taking hidden-camera footage that appeared to show employees repackaging food so they could sell it after its expiration dates. The company followed up with television commercials stressing the cleanliness of stores and stringent testing of employees to make sure they are following corporate policies.

AMERICAN STORES: A TECHNOLOGY LOVE AFFAIR

According to its 1990 annual report, American Stores consists of 270 Acme Markets, 213 Jewel Food Stores, 32 Star Markets, 75 Skaggs Alpha Beta, 5 Jewel Osco Stores, 503 Osco Drug Stores, 178 Sav-on Stores, 412 Lucky Stores, and 160 Alpha Beta Stores. This organization endeavors to maintain a competitive advantage by heavily investing in new technology including scanning, direct store delivery, labor scheduling, and inventory control systems. The direct store delivery system automatically receives, verifies, records, and pays for all merchandise and products delivered by outside vendors with minimum involvement of store personnel. The labor usage system has been structured to match employee schedules with peak customer traffic. American Stores is currently developing more superstores instead of conventional supermarkets.

Jewel Food was a leader in responding to the consumer movement. Jewel

tities of all active ingredients in nonprescription drugs and in all health and beauty aids carrying the Giant label, open dating, and care labeling, which helps the customer take better care of the product after the purchase. Giant has also been ahead of the competition in nutrition labeling. Giant pleased consumer advocates by stating a product's nutrients in units of ten rather than in percentages. The chain has also taken the lead in percentage-of-ingredients labeling in petitioning the government to establish definite guidelines.

Giant Food has a very aggressive promotion program. This includes eight to ten food one-half price specials and six to eight drug items each week, plus one-third-off specials on approximately ten grocery, drug, and frozen food items each week. Superspecials of one-third off are featured in the delicatessen, meat, bakery, and produce departments. Superdeals are offered on national and private-label broads at prices found only at membership warehouse stores. Moreover, over 2,500 schools participate in the Giant Food Apples for the Student program, which awards free computers, peripherals, and software for receipt tapes.

Giant Food is one of the leaders in the supermarket industry to implement strategies that have reflected new trends. These new strategies include a fresh-prepared food emphasis, an emphasis on perishables, in-store demonstrations and samplings, Sunday openings, an increased nonfoods emphasis, and more customer services. New and expanded divisions include pharmacies and florist departments. Moreover, Giant has constructed more superstores that have higher productivity ratios than conventional supermarkets.

Many supermarkets are offering seafood and bakery departments that have low profitability. Shifting competitive strategies seems to offer less emphasis on price and more on service, variety, and quality. The degree of price competition will depend on market area location. Although most supermarkets try to lower prices, there are only a few like Food Lion who are able to offer significantly lower prices than the rest of the industry.

A & P: NEW BUSINESS FORMATS

A & P has gained a variety of store formats with its acquisitions and increased profitability. A & P's net return on sales of 1.32 percent is much larger by comparison of 0.71 percent of average supermarket chains in 1990. Dominant market share has been achieved by buying up strong, family-owned regional supermarket chains such as Waldbaum/Food Mart with 140 units, Shopwell/Food Emporium with 53 units, Dominion Stores with 93 units, Eagle Stores with 11 units, and Pantry Pride with 20 units. These acquisitions have helped A & P achieve dominance in the East. More recently, Bormans', which operates as Farmer Jack, has been acquired in Detroit.

A & P has replaced the existing accounting system with one that gives management 50 percent more information than it had previously. A & P has also held store managers accountable for profitability. A & P has reduced costs by centralizing operations even though store divisions retain considerable merchandising autonomy. For example, warehousing facilities were consolidated in Canada after Dominion was acquired. In New York, purchasing and administrative costs were reduced because of shared personnel and facilities among A & P, Food Emporium, and Walbaum units.

A & P has also invested heavily in Sav-A-Center promotional superstores. A & P has also formulated plans to develop Futurestore upscale superstore outlets that will offer better-quality and higher-priced groceries than either conventional supermarkets or existing superstores. A & P is also investing very heavily in technology that will further reduce costs and provide better-quality information.

COMPETITIVE ADVANTAGE DIMENSIONS

The concept of differential advantage explains much of the dynamics of the supermarket industry. A & P, for a great many years, competed with a cost leadership strategy that appealed to a broad market. Later, A & P offered the "Where economy originates" (WEO) program of low prices but was unable to lower operating costs effectively. Food Lion has used a cost-focus strategy that appeals to a limited target market through low prices. Through operating efficiencies, Food Lion is able to control costs. So far, this strategy has enabled Food Lion to be an above-average performer in the industry. Giant Food has used a differentiation strategy by appealing to a broader market than Food Lion with services and products viewed as quite distinctive. Safeway assumed a cost leadership strategy through economies of scale and by superior management of new specialized departments, which helped to neutralize the strategies of A & P and American Stores.

LESSONS LEARNED FROM SUCCESS AND FAILURE

The reliance on price as a competitive weapon will diminish as the use of technology, such as supermarket scanners, provides management with better data on profitability. Price promotion will remain a significant variable, but emphasis will shift to nonprice variables such as product assortment and customer service. The goal will be total customer satisfaction. Competitive tracking and monitoring through market research to identify service gaps will become increasingly important in competitive environments. Market segmentation strategies will become more important in the future.

The dialectic process appears to offer an explanation for development

This may take the form of upscale and discount food stores targeted to precise consumer segments. Other food stores may try to develop a home shopping network that has been made possible by technological developments.

Fundamental to these lessons learned from success and failure in the supermarket industry are two paramount factors: management vision and how well change is managed.

MANAGING CHANGE

The evolution of A & P demonstrates the role of managerial vision—a vision that saw A & P branch out from its pre–Civil War location and go into a wide variety of food lines. Another vision saw the move into economy stores prior to World War I. Moreover, during the depression, thousands of A & P stores were closed, and A & P was transformed into a supermarket chain. It was the lack of this continued management vision by succeeding management that diminished the effectiveness of the A & P chain.

A & P was unable to respond effectively to the emergence of regional chains and local enterprises that could segment local markets. Many of these competitors not only were able to offer superior product assortments for these local markets but, because of economies of scale, also were able to offer lower prices. A & P did react positively to the King Kullen supermarket threat. Instead of perceiving this structural change as only temporary or a fad, A & P could envision that this competitive threat might prove to be disastrous. A & P had maintained only one-year leases for its unit stores and consequently was able to successfully implement the new supermarket structure.

The supermarket industry must respond to such forces as slow market growth, the growth of branded goods, increasing costs, and new forms of food institutions. Food retailers are confronted with increased competition from similar stores and from other types of stores that sell the same merchandise. Even take-out food sold at restaurants has taken away market share from the supermarket industry. Food retailers must focus on competition at the local level when designing marketing strategies. Price, location, and store atmosphere and service are three areas for food retailers to differentiate and try to gain a competitive advantage.

CONTROVERSIAL DECISIONS

Controversial decisions in the supermarket industry in the previous decade have focused on the concept of differential advantage and the development of different types of food stores to satisfy changing consumer consumption patterns. A supermarket organization can avoid direct competition by providing unique benefits to the marketplace. Giant Food has chosen to bring unique benefits to the marketplace by implementation of a fresh-food emphasis and in-store demonstrations. Expanded divisions include pharmacies and florist departments. The concept of developing a differentiation strategy with moderate cost in an industry noted for its oversaturation of supermarkets in numerous geographical markets is not an easy task.

Food Lion, in contrast, has been able to mitigate the effects of competition through its low-cost position. Consequently, Food Lion has been able to assume a strategy of overall cost leadership in the supermarket industry. The nature of the target market for Food Lion might vary from the market segment for conventional supermarkets. The structural nature of Food Lion, due in part to its distribution centers, reduces the possibility of the imitation of other supermarket chains.

Conventional supermarkets are confronted with intense competition from other types of food stores. Some of these conventional supermarket chains have made decisions to develop new forms of food stores in order to effectively compete. For example, Safeway has developed superstores. Jewel has developed box stores.

Inasmuch as new warehouse stores such as Cub Foods (Super Value) and Food 4 Less (Fleming Corporation) have been developed to appeal to one-stop food shoppers, conventional supermarkets need to respond to these changing patterns. A & P has responded with the Sun Food Market. However, there is an imminent danger of cannibalism of sales present.

Controversial decisions involve risk as the competitive positions of the larger chains deteriorate. There is a growing necessity to rapidly adapt to environmental or competitive changes or be confronted with the danger of financial disaster, no matter how established or dominant the supermarket chain had been in the past. The continuity of traditional successful practices will not sustain conventional supermarket chains. The degree of responsiveness to environmental and competitive change will determine the success or failure of the conventional supermarket chains. Jewel, for example, has developed many innovations under varying degrees of uncertainty such as the development of superstores, the franchise of smaller stores, the development of joint food and drug stores, and the opening of additional merchandise drugstores. Controversial decisions involve risk and innovations.

Discount stores have not been very successful in either the past or the present. Such organizations as White Front, Woolco, J. C. Penney Treasure Island Stores, Allied's Almart, Arlen's, Giant Stores of New England, Mammoth Mart, Parkview Gems, and Zayre, all discounters, have departed for one reason or another. Other discounters, such as Ames, Nichols, Bradlees, and Lechmere, are experiencing varying degrees of difficulties. Only Wal-Mart and Kmart have had outstanding success stories. Target, an upscale discounter, has found its market niche and does well serving this market, but Target does not compete head-to-head with Wal-Mart or Kmart. The scenario of Korvette, its early success and its later failure, provides many insights into the competitive marketing strategies of the discounters. Based upon past history, it is possible that Wal-Mart may be repeating some of the errors of Zayre's.

The general merchandise discount stores represented by Kmart, Wal-Mart, and Target incorporate a low-cost, high-volume, low-markup, fast-turnover operation that extends limited customer services. Merchandise assortments offer considerable breadth and depth with average- to good-quality goods. These discounters are sometimes referred to as *mass merchandisers* and are stripped-down, low-cost versions of the old-fashioned department store with a much greater merchandise assortment. Discounters make purchases in high quantities frequently direct from manufacturers and provide a no-frills, self-service environment. Both store and national brands are featured. Apparel departments do not necessarily provide trendy fashions. Instead, casual clothes, undergarments, and sports apparel are offered. When shopping for clothing items, shoppers need to look closely to find value and bargains.

It is likely that specialty category discounters such as Home Depot, Toys "R" Us, and Circuit City will grow dramatically in the future. However, the general merchandise discounters may not fare so well. The greatest competitive threats to discounters are strong intertype competition from

Eugene Ferkauf in the early 1950s assembled a group of 38 men, almost all of whom were Brooklyn high school friends of Ferkauf, to operate the company. This hiring approach had both advantages and limitations. In the long run, the limitations overshadowed the advantages. Many of Ferkauf's friends lacked the talent to direct activities as high-level retail executives. Ferkauf, in many respects, was blinded by friendship, and this was to be detrimental to successful operation of the business.

Over 30 state fair trade lawsuits were pending against Korvette when the company went public in 1955. Led by General Electric and other major manufacturers who desired to protect their conventional dealers from price cutting, Korvette became vulnerable to lawsuits. Manufacturers were prepared to resort to legal measures that would allow them to establish minimum prices for which their goods could be sold by retailers. This power struggle between Korvette and the manufacturers proved expensive. However, since there were few severe penalties for violating fair trade laws, Korvette did not really feel threatened.

By 1966, it became apparent that Korvette was unable to cope with its overexpansion of retail units and also had failed in its repositioning effort to upgrade its image. Korvette had developed a three-year expansion program, begun in 1962. As a result, the organization consisted of five stores in Chicago, three in Detroit, two in St. Louis, four in the Baltimore-Washington area, five in Philadelphia, and ten in the Metropolitan New York area. Korvette also developed a supermarket operation that management had little experience in and virtually no knowledge of how to operate. After adding over 20 supermarkets to the organization, a merger took place with Hill Supermarkets, a 42-unit Long Island, New York, chain. Experiencing heavy losses, Korvette sold the food division in 1968.

Korvette unsuccessfully attempted to change its image from that of a discount chain to a promotional department store chain. In accord with this new strategy, a new store was opened on Fifth Avenue in New York. The building was completely modernized with new show windows, a double set of escalators, all-new fluorescent and incandescent lighting using elaborate lighting fixtures, carpeted floors, and new display fixtures. Korvette, in short, resembled the traditional department stores that it once competed against. Financial ratios were ominous. Stock turnover decreased from about 11 to 7 times during the year. Sales per square foot of selling space declined from approximately $360 to $260. Markup margins increased from about 18 percent to 26 percent. In order to change its image completely, apparel and other soft goods, which afforded higher profit margins, were added to the merchandise assortment. Management found that apparel merchandising was more complex than merchandising appliances. Seasonal obsolescence presented high risks, and markdown practices were tricky. Some inventories became virtually unsalable due to accelerated fashion changes. Korvette executives were inexperienced in apparel merchandising, and therefore losses from this aspect of the operation were heavy.

Another problem that confronted Korvette was its furniture department. The furniture department was leased by the H. L. Klion Company. Klion was undercapitalized, and serious management problems regarding inventory control, accounting, and deliveries launched the company into a sea of red ink. Two labor strikes in 1964 ultimately caused customers to cancel $2 million worth of orders and further tarnished Korvette's image and reputation among consumers.

Finally, in 1966, Korvette was forced to merge with Spartans discount stores. Eugene Ferkauf was eased out of his management role, and a new chapter in Korvette history was to open. The lack of well-defined policies, objectives, strategic long-range plans, and controls was part of the reason for Korvette's downfall. Short-range plans regarding markups, markdowns, and merchandise turnover, especially in fashion merchandising, tarnished the image of Korvette. As well, customers were confused by the store's unclear market positioning. To consumers, Korvette was neither a discount house nor a viable, effective department store. Korvette thus found itself "stuck in the middle" with no sustainable competitive advantage and a blurred consumer image.

DISCOUNTERS: TODAY

Discount stores develop a differential advantage by pricing their merchandise lower than their competitors in order to attract price-sensitive shoppers. Kmart and Wal-Mart are full-line discounters that have very successfully followed this strategy. Ames and Zayre are examples of general discount stores that for various reasons have failed in the implementation of this strategy. Failures in the discount store category abound, while the survivors in the market are fewer and far between. Some successful discounters specialize in particular merchandise categories such as electronics. Crazy Eddie, The Wiz, Circuit City, and 47th Street Photo are some examples of cost-focused category killers that target a price-sensitive shopper in electronics merchandise lines by offering wide and deep assortments. As the brands these outlets sell are well known and widely available, price-sensitive customers patronize the store with the lowest price.

T. J. Maxx, Marshalls, and Syms are off-price apparel retailers who also follow price differentiation strategies. Branded or designer merchandise is offered at prices 30 to 40 percent below prevailing department store prices. Off-price outlets are typically located in freestanding locations along important suburban traffic arteries. Rentals are considerably less than at mall and downtown locations of competitors. Word-of-mouth communication is an important prepurchase information source, and like the electronics discounters, relatively spartan store interiors are maintained. Costs are fur-

Here was where Sears hoped to regain market share previously lost to the discounters.

Sears competes with discounters such as Kmart and Home Depot and also with specialty retailers like The Limited and The Gap. Sears' merchandise lines were divided into seven business units: home appliances and electronics, automotive supplies, home improvement products, home furnishings, and men's, women's, and children's apparel. This structure allows Sears to measure how profitable each category is in comparison to both discount and specialty competitors. Although improving, Sears is still far behind Wal-Mart and Kmart in cost control, information processing, distribution capabilities, and merchandising techniques. Sears' higher costs rule out a strategy based on cost leadership and low prices. Instead, Sears pursues a differentiation strategy.

Sears has, for example, moved into the area of financial services. The aim would seem to be to cultivate a market that because of time constraints desires not only a comprehensive merchandise assortment but also access to comprehensive financial services. Sears envisioned that a customer could purchase a home through its Coldwell Banker realty division, insure it through its Allstate Insurance division, and furnish the home through its retail stores. Sears had also moved into banking with its Discover credit card in 1986 and because of deregulated banking legislation aimed to convert its credit accounts into savings and checking accounts. In 1992, however, financial constraints caused Sears to largely abandon the financial services business units, and it is trying to divest itself of everything not retail, including Allstate, and concentrate on its primary business, which is retail stores.

J. C. PENNEY: AN EFFECTIVE COUNTERPUNCHER

During the 1960s and 1970s, J. C. Penney tried to establish a reputation in hard merchandise lines that would counter the strength of the discounters and Sears in this area. Accordingly, an alliance was formed with General Electric to sell its washers, dryers, and other appliances in its retail stores. This effort failed, and Penney discontinued its large appliances, its auto accessories department, and even children's toys in 1985. Instead, Penney refocused its efforts to selling apparel and household furnishings such as towels and sheets.

The Penney strategy was not to compete directly with the discounters but to establish a quality reputation in selling soft goods merchandise lines. The strategy was to offer private-label or store brands that would be as fashionable as national brands. The Penney Stafford line of men's suits was developed to compete with Botany, Palm Beach, and Cricketeer. A design/licensing contract was signed with Halston Enterprises to distribute fragrances and cosmetics to Penney stores. Household lines and bedding were

added under the brand names of Halston III, Lee Wright, and Kathy Hardwick. Furthermore, such national brands as Nike, Adidas, and Levi Strauss
were offered. Major appliances, paint and hardware, and lawn and garden
supplies were eliminated. This strategy not only provided additional floor
space for the expansion of apparel departments but also eliminated many
of the merchandise lines that competed directly with the discounters.

MONTGOMERY WARD: DEVELOPS NEW TURF

Montgomery Ward at one time was a clone of Sears. As such, it, too,
competed with the discounters but with little success. No longer under the
control of Mobil, Montgomery Ward has attempted to change from a general merchandise retailer to a specialty retailer. The new strategy attempts
to discard the image of a "me-too" Sears and also seeks to avoid direct
competition with the discounters. This repositioning effort led to the development of large departments in such important areas as appliances,
home furnishings, apparel, and auto parts. A new target market, composed
of younger, more affluent customers, has been selected. A store-within-a-
store strategy seems to have been developed successfully. However, Ward
is not competitive in such areas as cost control, distribution capabilities,
and merchandising skills.

Each of the mass merchants—Sears, Penney, and Ward—have tried to
avoid direct competition with the discounters. Penney appears to have been
the most successful in this task. Ward's has been moderately successful, but
Sears, unable to develop an image for selling fashion merchandise, has fared
poorly. The discounters have significantly eroded the market share of the
mass merchants. Cost control, distribution capabilities, and management
information systems have been weaknesses of the mass merchants and important strengths of the discounters. The discounters have maintained a
stable and clear-cut image in contrast to the mass merchants, who all went
through transition periods. Well-thought-out objectives, positioning, and
long-range planning and control are critical to developing successful retailing strategies. For retailing strategies to be effective, target market
segments must have clearly perceived images of the retailer regarding pricing, merchandise assortment, and services.

R. H. MACY AND ALEXANDER'S: THE DEFEATED

For some years, R. H. Macy promoted the reputation that it would not
be undersold and would match prices that customers obtained elsewhere.
Alexander's, a New York City department store chain, positioned itself as
a low-price or "bargain" department store. Between the general merchandise and specialty line discounters, the images of both Macy's and Alexander's became blurred. Macy's was all things to all people, and while this

and modernization, increased emphasis on pricing leadership, heavy investment in retail automation, and a pronounced focus on lifestyle departments. The company's marketing strategies target a broad customer base
from ages 22 to 55, with a family income between $35,000 and $55,000
a year. The point-of-sale (POS) scanning and satellite system initiated in
1986 allows for more accurate customer checkout, provides data for improved replenishment of merchandise, and therefore has helped make
Kmart more competitive.

Today, a parallel supercomputer helps store executives decide, with pre-
cision, when to cut prices, what to buy, and where to stock it. The supercomputer enables Kmart to gather data from every transaction in every
store for the past year or more. Sales data can be analyzed almost immediately in on-line searches. This information-processing capability can be
very helpful, for example, in targeting price reductions on certain products.
In the past, a slow-moving item might be marked down throughout the
Kmart chain. Today, markdowns will be taken only in those stores where
the item is known to be moving slowly. In addition, information gleaned
from parallel supercomputing can help management to redistribute items
from stores with slow sales to stores where the items are selling.

Kmart has been unable to match the sales productivity per square foot
of store space of Wal-Mart and is in danger of losing its low-price focus
appeal. As a result, Kmart will close about 110 stores, about 5 percent of
its discount stores, in 1995. In addition, by the end of 1996, the company
expects to reduce expenses by $800 million. Kmart has recognized that
these stores of about 40,000 square feet are too small to compete in today's
fierce competitive environment. New stores will average about 110,000
square feet and will be supercenters that combine grocery and discount
operations. Depending on competition, many of these supercenters may
remain open on a 24-hour basis. Kmart is divesting its specialty divisions
in favor of concentrating on its discount operations, which is viewed as a
positive strategy.

WAL-MART: A NEW CHAMPION

The first Wal-Mart store was opened in Rogus, Arkansas, by Sam and
Bud Walton. Two years later the next Wal-Mart store was opened in Har-
rison, Arkansas. Wal-Mart's development illustrates the risk-taking and pi-
oneering attitude that is demonstrated in its contemporary business
strategies. Wal-Mart's early beginnings were in markets where opportunity
was not as great as in contrast to the metropolitan markets where Kmart
units were established.

In October 1970, Wal-Mart stock was traded publicly over the counter.
In August 1972 it was listed on the New York Stock Exchange. There were
276 stores located in 11 states by 1979. Stores were primarily situated in

towns of 5,000 to 25,000 population. Average store size was 45,000 square feet. Wal-Mart opened its first major distribution center in 1978. Moreover, operations commenced for a Wal-Mart–owned pharmacy, auto service center, and jewelry divisions.

The 1980s were a new era of expansion for Wal-Mart. Stores were now situated in 24 states. By 1990, Wal-Mart had expanded to 34 states. First store openings were made in California, Nevada, North Dakota, South Dakota, Utah, and Pennsylvania. Wal-Mart by 1990 was no longer a southern-based discount chain but could be considered a national one with great growth potential. New store units averaged 100,000 square feet.

Wal-Mart's success can be traced to three important guiding fundamentals. The first relates to its employees. Each employee is called an *associate*. Employees are well motivated, there is high esprit de corps, and principles of teamwork are integrated into performance standards. Wal-Mart has been the most successful retailer in motivating employees.

The second fundamental is an extremely successful transportation and distribution system. More than 75 percent of incoming merchandise is received by 1 of 17 distribution centers within one day of the order, serving from 100 to 150 stores. The balance of merchandise is received by the individual store direct from the vendor within seven days of the initial order. A very sophisticated satellite communications system links Wal-Mart with suppliers. Parallel-processing supercomputers allow Wal-Mart's management to track the sales of every item in every store on a daily basis. This information can help managers know what items to mark down and what items to redistribute to other stores.

Finally, Wal-Mart uses a total-quality concept in managing executives and employees. The approach is unconventional in the retailing industry and has extraordinarily improved performance. Wal-Mart department heads are able to review financial figures such as costs, freight charges, and profit margins, which are typically not seen by their counterparts in other retail organizations. Wal-Mart has emphasized a commitment to recycling and promoting products that would improve the environment. The shopping experience is made as pleasant as possible for customers.

Wal-Mart has encountered a powerful and well-publicized antimovement in New England. In Massachusetts alone, communities such as Quincy, Plymouth, Sturbridge, Lee, Greenfield, and Westford have opposed new Wal-Mart store openings. Critics claim that tourism, small business, and other shopping malls will be adversely affected, causing job losses and business failures that would nullify any gains. Wal-Mart is pressing ahead but may need to modify existing strategies.

The April 5, 1992, death of Sam Walton, who built the Wal-Mart organization and who developed the guiding fundamentals that have been so successful, is bound to have a profound impact. Sam Walton was very effective at motivating employees. His merchandising vision will be missed by the Wal-Mart organization. No other merchant in the latter part of the twentieth century has been able to duplicate his merchandising successes.

TARGET AND MERVYN: COMPLEX POSITIONING

Target Stores is a division of Dayton Hudson Corporation and is the largest and most successful upscale discounter in the United States. Target operates more than 550 stores in 32 states, with a larger number of outlets in California, Indiana, Michigan, Minnesota, and Texas. The first Target store was established in 1962. Target's main emphasis is on basic merchandise—staple, everyday items with approximately one third devoted to fashion merchandise. Market segmentation and targeting strategies are directed to young, well-educated adults with children and above-average incomes. The lifestyles of this market segment include a desire for sporting goods, leisure clothes, and convenience appliances. This market segment perceives Target as a shopping alternative to conventional department stores, mass merchandising chains, as well as traditional discounters.

The typical Target outlet is approximately 100,000 square feet and derives 65 percent of its sales volume from housewares, toys, and white goods. Emphasis is placed on carrying brand-name merchandise and the cultivation of the midrange fashion market that competes with stores like J. C. Penney. Information-processing systems are constantly upgraded and are instrumental in the implementation of a tight inventory control system that generates complete sales histories of the merchandise that are far superior than competitors' systems. In the few locations where Wal-Mart and Target compete directly, Target has reported favorable results.

Mervyn's is another division of the Dayton Hudson Corporation. Although also a discount operation, it does not compete directly with Target since Mervyn's specializes in selling nationally branded and top-quality private-label active and casual apparel. Mervyn's consists of about 275 stores located in 15 states. Mervyn's merchandise assortments in children's wear are broader than most competitors' assortments. The Dayton Hudson organization was now able to broaden its geographical base with a California-situated chain. Mervyn's is a limited-service department store. Mervyn's is not really a discount chain but sells merchandise at reasonable prices, lower than many conventional department stores, but also offers fewer services than a conventional department store. Thus, the Dayton Hudson organization is using a strategy known as *store portfolio management*, whereby one company holds several marketplace positions in an attempt to stabilize the institutional movement described in the wheel-of-retailing hypothesis.

A STORE FAILURE: ZAYRE

When Kmart upgraded its image to serve higher-income customers in 1978, Zayre Stores remained with its traditional customer base and became one of the few discount chains to successfully cater to inner-city market segments with strong ethnic preferences. Chicago, by 1983, was Zayre Stores' largest market.

Zayre Stores, by 1985, had changed markedly. There were approximately 300 Zayre Stores, 150 T. J. Maxx units, and 400 Hit or Miss units, which were all divisions of the Zayre organization. T. J. Maxx was an off-price retail operation, and Hit or Miss focused on the somewhat conservative, youthful, career woman who was very fashion conscious but was on a limited budget. Hit or Miss lacked a distinctive image and was not successful.

Zayre also established BJ's wholesale club with a limited membership and Chadwicks, a direct-mail operation. Both of these operations did well in the beginning, but as these other areas of the Zayre organization expanded, the core discount business suffered from neglect.

The Zayre discount organization developed problems from inventory buildups, poor maintenance, technological obsolescence, and disastrous pricing strategies. Half of Zayre outlets were located in inner cities, and customers there had limited shopping alternatives. Other units were located in the suburbs and small towns. However, Kmart in the Northeast and Wal-Mart in the South were too-formidable competitors. When Wal-Mart and Kmart were installing electronic scanning devices at checkout counters and sophisticated inventory-control systems in 1985, Zayre was just beginning to investigate these innovations. By 1988, Ames acquired the discount department stores operated by Zayre. Although Zayre tried to shift its focus away from low-margin appliances and electronics to more profitable clothing, it was all too late.

Wal-Mart, too, is developing other retail formats such as supercenters. These superstores are not fairing as well as expected. With the death of Sam Walton, there is a danger that the core discount business may become neglected. Since Wal-Mart has retained its cost leadership strategy, this may effectively help the firm to avoid the mistakes of Zayre.

DISCOUNTERS: SEARCH FOR A DIFFERENTIAL ADVANTAGE

The wheellike or cyclical evolution of retail institutions is an inadequate explanation for all retail change, but it does provide valuable insights into the marketplace entry of low-margin, low-status establishments such as Kmart and Wal-Mart. These types of institutions enter the market by reducing operating expenses to a minimum and consequently can offer gross margins substantially below the required gross margins of conventional retailers in the market. Operating expenses are reduced by offering minimal customer service, by providing modest shopping facilities, by occupying low-rent locations, and by offering limited product mixes. The wheel hypothesis maintains that competitive pressures over time force these discount institutions to add services to gain a differential advantage. As the institution matures and emulators enter the market, the institution responds by trading up, and this usually means providing more elaborate facilities and services and locating in more expensive locations. Fashion product lines may be added in this stage. Eventually, these discount operations will become vulnerable to discount warehouses, catalog showroom operations, and off-price retailers.

Wal-Mart and Dayton Hudson seemed to have gained insights from the wheel hypothesis and have attempted either to slow down the cycle or to take advantage of the cycle. Wal-Mart has opened Sam's Wholesale Clubs, a wholesale/retail cash-and-carry membership warehouse operation, and has opened Hypermarket, U.S.A., a combination grocery and general merchandise operation in excess of 200,000 square feet.

Dayton Hudson has also tried to inhibit the wheel hypothesis by controlling Target Stores, Mervyn's (another discount operation), and conventional department stores. Dayton Hudson attempts to stabilize the upscale movement of Target, the conventional discounting of Mervyn's, and the downscale of its department stores. Strategic planning considers new competitive threats as former marketplace niches are abandoned, and both Wal-Mart and Dayton Hudson respond to the inevitable changes dictated by the wheel hypothesis. The wheel hypothesis does suggest that discounters should be cautious in adding services or upgrading their locations and facilities. Since price-conscious consumers are not likely to be store loyal when purchasing national brands, or what they perceive to be homogeneous products, there is a strong propensity for them to switch to lower-priced competitors.

The Porter model suggests that competitors in an industry must choose a sustainable strategy based on cost leadership, differentiation, focus, or some combination of these generic strategies. The selection of a strategy is contingent upon a firm's strengths and the importance of several environmental factors including the threat of new industry entrants, the bargaining power of suppliers and customers, the availability of substitute products for customers, and intensity of rivalry among industry competitors. It is critical for a firm to make a clear strategic choice or run the risk of being "stuck in the middle" by trying to be all things to all people. The latter is believed to be a recipe for mediocrity or even failure in an intensely competitive industry where substitute products are readily available.

Kmart, for example, began with a cost leadership strategy to compete against mass merchants such as Sears and conventional department stores.

Wal-Mart, too, built its business on a cost leadership strategy but differentiated itself from Kmart by increasing the value added to its customers by offering slightly more customer service and somewhat more fashionable apparel.

Other discounters employed more focused strategies. Herman's in sporting goods and Circuit City in home electronics are examples of retailers that, like Wal-Mart, enjoy considerable bargaining power with manufacturers but, unlike Wal-Mart, have combined cost leadership with a focused strategy in narrowly defined merchandise groups. By carrying nationally recognized brands and offering specialized sales assistance, these stores pose a threat to the general merchandise retailers who offer less specialization and slightly higher category prices. The cost-focused discounters are thus able to offer more value to price-sensitive consumers.

MANAGING CHANGE

Very few of the top discount operations around a decade ago have survived. All indications point to consolidation in discount department stores as two more regional discount department store chains—Ames and Hills—have filed for bankruptcy. Kmart, Wal-Mart, and Target have survived, but if the history of discounting is understood, there are indeed ominous clouds on the horizon, should these organizations not respond effectively to a changing retailing environment.

Kmart has responded to a changing retailing and competitive environment by renovating its existing stores and implementing these changes in newly constructed stores. Specifically, there is an attempt to break away from dowdy-looking stores and an image of cheap merchandise. Stores are made larger; there are extrawide aisles, bright displays and graphics, more brand-name merchandise, and additional use of advanced information technology such as parallel supercomputers. The bargain basement image has been rejected in favor of a more attractive and a more sophisticated shopping environment. Moreover, Kmart is endeavoring to attract customers by emphasizing more merchandise offerings in fashion apparel and kitchen, bed, and bath items. This is one of the strategies Korvette attempted earlier that failed. Will customers accept a fashion-oriented Kmart? Costs have increased, and a cost-focus strategy has not been fully reaffirmed. Kmart was successful largely because of a cost leadership strategy, but now that strategy has been modified. Hopefully, a repeat of the Korvette failure will not arise, but warning signs are present. Another potential problem is that a new store might generate added volume in the short run, but eventually sales may diminish. New stores and refurbished stores add expenses that must not be passed on to customers in a discount house operation.

Kmart has more than 1,800 retail stores, including Office Max, Builders Square, The Sports Authority, and Waldenbooks. Many of these stores are situated in strategic suburban locations throughout the country, and these sites give Kmart an important advantage over competitors such as Wal-Mart and Target.

Still, the specter of Wal-Mart can be menacing. In 1991, Wal-Mart became the number-one retailer in the United States in sales volume. However, Wal-Mart's success has been established by its stores situated in primarily rural areas in the South. Wal-Mart has about 1,500 stores, and plans are already under way to develop the California and northeastern markets. The same formulas of operating on exceedingly low overhead costs and offering the lowest possible prices, with relatively high levels of customer service, will be followed. Wal-Mart will try to adhere to its success formulas. Many of the newer stores, however, will abandon Wal-Mart's simple, down-home image in favor of offering more expensive displays and wider aisles in order to compete with Kmart's new image.

Both Kmart and Wal-Mart, in 1992, ventured into the grocery field. Kmart has opened six superstores, called Kmart Super Centers, which stock grocery products along with the usual inventory of Kmart merchandise. Wal-Mart has taken a more aggressive assault on the $375-billion-a-year grocery industry, having opened 17 180,000-square-foot supercenters in 1992 with 37 more under construction, located mostly in Arkansas, Missouri, Oklahoma, and Texas. A total of 300 Wal-Mart Supercenters are planned by 1997.

Although Wal-Mart has successfully undercut the prices of the general merchandise retailers, especially in smaller towns, the competition is expected to be stiffer in the grocery industry, which already operates on low margins. Food Lion, for example, built its low-cost, low-price reputation in small towns. Even the Mom and Pop grocers that are affiliated with voluntaries and cooperatives buy their merchandise in truckloads and trainloads, helping to keep costs and prices low. Moreover, some consumers dislike shopping for groceries at large stores that lack the personal touch and services such as help in carrying groceries to shoppers' cars.

Still, Wal-Mart has had considerable success in grocery sales in its 428-unit Sam's Club warehouse chain. Wal-Mart's financial clout is expected to help the company expand in the grocery business, and Wal-Mart's high level of confidence with the consumer should not be overlooked.

Target has about 550 stores and is the most upscale of the discounters. Target stores are located nationwide except in the mid-Atlantic and northeastern states. Target stores are the most attractive of the discounters. Future stores will include such innovations as larger size, wider aisles, more spacious carts, a larger food court, and expanded sitting areas. Target's largest threat besides Wal-Mart and Kmart would seem to come from specialty retailers such as Toys "R" Us and Herman's in sporting goods.

The discounter's managerial vision has focused on the development of new forms of retail outlets, the implementation of sophisticated information and distribution technology, and the changing of merchandise assortments. Sophisticated technology and merchandise assortments address short-range objectives much more than long-range objectives. Wal-Mart has been the leader in introducing new forms of retail establishments. Sam's Wholesale Clubs, Hypermarket, U.S.A., and Wal-Mart Supercenters are illustrations. However, Hypermarket, U.S.A., has not lived up to expectations and is still undergoing modifications in strategy, including the closing of four of the 225,000 square foot stores. Wal-Mart has left its traditional small-town southern base where its strength lies for other markets in the Northeast and California. It remains to be seen if Wal-Mart can successfully develop these new markets, which are heavily saturated with competitors.

Kmart has developed or acquired The Sports Authority, Builders Square, Payless Drug Stores, Office Max, Waldenbooks, and Kmart Super Centers. The present strategy is to renovate existing stores, construct larger new stores, and upgrade existing technology for inventory control purposes. Kmart maintains its dominance in prime store-site locations. Emphasis is on providing a more fashionable Kmart. Kmart in the past acquired Bishops Buffet, a chain of cafeterias, and initiated Designer Depot, a chain of off-price quality apparel stores. Neither project was successful. Specialty divisions have strained the Kmart organization, and Kmart is returning to concentrating on its core business, which is the discount store.

A contrary opinion is that consumers really do not desire a fashionable Kmart. Consumers developed loyalty to a low-price Kmart, and this change in image may hurt more than help in the future. Korvette was unsuccessful with a similar change in image, and unless this strategy is very carefully implemented, Kmart may fail as well.

Although executives in both Kmart and Wal-Mart are exercising managerial vision and leadership, traces of the Zayre experience are present. First, Kmart may find that its market does not want more fashion but just low prices. Second, Wal-Mart has lost Sam Walton, the great people motivator, and implementation of its strategies may become more difficult. Department stores are fighting back by offering low prices, private-label brands, and rebate credit cards through Visa and MasterCard, and the competitive wars continue.

LESSONS LEARNED FROM PAST MISTAKES AND FAILURES

The question remains if Kmart, Wal-Mart, and Target can learn from the past mistakes of Korvette, Zayre, and other discounters no longer in existence. Although retail history is filled with case studies of initially successful discount retailers, very few of these organizations have survived over time.

The wheel-of-retailing explanation for the evolution and eventual demise of retailers has held true over the years. Short-term decisions that, over time, increase costs seem to be innovating retailers' fatal flaw. Although Wal-Mart has expanded beyond its southern stronghold, costs have been maintained at the lowest possible level. Kmart has made several decisions, each of which may increase expenses only slightly, but collectively these added costs may modify its image and lead to new competitive threats. Former marketplace niches have been abandoned, and specialty discounters and specialty category superstores have moved in to fill these gaps. Both Kmart and Wal-Mart have progressed far enough in the wheel cycle so that they are becoming increasingly vulnerable to discount warehouses, catalog showroom operations, and off-price retailers.

Discounters have also been subject to Darwin's theory of natural selection. Environmental suitability and adaptive behavior have been necessary conditions for the survival of the discounters. To illustrate, the importance of some retailers for certain types of products has declined, and other types of retailers have become more important. Hardware and infants' wear stores declined in importance as discount stores gained prominence. Food stores, discount stores, and drugstores have become important channels for the distribution of toys in the past 20 years. During the process of change and survival of the fittest, some institutions prosper; others fail. Now, the discounters are challenged in the children's wear and toy lines by Toys "R" Us, Gap Kids, Kids "R" Us, and Lionel Toy Warehouse.

Population shifts also help the natural selection theory to explain the rise or decline of discounters. When population shifted from the central cities to the suburbs, gigantic shopping centers were constructed to accommodate the needs and wants of new homeowners. Kmart has some excellent locations in these shopping centers or near these prime locations. Many downtown department stores had to close their doors because of population shifts that they had not anticipated.

Many of the failures among discounters stemmed from their inability to both recognize and respond to changing needs of customers. Institutions that did not recognize and respond to these changed needs did not survive. The downtown department store, for example, adapted slowly to the environmental changes of the 1950s, and this inertia contributed to the rise of discount stores. Downtown department stores could have anticipated this competitive threat by the expansion of basement merchandise lines for price-sensitive customers and by recognizing the importance of self-service and scrambled merchandising strategies. In the same vein, discounters will need to combat the competitive threats of home shopping, off-price store clusters in strips and malls, and specialty superstores such as Toys "R" Us. Discounters must continue to implement important changes in technology such as scanners, parallel supercomputers, and other sophisticated means of managing information. Discount stores rose to prominence with low-price strategies. Only Wal-Mart seems to have remembered this lesson of the past as rising costs have overtaken many discounters and contributed to their failure.

CONTROVERSIAL MANAGERIAL DECISIONS

According to Webster's dictionary, *metamorphosis* means a change of form, shape, or structure or a marked change of character, appearance, or condition. Both Kmart and Wal-Mart have changed since their early beginnings. Target is still in the entry stage. Kmart's decision to focus on fashion rather than concentrating on cost control procedures and not offering a merchandise assortment more in accord with the character of a discounter might be deemed a controversial decision. Wal-Mart's decision to leave its southern base and expand into the Northeast might also be considered a controversial decision. Some of these northeastern locations, while in small towns, are close to larger shopping centers containing established rivals. Wal-Mart has also broken from its general merchandise tradition to enter the grocery industry with its less-than-successful hypermarkets and its new Wal-Mart Supercenters. Hypermarkets, as retail institutions, have previously failed in the United States. The supercenter stores are expected to meet strenuous competition from large, established low-cost food retailers such as Food Lion and Winn-Dixie. Both Kmart and Wal-Mart are going in directions that are unfamiliar to them.

Discounters in the past have failed when attempting to change their character, structure, appearance, or condition. A modification of store image had confused their customers. A blurred image, over periods of time, is deadly for discounters. Unless Kmart and Wal-Mart can successfully adhere to previous strategies such as the low-cost focus that has helped create a successful image for these organizations, they, too, may become fossils of retailing history such as Robert Hall, W. T. Grant, and other formerly great retail institutions. Discounters must be able to anticipate environmental change, but strategic modification of policies must maintain their original image.

CHAPTER 6

Specialty Clothing Stores: Battling the Giants

Customer-Driven Strategies
- Development of precise customer segments
- Image development with physical store attributes and fixtures
- Narrow merchandise assortments with breadth and depth
- Development of quality store-label merchandise
- Selective site locations
- Appeals to cross-shopping behavior
- Diversification of store divisions
- Splendid information systems

Specialty Store Mistakes
- Reacting to trends rather than developing proactive strategies
- Slow to grasp changes in customer demographics
- Poor observation of changing consumer shopping patterns
- Use of market-driven rather than customer-driven strategies
- Slow to change physical environmental elements
- Inadequate information systems

Specialty stores in the United States have evolved from the old general store. General stores carried just about everything from groceries to clothing and were characterized by their non-departmental nature and their lack of product specialization. The earliest specialty stores were manufacturer-retailer organizations where the craftsman sold wares in a store as contrasted with wagon peddlers who traveled from house to house or village to village. The general store lacked the space to accommodate the wide variety of goods being produced, and markets became large enough that they could be divided into submarkets.

The specialty store acquired a broad assortment in a particular product line and an in-depth knowledge of the product that was useful to, and wanted by, the consumer. A number of social and economic conditions were responsible for the development of specialty store retailing. The rise of population centers such as towns and cities that evolved from an agrarian society reflected the diversity of tastes and requirements necessary for retail specialization. Moreover, advances in production and the evolution of the factory made available more goods in greater variety and assortments necessary for specialization.

The term *specialty store* has been applied to a wide variety of retailers. For example, shoe stores, toy stores, sporting goods stores, bookstores, and women's apparel stores are all classified as specialty stores. These stores share a number of common methods of operation such as targeting a particular market segment of consumers, carrying a limited variety but wide assortment of merchandise such as men's apparel versus apparel in general, and offering services deemed important by their customers such as an experienced sales force, delivery, repair, alterations, demonstrations, and special orders. This chapter will confine itself to specialty clothing stores such as The Gap, The Limited, Lane Bryant, Brooks Brothers, Abercrombie & Fitch, and Marshalls.

Since apparel specialty stores usually carry a narrow but deep assortment of merchandise and target selective market segments, apparel stores are able to maintain better selections and sales expertise than their competitors, which are frequently department stores. This strategy also allows specialty apparel stores to better control inventory management and exercise a certain amount of flexibility. Some apparel stores have elaborate fixtures and upscale merchandise for affluent customers, while others have a discount orientation for price-sensitive consumers.

A new type of specialty store known as the *category killer* is gaining strength. A category-killer specialty store is an especially large store. There is an enormous selection in its product category, and it features relatively low prices. There is an enlarged trading area with customers drawn from greater geographic locations. The Limited and The Gap are examples of specialty clothing chains that are opening new category-killer stores to complement existing ones. Crown Books and Home Depot are other examples of category-killer stores in their respective merchandise lines.

Apparel stores can be adversely affected by seasonality or a decline in the popularity of a particular fashion. The fashion cycle in recent years also appears to be growing shorter in both women's and men's clothing. Specialty apparel stores may fail to attract customers interested in one-stop shopping. Moreover, killer-apparel stores may also fail to appeal to consumers interested in a small-store environment and uncrowded aisles. There is a trend toward a casual look and "dressing down," which means less money spent on apparel purchases.

Four key ingredients seem to be important for either success or failure among specialty store apparel retailers: innovation, target market segmentation and image, physical environmental resources, and human resources. Innovation in specialty apparel store retailing developed when The Limited redefined the definition of specialty retailing. The Limited also successfully changed the image of Lane Bryant and the Lerner stores. Lane Bryant developed an image for serving large-size women who are fashion conscious and Lerner's developed the image of serving women in an elegant environment but with budget constraints. The Gap successfully targeted those consumers who desired conservative and basic apparel of high quality. The Limited changed the physical environment of Lerner's by putting in marble floors and taking out the tile floors and using a peaches and cream decor instead of the inexpensive-looking orange paint that was present. The Gap has been very successful with Banana Republic, and its decor reflects originality, creativity, and the personality of its location. Leslie Wexner, founder of The Limited, has been both a visionary and a people motivator. Wexner has been credited with a great ability to motivate top-level managers to implement changes in strategies and policies with enthusiasm.

CHARACTERISTICS OF APPAREL CHAINS

Most responsibilities are centralized in the headquarters, regardless of the chain's geographic coverage. Decentralized responsibility for sales is an exception to this procedure. The apparel chain is usually divided into more main divisions than is typical of department stores. Trained specialized executives direct such divisions as real estate and maintenance, buying store operations, warehousing, and others. The personnel division has been elevated in status over the years and assumes an important role in operations. An elaborate report system keeps management abreast in the headquarters of developments in the field.

Usually an apparel chain is divided into geographic districts, with a manager for each store and a field manager or supervisor for each district. The store manager is responsible for the sale of merchandise that has been selected and purchased at the chain's headquarters. In some situations, a store manager may be allowed to purchase a small percentage of merchandise considered appropriate for the local target market. The store manager sells and also hires and trains a sales staff, arranges store displays, and reports daily sales to headquarters. The field manager is the connecting link between headquarters and the retail store. The field manager has responsibilities for supervisory inventories, checking displays, and hiring and training managers and will relay requests for merchandise that will satisfy local demand.

Merchandise managers and buyers at the headquarters purchase the apparel. Each buyer purchases a specific type of merchandise such as dresses or coats. Distributors then control the shipment of merchandise to the stores, with each one responsible for a number of stores generally ranging from 10 to 20. The quantities, colors, styles, and sizes sent to each store are based on the daily sales reports and an analysis of consumer buying trends in each store.

COMPETITIVE ASPECTS OF INDEPENDENT APPAREL STORES

Independent apparel stores generally operated by the owner or with a partner and a few employees have certain advantages over large department stores. There is personal contact with the customer, and in many instances, customers may be on a first-name basis with either the owner or employees. The store has a community base, and there is social interaction between the owner, employees, and customers. Services such as delivery and alterations can be adjusted to individual customer preferences. There is an image of a friendly, personalized retailer that provides a comfortable atmosphere in which to shop.

The independent store has the freedom to arrange store hours and to carry merchandise offerings in accord with customer desires and tastes.

These customer desires and tastes are frequently well known to the owner and can be flexibly adjusted as required. There is an opportunity to avoid some of the inefficiencies of large store operations.

The independent store has some limitations that can be glaring if not properly controlled. Specialized experts in buying, display, inventory control, or other specialties cannot be employed since costs would be prohibitive. This means that the owner must be a generalist with the ability to perform all specialties reasonably well. If a specialist is employed, then profitability is diminished. Furthermore, there are budget constraints, which means that only limited advertising and display promotions can be utilized. Since the owner cannot be frequently in the marketplace and the fashion cycle has accelerated more rapidly in recent years, important buying opportunities may be overlooked. However, independents would not be so common in retail trade unless these obstacles could be surmounted and have been by many entrepreneurs.

COMPETITIVE ASPECTS OF CHAIN APPAREL STORES

Chain apparel stores are able to turn stocks more rapidly than either independents or department stores and are therefore able to introduce price promotions. Operating services can be standardized in such a way as to effect lower costs. Centralized purchasing of fashion goods in volume performed by specialists should reduce costs and obtain better terms. A division of labor would allow greater expertise and enhance merchandise offerings. Generally, chain apparel stores can generate greater sales per square foot than independents.

Chain apparel stores are able to offer more personalized service than most department stores. Merchandise assortments are usually of greater breadth and depth than department store competitors. Moreover, chains such as The Gap and The Limited can offer good-quality merchandise in relation to price. Personnel in specialty chain stores can be better motivated than personnel in most department stores.

Chain apparel stores have a better opportunity to target a precise market segment. Fashion Bug, a chain with about 2,000 stores, for example, has grown by carefully cultivating its target customer. Its target customer is generally a working woman with a family income of $30,000 to $35,000, whose husbands are most likely blue-collar workers. The newer stores are located in small towns, emerging suburbs, and small cities such as Big Flats, New York, Seabrook, New Hampshire, Draper, Utah, and Chambersburg, Pennsylvania. Fashion Bug keeps prices down by stocking private-label merchandise, which accounts for about 75 percent of sales. The typical 10,000-square-foot Fashion Bug store competes with chains like Kmart by carrying a wide assortment of blazers, dresses, skirts, sweaters, and jumpsuits.

The Ann Taylor 200-store nationwide fashion chain for professional women has turned around a declining situation by developing its Ann Taylor private label. Store labels, if promoted correctly, can compete favorably with national brands. The chain in the 1980s offered stylish, well-made career clothes at better-than-department store prices. Subsequently, the quality was lowered to offer lower prices, and customers stayed away in droves. Efforts have been made to reverse this situation, but eventual success or possible failure is still a question mark.

Specialty chain apparel stores have made inroads into the department store market, but competition has intensified. Department stores have the inherent advantage of one-stop shopping, have lowered prices to compete with discounters, and have developed store brands of quality. Department stores have also devoted more space for apparel merchandise and more promotional advertising. To a certain extent, sameness has plagued apparel retailers, and sharper differentiation of merchandise is needed.

CONSUMER BEHAVIOR AND CROSS-SHOPPING

It has been found that consumers tend to shop at different store types, depending partly on their demographic characteristics, their attitudes toward shopping, and socioeconomic and lifestyle attributes. Traditional studies have characterized profiles of discount and department store shoppers. A relatively new consumer behavior phenomenon has developed that has had a profound impact on department and specialty store retailing known as *cross-shopping*. Cross-shopping means a highly confident young career woman would think nothing of wearing a blouse purchased at The Gap and a pair of jeans purchased at Kmart. A Banana Republic turtleneck sweater might cost $35, and a virtually look-alike turtleneck sweater might sell for $25 at Wal-Mart. The consumer, a cross-shopper, would have a high level of comfortability in making the purchase at Wal-Mart. Specialty discount chains such as Marshalls and Loehmann's take away market share not only from department stores but from traditional specialty stores as well.

The aging baby-boomer population and the increase of elderly population favor department stores over specialty stores. In contrast, the number of people ages 25 to 34 who are typical discount store shoppers, according to demographic studies, will decline. Many consumers prefer one-stop shopping and thus favor shopping in department rather than specialty stores. Department stores are making inroads against specialty apparel chains, such as The Limited. In 1994, The Limited announced that it plans to close 360 of its 4,481 specialty stores, which include Lerner's and Victoria's Secret. Kmart has posted lower earnings and has begun a broad restructuring. Department stores such as Frederick and Nelson closed in 1992 and I. Magnin in 1993 in downtown Seattle, and the battle with specialty stores, department stores, and discounters continues at a feverish pace. On the other hand, department stores have eliminated unprofitable stores and have modernized, making them more formidable competitors. Department store groups, such as Federated with Bloomingdale's and Abraham & Strauss in New York, Jordon Marsh in New England, Rich's in the South, Burdines in Florida, Bon Marche in the Northwest, Stern's in New Jersey and New York, Lazarus in the Midwest, and Macy's are using centralized buying techniques, and individual stores are exchanging information that should help lower prices, better determine customer demands, and increase inventory turnover.

There is a growing polarization that favors the low-margin, mass-volume retailers on one end and high-price, haute-service boutiques offering one-of-a-kind or unusual items on the other. Cross-shopping, or polarization, spells difficulties for The Gap, The Limited, Benetton, and Ann Taylor, and other merchants in the middle.

The bulk of the population is middle-aged and growing older, and as consumers grow older, more self-confidence is manifested, and there is less impulse shopping and less of a fashion orientation.

Consumers have expressed desires to purchase store-label fashion merchandise. This was not always the case in the past, as consumers had expressed a definite preference for manufacturers' national brands. Large retailers such as J. C. Penney, I. Magnin, and Neiman-Marcus, for example, have reduced their inventories of designer labels, such as Calvin Klein, Bill Blass, and Ralph Lauren, and have placed their own labels on their better-quality clothing. The reason for this development is that many designer-labeled products are now available at much lower prices in stores such as Target and off-price retailers. Moreover, store brands promote patronage loyalty, and manufacturers such as Ralph Lauren have established factory outlet stores. The Limited is heavily into private labels and exploiting them, since only private labels are carried. Dillard's, on the other hand, has specialized in carrying designers' or manufacturers' brands and does little or no private label. However, The Limited and other specialty stores offer store brands that reflect prestige, and traditionally this has been counter to the notion of store brands providing an inferior-quality image. Thus, specialty stores are in direct competition with national manufacturers' brands. Consumer acceptance of store brands of fashion goods has been high.

The concept of store image may be envisioned as a composite attitude that consumers in a particular market segment have about a retail store as related to their set of expectations. The perceived personality of the retail store is a development of the perceptions, emotions, and attitudes of consumers toward the various characteristics of the store. Market position is the sum of images that consumers have about the retail institution. These impressions consist of the retailer's merchandise assortment, ambience, personal communications, and internal and external nonpersonal communication. These factors must be coordinated to create a favorable store image that will attract the patronage of consumers in defined target market segments and create a competitive differential.

Specialty stores caught the demographic wave in the 1980s and were the fastest-growing sector in retailing. Even Sears has joined the specialty store wave by opening McKids, a licensing venture with McDonald's, and has acquired Pinstripes Petites, a women's apparel chain. Consumers desired name brands and a greater selection of specialty merchandise. Therefore, retailers offered more limited lines of specialty merchandise in deeper assortments. Specialty apparel stores such as The Gap offered more personalized service in a small-store environment. Other mass merchants opened specialty stores like Plums (owned by Dayton Hudson) or acquired units like Loehmann's (owned by Associated Dry Goods).

Traditional shoppers—such as the American family of husband in the workforce, wife at home with two children—have been replaced by singles purchasing for themselves, young couples sharing many expenses, midlife families with empty nests, and households headed by the elderly. Strategies once directed to traditional shoppers have been severely challenged by new forms of competition that have precisely addressed themselves to market positioning. The specialty apparel retailer has cultivated successfully narrow segments of consumer markets. Many of these specialty apparel retailers are located in shopping malls and not only are in convenient locations but also offer one-stop shopping for particular clothing items.

The retail store choice decision can be one of high involvement or low involvement. At times the decision may be highly important, and at other times, especially with convenience items, the decision may be one of low involvement. For example, a men's or lady's suit to be worn for a job interview may have high relevance because of its high price, complex features, large differences between alternatives, and high perceived risks of making a wrong decision. Consumers engage in a decision process approach for store choice as well as for product and brand choices. These decisions may be of a complex or of a routine nature. Demographic and lifestyle characteristics and other purchaser characteristics, such as perceptions of store attributes, lead to general opinions and activities related to shopping and search behavior.

THE LIMITED: KING OF APPAREL SPECIALTY STORES

The Limited, a women's ready-to-wear store chain, was first started in 1963 in Columbus, Ohio, at Kingsdale Mall. The store's name, The Limited, denoted its limited assortment of merchandise of women's sportswear, which it carried only in its first two years of operation. One of the reasons for the success of The Limited has been the display of fashion. Displays are coordinated and presented as a total look, beginning at the windows and pervading the entire store. Displays vary with the season and are changed weekly in each store. In the 1980s, The Limited acquired the 800-store Lerner chain, which sells lower-priced women's clothing; the 200-store Lane Bryant chain, which specializes in clothes for large women; Victoria's Secret, a chain of 545 lingerie shops; and the Henry Bendel upscale clothing store in New York.

The original Limited stores offered trendy women's sportswear such as blouses with Peter Pan collars, madras shorts, and Shetland sweaters. Customers of The Limited are typically young women who are on the forward edge of fashion and spend a higher percentage of their disposable income on their clothing than counterpart traditionalists. These customers shop for a total fashion image and are strongly influenced by social forces, especially reference groups such as professional organizations. Projecting and reflecting attitudes, lifestyle, and appearance are of paramount importance to these customers. The Limited Express's customers are generally young teenage girls who are fashion and fad conscious and also strongly influenced by reference groups.

The Limited chain has about 4,600 units, but The Limited stores themselves comprise approximately 800 units, the majority of which are located in regional malls. The stores are divided into six categories: (1) flagship stores, which are very upscale, with 75 percent of the merchandise upscale or designer; (2) best stores, located in better neighborhoods, with 50 percent of the merchandise consisting of designer labels; (3) better stores, with designer labels making up only 25 percent of the merchandise assortment; (4) typical stores, which carry the basic merchandise assortment; (5) downtown stores, which appeal to the working woman; and (6) ethnic, which are the most fashion-forward stores.

The Limited strongly motivates its sales associates and the sales management team. The company maintains a department whose major function is to devise contests within each season to promote the motivation to obtain maximum sales. Limited employees are among the highest paid in retail trade, and therefore expectations of performance of both managers and sales associates are high.

Change, and the anticipation of change, is uppermost in the mind of Leslie Wexner. Leslie Wexner founded The Limited on a precise philosophy. The philosophy was that a specialty store should focus on a narrower, more limited assortment of merchandise than was traditional up to that time. This concept helped redefine specialty retailing, and Wexner has constantly through the years further delimited the definition of specialty retailing. Leslie Wexner is perhaps one of the most visionary merchants in the history of retail trade. Wexner has an uncanny ability to identify the potential of a niche market and either to develop a new retail format or to take a failing enterprise and turn it around. When first acquired, Lerner's, Lane Bryant, Victoria's Secret, and Abercrombie & Fitch were failing institutions and needed revitalization. Leslie Wexner was one of the first merchants to recognize that larger stores would have higher productivity than traditional-size stores. Moreover, he has the ability to sense trends and how events will impact fashion trends and how to implement changes that will reflect these trends. Each division of The Limited has been decentralized, which allows each business to move faster and have more control over its operations. Wexner is not the people motivator of the same caliber as the late Sam Walton, but, nonetheless, he is highly respected by his managerial associates, and his judgment is unquestioned.

The Limited is not without problems and challenges. Two of its largest divisions, Limited Stores and Lerner's, have been losing traditional customers. Limited Express is luring customers away from The Limited. Limited Express carries hip sportswear at reasonable prices, and younger customers are more attracted to it. Lerner's once-loyal customers now spend more at Wal-Mart, Kmart, and other discounters that sell the same type of clothes as Lerner's but at more reasonable prices. A confusing fashion message has cannibalized Limited Stores by Limited Express. Many stores were upgraded with high-tech lighting, chrome, mirrors, and marble floors. This led to a gap between the quality of the merchandise and the store environment. The solution has been to compete with better merchandise quality. Another decision has been to take advantage of looser corporate dress codes and sell sportswear and casual clothing through Structure, its 426-store men's chain. However, it is doubtful that more attention to men's fashions will sustain growth in many Structure store locations since sameness seems to plague apparel retailers. The expansion of the Structure stores would seem to be more of a short-term expedient than a long-term solution.

The strategy to target a more upscale customer by Lerner's is a big gamble. Lerner's is no longer offering hats, socks, sleepwear, and other low-priced items and is offering more expensive sportswear such as wool-and-cashmere-blend sweaters. This means that Lerner's is abandoning its once-loyal customer base and trying to cultivate a new target segment. There is a danger that this will lead to cannibalization and also that a radical change of image, difficult to achieve, will not be accepted by consumers.

LANE BRYANT: A REVAMPING STRATEGY

The history of Lane Bryant can be traced back to 1904 when its specialty was designing maternity clothes. A mail-order business was started in 1910. Lane Bryant's maternity business grew tremendously, and the company's sales passed $1 million for the first time in 1917. Soon Lane Bryant also began to specialize in selling large-size clothing. Initially, half sizes were first developed to eliminate excessive alterations for the average woman. Lane Bryant gradually added extra sizes in foundation garments, suits, blouses, sweaters, skirts, shoes, hosiery, coats, gloves, sportswear, and bathing suits. In the mid-1920s, Lane Bryant turned its attention to satisfying the needs of tall women and chubby girls. By 1923, Lane Bryant had stores in Manhattan, Brooklyn, Chicago, and Detroit. By 1955, stores were established in Pittsburgh, Cleveland, Miami Beach, Minneapolis, Beverly Hills, Milwaukee, and Houston.

Double-knit polyester pants and black tents represented the fashion apparel of Lane Bryant in the 1970s. The Limited's 1982 acquisition of the chain and commitment to an upbeat image have changed an image of staleness to one where merchandise offerings are actually attractive and stylish. Large-size women's clothing is a hot retail category and has grown from an industry of $2 billion to over $8 billion in the 1990s. During this period, Lane Bryant expanded from a total of over 200 stores to more than 600 stores. Many new competitors, ranging from off-price to designer goods, have entered the field. J. C. Penney also entered the field and has been successful with a specialty large-size catalog that was introduced in 1983. Bullock's, a Los Angeles–based department store chain, also launched a separate specialty chain for large women known as Bullock's Woman.

Lane Bryant believes that its customer is the sister or the mother or the daughter of the woman who shops in the other Limited divisions. These women frequently shop together. It is estimated that the large-size market will continue to grow as the baby boomers mature.

THE LIMITED'S OTHER TURNAROUND SITUATIONS

Lerner's was founded in 1918 and purchased by The Limited in 1985. Lerner's, at that time, was a struggling budget-priced store with a grim decor that was serving lower-income working women. A sweeping renovation effort was made to create elegant shops that still offer low prices but boost the customer's self-esteem. The old design used a cheap-looking orange paint and tile floors. The new design featured a peaches and cream decor, marble floors, and private fitting rooms. The objective was not to remind customers of budget restraints. Once primarily directed at juniors, Lerner's is directed toward more fashion-conscious but budget-minded baby-boomer women.

Lerner's now consists of more than 800 stores, and its decision to change its target market was a big gamble. This new strategy still remains a question mark. Lerner's has abandoned its regular customers in an upscale effort and is competing to obtain new ones. Low-priced merchandise lines such as hats, socks, sleepwear, and other low-priced items have been withdrawn in favor of offering more expensive sportswear.

Although Lerner's is more upbeat, the chain continues to perform below potential. Lerner's appears to obtain a low share in a high-growth market. For example, discounters such as Kmart and Wal-Mart seem to be serving the budget-conscious customer better. The Limited needs to think hard about the strategies used by Lerner's and how to make them more effective. One advantage of this downscale market is that although customers do not have much money to spend, profit margins on the goods purchased are very profitable. Even Bloomingdale's and Bergdorf Goodman are giving more floor space to low-priced scarves and other lower-priced items.

Abercrombie & Fitch, founded in 1892, was once considered one of the outstanding sporting goods stores in the United States. Its prestigious Madison Avenue, New York, location attracted such customers as Admiral Byrd, Amelia Earhart, Ernest Hemingway, and Theodore Roosevelt. Today, Abercrombie & Fitch has to make up its mind whether or not it is a fashionable menswear store or a gift shop. Once Abercrombie & Fitch was considered a legend, but now it may just be a relic.

In 1977, the nine-unit Abercrombie & Fitch chain filed for bankruptcy protection. According to The Limited, other men's retailers envision themselves as merchants selling menswear. At a time when niche merchandising has gained in popularity, Abercrombie & Fitch has been unable to establish an identity. Competition from off-price retailers has eroded the image of merchandise offerings. Apparel sold by L. L. Bean and Eddie Bauer includes larger and better selections.

Abercrombie & Fitch competes directly with the highly successful Banana Republic operated by The Gap Stores. Banana Republic offers the same safari clothing, and the Sharper Image also sells expensive gadgets like electronic chess sets. The Banana Republic is also giving a strong emphasis to women's fashions that are current but not trendy. Banana Republic stores are exceedingly imaginative and offer a merchandising mix that is exciting. Abercrombie & Fitch would seem to be a poor imitation of the Banana Republic but does compete favorably with other competitors by targeting a small, viable customer segment.

The Limited has recognized that the environment is dynamic. In a changing environment, which opens up new opportunities as well as problems, The Limited has proven to be adaptable with Lerner's and Lane Bryant strategies. Leslie Wexner and his staff are close to customers, satisfying customer needs, and stress enhancement of customer relations. The Limited is constantly considering the advent of change, and this is one of the more important factors instrumental in turnaround situations.

THE GAP: A MASTER OF THE BASICS

The Gap, Inc., is a specialty retailer selling apparel under five trade names: Gap, Gap Kids, Banana Republic, Baby Gap, and Old Navy/Warehouse, which is still in the beginning stages. The Gap, composed of more than 875 units, was started with the original concept of selling a few single items such as jeans and T-shirts of well-made construction at not-so-cheap prices in an attractive store environment. The midteen market was cultivated by also selling records and cassette tapes. The Gap, established in 1969, added Gap Kids in 1986 and now has more than 350 stores. The Banana Republic was acquired in 1983 and was originally a two-store chain with a small but thriving catalog business. The company became known for the multipocketed photojournalist's vest, versatile Kenya convertibles, and the traveler's raincoat and has more than 180 stores. The Old Navy/Warehouse division, with over 80 stores, sells competitively priced casual clothing.

While there are similarities between The Gap and The Limited, there are pronounced distinctions. The Gap sells a simple, practical, conservative product in contrast to The Limited, which stresses fashion that is more trendy and stylish. The Limited is much more creatively and modernly decorated and is on the cutting edge of each fashion that is offered. The Gap carries basic merchandise items in large assortments of sizes and colors, necessitating a significant inventory prior to peak selling seasons. Therefore, The Gap needs to place orders well in advance and is vulnerable to demand-and-pricing shifts.

The Gap is trying to add a new merchandise line that goes beyond the basics, which would encompass stretch pants and leather vests. The old strategy worked because of slow-reacting competitors, consumers' desire for plain, simple clothes, and most important, a powerful promotional image. Sharp black-and-white ads featuring celebrities like Lenny Kravitz and Winona Ryder in jeans and T-shirts helped sell the concept that Gap clothes were responsive to the youth culture. Competition from J. C. Penney and Kmart has forced The Gap to reconsider its former strategy. Basics still occupy about half the space in Gap stores, but with the change in merchandise mix, there is a need to attract older shoppers. The Gap has deviated from its all-cotton look by including some polyester blends. The Gap in the past has offered reasonably priced casual clothing that does not go out of style in a single season. Tight cost controls have kept prices reasonable, but new competition from Penney, Kmart, and other discounters has necessitated a change that is indeed risky.

The Gap continues to offer a brand that reflects integrity and quality and fastidious attention to color, style, and detail. The Gap has made its store label a brand of good taste and dignity.

The Gap is going through a transition period as it ventures into new pastures. Target stores and Mervyn's have with some success copied the Gap style while undercutting it in price. Today The Gap caters to an older, more affluent clientele. However, "if you can't beat them, join them" has become part of Gap strategy as Gap Warehouse stores now compete with the discounters. Gap Warehouse apparel will generally be constructed with lighter-weight fabrics and will sell clothes for children, which is a departure from Gap stores' usual policies.

The success story of Gap stores in the past is a chain where its culture is preoccupied with the most mundane details, from cleaning store floors to rounding counter corners at Gap Kids stores for safety's sake. A high-tech network maintains over 1,200 Gap stores constantly stocked with fresh merchandise. The Gap designs its own clothes and has made its store label a serious rival of manufacturers' brands. The most pressing challenge for The Gap is to compete with discount house competitors. One strategy for accomplishing this objective is to open stores of about 8,000 square feet from the average Gap store of 4,000 and add new adult merchandise lines. The Gap is also phasing out national brands in favor of promoting its own brand. The trend toward wearing more casual basic clothes should enhance The Gap's merchandising offerings. In contrast, The Limited offers more trendy apparel, and the trend toward wearing more casual clothes may be detrimental to The Limited.

The challenge is especially critical for The Gap since it must attract older shoppers as well as teens. Apparel offerings must appeal to all age groups. Therefore, fashion items such as ribbed, sleeveless turtleneck sweaters are a gamble for The Gap to offer, but cutting prices on basics to compete with discounters such as Kmart is also a serious competitive situation. The Gap is trying to use fewer vendors and to do more manufacturing in low-cost countries such as Mexico in order to decrease costs. Research has also revealed that there is a significant pattern of cross-shopping between Gap and Banana Republic customers. Therefore, Banana Republic, Gap Stores, and Old Navy/Warehouse are positioned based on price-point and fashion content. Banana Republic assortments are at the higher end of the company's price and fashion spectrum; The Gap, in the middle; and Old Navy, at the lower end. This strategy in the short term is working, but there is a danger that a blurred image in the perceptions of consumers may develop between the offerings of The Gap and Old Navy. Duplication might constitute a serious problem if not carefully monitored.

BROOKS BROTHERS: WALKING A TIGHTROPE

Brooks Brothers is steeped in tradition and fierce customer loyalty. Brooks Brothers was founded in 1818 and has the distinction of being America's oldest clothing store. Theodore Roosevelt, Ulysses S. Grant, and Woodrow Wilson all wore Brooks Brothers suits upon taking their oaths of office. Authors such as Ernest Hemingway, F. Scott Fitzgerald, and Somerset Maugham depicted characters in their novels who wore Brooks Brothers suits. Among the male movie stars that have worn Brooks Brothers suits have been Fred Astaire, Burt Lancaster, and Gary Cooper. Female movie stars such as Elizabeth Taylor, Katharine Hepburn, and Audrey Hepburn have purchased dressing gowns, slacks, and sweaters, among other items at Brooks Brothers.

Brooks Brothers has vertically integrated and makes all of its suits and shirts. The conservatism that has characterized apparel made by Brooks Brothers is one of the factors that has made the firm a legend. Personal service is outstanding, and it is not uncommon for a few generations of one family to patronize Brooks Brothers throughout the years.

Customers feared that this conservatism and personal service would end when the firm was purchased by Julius Garfinckel & Company of Washington, D.C., in 1946. The firm's dignity continued, but even minor changes were resisted by loyal customers. The tradition for the most part was continued, but production efficiencies and other effective measures were instituted. Finally, in 1988, Marks and Spencer, a firm based in Great Britain, purchased Brooks Brothers.

Marks and Spencer, since its purchase of Brooks Brothers in 1988, has continued to walk a tightrope. The rigid Ivy League customer is becoming an endangered species. The perception that Brooks Brothers sells only three-button "sack suits" with a center-vested jacket and boxy fit had to be changed. Brooks Brothers now offers more two-button versions and suits with a tapered fit and suits cut for athletic men with broader upper bodies. Brooks Brothers agonized when it widened the width of the trouser legs on its suits from 16 to 17 inches. Even the installation of escalators in its flagship store on Madison Avenue in New York was jarring to many customers. These older customers liked things the way they were in their college days. However, the store still retains its signature wood-and-brass look, but it is less intimidating. The challenge confronting Marks and Spencer is how to attract new customers without losing extremely loyal customers who are diminishing in numbers. Meanwhile, the flagship store has lost customers to stores that offer more variety such as Paul Stuart and Barneys of New York.

Brooks Brothers in the past had represented the Eastern Establishment, but all of this has changed. Brooks Brothers has expanded and now has stores throughout the United States in such cities as Atlanta, Birmingham, Chicago, Cincinnati, Cleveland, Dallas, Denver, Ft. Lauderdale, Houston, Indianapolis, Los Angeles, Minneapolis, New Orleans, St. Louis, San Diego, San Francisco, Seattle, Tampa, and Tulsa. Years ago, Brooks Brothers located in only downtown locations, but now enclosed shopping malls have gained importance in selection criteria. Brooks Brothers is indeed doing a balancing act on the tightrope.

OFF-PRICE APPAREL RETAILERS: THE DIFFERENTIATION TRIANGLE

The emergence of off-price apparel retailers in the 1980s changed the nature of competition since new strategies and policies and new ways of implementing old ones developed. Competition from off-price retailers forced department stores to reconsider their relationships with suppliers who traded with these competitors. Many department stores, as a result, reduced their reliance on designer brands in favor of their own store brands. Others declined to make purchases from suppliers who sold goods through off-price retailers.

An off-price apparel chain features brand-name or designer-label apparel and accessory merchandise. Prices are frequently 40 to 50 percent below department store prices. Off-price apparel chains such as Loehmann's and Marshalls are targeting department store shoppers. Off-price chains try to establish long-term relationships with suppliers and must have a regular flow of goods into their stores.

Manufacturers are sometimes induced to make merchandise during the off-seasons. At other times, off-price retailers purchase closeouts and canceled orders. Off-price chains are less demanding than department stores in terms of advertising allowances and may not even advertise specific brands, do not return merchandise, pay promptly, and sometimes pay even in advance to obtain prices lower than wholesale.

Marshalls, an apparel chain, stocks an unpredictable assortment of merchandise, in humble surroundings, with no personal service, and frequently has long checkout lines. Branded family apparel and accessories are offered at 20 to 60 percent less than department and better specialty stores. Marshalls has more than 400 stores in about 40 states. A greater emphasis on quality has helped Marshalls and other off-price apparel retailers to succeed. Many shoppers looking for brand names and designer labels as a guarantee of quality abandoned the department stores. Both Marshalls and Loehmann's buy manufacturers' overruns or orders canceled by department stores.

Marshalls has learned the hard way that off-price retailers do not sell goods of lower quality at low prices. This tarnished image is now a memory of the past, and Marshalls has reestablished its image by emphasizing quality brand names, renovating stores, and redesigning merchandise displays. Marshalls is a part of the Melville organization, which also controls Stride-Rite Shoes, CVS Drugstores, and Kay-Bee Toy and Hobby Shops.

Independent off-price retailers either are owned and operated by entrepreneurs or are divisions of larger retail corporations. Although many off-price retailers are owned by small independents, most large off-price retailers are controlled by large retail chains. Examples include Loehmann's, operated by Associated Dry Goods, owner of Lord & Taylor; and Designer Depot, controlled by Kmart. Factory outlets are also off-price retailers, owned by manufacturers, and carry manufacturers' surplus, discontinued, or irregular goods. Examples are Burlington Coat Factory Warehouse and well-known factory outlets of Levi Strauss, London Fog, and others. Many of these new outlets are now located in factory outlet malls. Even swank establishments such as Gucci, Anne Klein, Dansk, and Charles

Jourdan have located in factory outlet malls, offering trendy merchandise at discounts of 40 to 60 percent off department store prices such as Lord & Taylor's. Since consumers continually quest for value, these factory outlets and off-price retailers remain formidable competitors for traditional specialty apparel retailers, department stores, and discounters such as Kmart. Already, Kmart and Mervyn's have demonstrated disappointing results, but department stores remain strong competitors.

ROBERT HALL: UNCHANGING STRATEGIES AND POLICIES

The beginning of the Robert Hall Clothing chain can be traced back to 1937. At first, only men's clothing was carried. In keeping with the low-overhead, low-markup philosophy, these garments were displayed on pipe racks; no show window or decorative displays were used. Sales were made on a cash-only basis. The store was quickly a success among price-conscious consumers and soon additional stores were opened and women's and children's apparel were added.

In 1946, United Merchants and Manufacturers, Inc., a major textile manufacturing and factoring company, acquired Robert Hall. In 1948, Robert Hall vertically integrated by opening its own men's clothing factory in order to ensure a supply of lowest-cost merchandise of consistently good quality. The women's and children's lines were purchased from clothing manufacturers who cut the orders to Robert Hall's specifications using materials bought by Robert Hall. At its peak, Robert Hall operated over 430 stores and boasted that it was the largest apparel chain in the United States. However, sales plateaued by 1971, and steep losses were incurred by 1975. A new management team made an effort to close some 150 unprofitable stores and to renovate some 100 to 150 older stores. Plans were made to locate 25 new stores in shopping malls by 1977. This move would allow Robert Hall to better compete with Sears, Ward, and Penney, which were its main competition.

In the early years of the operation, the merchandise and target market objectives were at least generally stated. The company identified its target customers as price-conscious blue-collar Americans who were seeking good-quality tailored clothing. These objectives, however, were too vague to be useful for control purposes. As time passed and the economic and social environments changed, it should have been apparent, through performance analysis, that changes in company direction were in order.

When Robert Hall tried to develop a fashion image in the late 1960s, the firm seemed to be reacting to shifts in market tastes and preferences—but only in a halfhearted way. In the mid-1960s, the company should have redefined its purpose and objectives in light of the changing environment and continued to monitor its performance toward achieving those objectives.

Changing social trends, which placed a greater interest in the casual life-style, and higher personal incomes made it possible for many consumers to upgrade their wardrobes and helped to rekindle the public's interest in fashion. Robert Hall's merchandise mix was not well positioned to adapt to these changes. Robert Hall could have continued to serve the lower-income market where it was established but would need to extend credit to its customers and add new styles. Moreover, consumers quickly accepted shopping centers and enclosed malls for shopping and social activities, but the great majority of Robert Hall stores were freestanding stores. Robert Hall identified this trend too late to relocate to shopping centers and malls. Competitors such as Sears and Penney were much faster in recognizing the shift in shopping patterns and the shift toward more fashionable apparel.

In the late 1960s, Robert Hall attempted to establish a fashion image by hiring Countess Antoinette Riva Ninni of Milan to design 18 fashions a year exclusively for Robert Hall. The countess also served as a general fashion consultant to the chain and, as well, made personal appearances at individual stores. Unfortunately, Countess Ninni was not well known, and the effort to develop a fashion image was largely unsuccessful.

There seemed to be little or no coordination between Robert Hall's merchandising and financial management departments. If a functioning internal information system had been in operation, the financial impact of carrying aging inventory would have been apparent. The deteriorating financial performance also reflects the lack of attention directed to setting performance objectives and establishing control procedures.

Finally, in the summer of 1977, the 366 remaining stores in the Robert Hall chain were closed, never to be reopened. In August 1977, Robert Hall's $125 million inventory was auctioned off in unit lots at Madison Square Garden in New York City.

MANAGING CHANGE

The Limited has been successful because management was able to perceive and manage change. Conversely, Robert Hall failed because management could not perceive and manage change. Although these statements sound simplistic, change is an integral part of the retailing environment and must be perceived and acted upon. Many of the divisions of The Limited such as Lerner's and Lane Bryant were performing poorly and thus have been remarkable turnaround situations. Target markets were modified, decor was changed, and store images were successfully upgraded. Both merchandise lines and service had to reflect these changed store images.

The Gap developed a creative strategy to enhance the image of the Banana Republic. When Banana Republic's popularity began to decline because safari-type clothing had fallen out of favor, theme park fixtures were replaced by more subdued displays. Basic clothing such as khaki slacks and simple cotton dresses continued to dominate the merchandise offering, but more upscale European-style casual clothing was added.

Robert Hall did not anticipate consumer shopping preferences for malls and shopping centers. Most of Robert Hall's stores were freestanding stores. Robert Hall did not perceive changes in apparel tastes due to the surge in the number of double-income families. Penney had correctly envisioned the upgrading of consumer fashion preferences, but Robert Hall had not changed its merchandising mix. Moreover, bank credit cards revolutionized consumer purchasing habits, and Robert Hall resisted credit extensions to its customers. Finally, Robert Hall did not have an adequate information system and therefore failed to anticipate customer changes in fashion demands.

Department stores, in recent years, have established many boutiques, theme displays, and designer departments to compete with specialty stores and discounters. Many department stores have concentrated on the sale of fashionable apparel with moderate prices. Other department stores have modified their markets, targeting middle-income and upper-middle-income consumers. Discounters such as Kmart have also invaded the apparel market. Specialty stores will need to respond to all of these competitive changes and to sharper differentiate their merchandise from competitors'.

CONTROVERSIAL RETAIL MANAGEMENT DECISIONS

The decision by Wexner of The Limited to redefine the definition of specialty retailing was indeed a controversial decision. This new definition helped to direct the organizational mission of The Limited. The organizational mission of The Limited was to offer a very narrow merchandise assortment with both breadth and depth to a selective target market. In turn, each division of The Limited such as Lane Bryant and Lerner's was to offer a different narrow merchandise assortment with both breadth and depth to a different target market. Lane Bryant and Lerner's were each drifting and had to renew their search for purpose. What is our business? Who is the customer? What should our business be? These simple questions are among the most difficult that a company will ever have to answer. The Limited decided to phase Lane Bryant out of the maternity business and serve large-size women. Lerner's, once serving a lower socioeconomic class, was redesigned to target a more upscale customer.

Off-price specialty retailing also involved controversial decisions. Stores such as Marshalls and Loehmann's created a differential advantage by pricing their merchandise below their competitors' in order to attract price-sensitive shoppers. To decrease their costs, off-price outlets are frequently located in freestanding sites, and consequently rents are considerably lower than at the mall and downtown locations of department stores. These off-price retailers buy in large quantities from manufacturers at prices lower than those paid by discounters. Therefore, negotiations with suppliers are critical, and success or failure is dependent on successful supplier relations. There are many critics who maintained that off-price retailing would not endure very long because it is dependent on tricky negotiations with suppliers. Purchases include factory overruns, end-of-season and last season's styles, closeouts, irregulars, and samples. Consumer acceptance has been dramatic as they search to buy designer labels or well-known brand-name clothing at regular wholesale prices or less, making off-price retailing an important growth trend in specialty store apparel retailing.

The off-price apparel chain is in the maturity stage of the life cycle. Sales are continuing to increase, but at a much slower rate than in previous years. The decrease in sales growth has been due to overexpansion, competition from other retailers, and saturation of the market niche. Management can be faulted for some of these reasons for decline. A more serious reason is an inability to ensure continuous merchandise availability, and this reality reinforces what earlier critics thought about future potentials of off-price retailers.

LESSONS LEARNED FROM PAST MISTAKES AND FAILURES

The Limited developed a sharply clear and defined organizational mission in contrast to Robert Hall's general objectives. Over time the mission may remain clear, but some managers may lose interest in it. Not only has Leslie Wexner been able to inspire managers to renew their interest; he has also been able to generate enthusiasm for changes. An organizational mission should specify the type of customer it desires to target, the specific wants of these customers, and how the firm will satisfy these wants. This definition impacts the firm's growth potential by establishing guidelines for selecting opportunities that will satisfy customer needs and wants, the organization's resources, and changes in environmental factors. The Gap also has developed a very clear organizational mission that has been successful. The advantages of these organizational mission statements are that they are expressed in simple language that can be understood by all. A simply expressed organizational mission stands a better chance for successful implementation than one that is complex and therefore difficult to decipher.

A clear organizational mission in itself is not necessarily tantamount to achieving a successful operation. In the early 1980s, for example, Sears found that discounters and specialty stores were taking away its traditional middle-class customers, and therefore Sears needed to discover an appropriate market niche. Sears endeavored to promote itself as a fashion-oriented department store for more upscale customers. This effort failed. Sears then attempted to offer budget products and slashed prices. These efforts were also unsuccessful. Finally, Sears is trying to offer functional, rather than fashionable, goods and services that offer value to middle-class, home-owning families. The organizational mission needs to be well coordinated with the organization's goals, opportunities, the situation analysis, and the development of the merchandising mix.

An organization mission and objectives need adjustment over time. The Gap has found that its safari image in its Banana Republic division and its theme park appeals have faded from popularity, and the Banana Republic is now trying to reflect the personality of its locations. For example, a Banana Republic store has been individually designed to reflect a converted dairy barn in Pittsburgh, a vintage storefront in Vermont, and an erstwhile trolley barn in Salt Lake City. Banana Republic stores are exceedingly imaginative, and they are stressing more casual clothes rather than a safari fashion image.

The Limited is confronted with the challenge of fashion change. A theme of the 1980s was the belief in endless upward mobility. Upward mobility would seem to have evolved into downward mobility. Stagnant incomes bring frugality and savings into fashion selection. Fashion items once sold as enhancements to personal style are repositioned to emphasize their practical value. Cross-shopping behavior now allows the purchase of apparel items in discounters such as Kmart, Wal-Mart, and Target. The Gap has profited from this trend to some extent, and The Limited flagship chain of almost 800 stores has lost ground. Moreover, the casual look has become popular, and even offices on Wall Street allow employees one day a week to arrive at work in informal wear such as jeans. The fashion trend would seem to be "dressing down," and The Limited must adjust and modify its strategies accordingly. The question remains, Can The Limited profit from the past mistakes and errors made by other organizations in retail trade and surmount these new challenges?

CHAPTER 7

Home Improvement Centers: A New Powerhouse

Environmental Changes

- The do-it-yourself trend
- More women shoppers
- Blurring of gender roles
- The home building market
- The economic environment

Responses to Environmental Changes

- Home centers versus home improvement centers
- Scrambled merchandising
- The warehouse concept
- Superior customer service
- One-stop shopping strategies
- Geographic cluster segmentation strategies

What constitutes a home improvement center? The stereotype picture is an operation that carried hardware and lumber and sold primarily to building contractors. The modern home improvement center sells primarily to the do-it-yourself market sector of home owners and combines the traditional hardware store and lumberyard with a self-service home improvement center. The typical home center carries a wide variety and deep assortment of building materials, hardware, paints, power tools, garden and yard equipment, plumbing and heating equipment, electrical supplies, and other home maintenance supplies. Some home improvement centers have expanded their offerings to include home furnishings and household appliances. Home centers offering upscale merchandise have favorable niche market opportunities.

The primary growth sector is the warehouse home improvement center concept, pioneered by Home Depot. Stores buy directly from the manufacturer and are heavily technology driven through advances in the latest scanning equipment and bar coding. Home improvement centers usually maintain large showrooms that display sample merchandise. Customers purchase merchandise by placing merchandise requests at the order desk, and clerks pull the orders from adjacent warehouse stocks. Customers also serve themselves with showroom stock. Since home improvement centers provide customers with information and advice on the use of materials and equipment, there is a strong possibility that a customer loyalty base can be promoted. The most prominent home improvement centers are Home Depot, Lowe's, Payless Cashways, Builders Square, Hechinger, and the Home Club. In the 1980s, Wickes Lumber and Grossman's both occupied important positions in the home center sector, but both have encountered difficulties.

The home improvement center market is affected by environmental trends. Economic trends in the past decade reflected recession, fewer housing starts, and a slowdown in do-it-yourself remodeling work. The economic recovery in the mid-1990s should release considerable pent-up demand. Baby boomers, although marrying at a later age, are in a better financial position and are likely to increase spending on home decor and do-it-yourself products. Home ownership has been the American Dream in the past, and this attitude is likely to continue. Home ownership should be more affordable in the 1990s than in the 1980s. Mortgage interest rates are much lower than in the 1980s, when it was not unusual to pay as much as 12 percent on a first mortgage. Moreover, the upward spiral in home prices has declined, with median prices rising no more than 3 to 4 percent. Thus, the potential home improvement center market appears much more promising in the future than it was in the past.

As the 1980s unfolded, it became apparent that pronounced changes would occur in the home improvement market. New store formats developed to satisfy rapid growth. The warehouse store with its huge breadth and depth of merchandise assortments, self-service, and high sales volume became a formidable competitor. Superstores proliferated, and drive-through lumberyards were tried. Some retailers attempted to combine different store formats, while others tried to defend their market. Retailers that failed to adapt to the changing environment have continued to lose market share.

Ten years ago, power tools were sold by Sears and other mass merchants. Decorating items were sold by specialty stores such as paint and floor covering retailers. All of this has changed, as the home center sector has not really evolved but has undergone a revolution.

Four key ingredients in the home improvement center industry seem to be important for either success or failure: innovation, target market segmentation and image, physical environmental resources, and human resources. Innovation in the home improvement center industry developed when Home Depot effectively implemented the warehouse store concept and when Lowe's instituted scrambled merchandising. The warehouse concept was to revolutionize customer service, and the policy of scrambled merchandising broadened the merchandise offerings so that home centers previously called lumberyards could be referred to as home improvement centers.

Both Home Depot and Lowe's have developed effective strategies of market segmentation and have promoted clear store images to consumers. Home Depot targets consumers who desire low prices and a high level of service. Home Depot has promoted an image as a destination store that serves as a magnet for customers because of merchandise assortments, displays, price, and other unique features. Lowe's segments customers in small towns, satisfying their wants and needs. Lowe's has effectively promoted an image as a one-stop home improvement center because of its effective policy of scrambled merchandising.

Home Depot has used physical environmental resources to effectively create its image as a low-price store. Merchandise is displayed on the selling floor in cut cases, on floor-to-ceiling open shelving, or stocked on pallets. Bernard Marcus, of Home Depot, with outstanding leadership qualities, has also used manpower resources effectively. Bernard Marcus participates in the training of store managers. Marcus is very tolerant of mistakes, encourages initiative, and avoids the red tape of bureaucracy. Marcus has been compared favorably with Sam Walton as a people motivator.

ENVIRONMENTAL TRENDS

The home center market is composed of individuals and organizations with the purchasing power, the interest, and the desire to purchase a specified product. Therefore, the demographic factors of markets and the lifestyles of the people who compose these markets are an important consideration. The extent of the purchasing power of target markets and how they desire to spend their discretionary income are paramount considerations for understanding the home center market.

There is a vital link between geographic preference and economic opportunity for home centers. The Sunbelt states in the South and West have attracted population growth from other regions with much harsher climates. The housing market in the Sunbelt states consequently has provided much better market opportunities for home improvement centers. Geographic mobility is a potentially useful market segmentation dimension. From 17 to 21 percent of the population moves at least once a year. This market segment generally has more income and lives in costlier homes. The mobile segment tends to be an attractive market for furniture, appliances, paint, garden and yard equipment, and other home maintenance supplies.

Regional distribution of population is important to home center retailers since regional differences lead to variations in demand for many products. These differences develop because of climate, social customs, and other factors. For example, the sale of outdoor furniture will soar in the Pacific states as this region increases in population. Due to climate, those in the Pacific states spend many more hours outdoors than those in the eastern states.

Although there have been large differences in regional growth rates, distribution of the total population has only been slightly altered. The states with the fastest growth rates, with the exception of Texas and Florida, still remain very small. For example, the Mountain states have developed more rapidly than any other region yet constitute only 5 percent of the nation's population. There are a number of well-known reasons for the growth of the more popular regions: the attractiveness of climates and lifestyles of Sun Belt areas; the lower costs of establishing business organizations in the South; the energy production boom in the Rockies and Southwest regions; and the increasing expenses of energy in the eastern states. Slower population growth has important implications for home improvement center retailers inasmuch as they will not be able to count on a rapidly growing population to increase their customer base. Home improvement center retailers will need to win new customers away from the competition. Those retailers who will grow are those who can best anticipate and respond to changing customer demand patterns.

The most notable trend concerning age distribution and projections is the aging of the U.S. population. The elderly consumer represents an attractive market for housing. Many elderly market segments are selling their homes in harsher climates and reestablishing themselves in warmer geographical locations. Home centers that can provide household items for this market will stand to profit. This market may even furnish their new homes with the help of professional interior decorators and therefore constitute, in some geographical areas, an upscale market.

Short-term trends in disposable personal income, savings, and discretionary spending can disguise, but not reverse, long-term trends. Home ownership is an integral part of the American Dream. The traditional family may not necessarily remain the target market as singles and other nontraditional units also desire housing appropriate for their needs.

Home ownership has become more affordable than in the past. The growth of the multiincome or double-income family has contributed to new demand patterns. Moreover, as income levels increase, increasing mortgage interest rates represent a smaller percentage of disposable personal income. Purchasers also obtain many more features in modern homes than did home buyers a generation ago. Built-in features such as microwave ovens and higher standards for insulation and energy efficiency have become important elements of value.

Lowe's, Black & Decker, Color Tile, Masco, The Stanley Works, and W. R. Grace have formed the Home Improvement Research Center. This organization provides reports to the home improvement industry on future developments and trends. Such developments and trends as consumer savings, housing and construction, and population and American household characteristics inform the home improvement industry about future demand patterns.

THE HEART OF HOME IMPROVEMENT CENTERS

Two concepts have been at the heart of the revolution from home centers formats to home improvement center formats. Each concept has complemented and reinforced the other to make home improvement centers a viable and functioning competitive force in retail trade. Scrambled merchandising has had a profound impact on the merchandise offering, and the warehouse concept has had a significant impact on merchandise display and inventory management.

SCRAMBLED MERCHANDISING

Whether the home improvement center is large or small, policies must establish the type and assortment of merchandise it will offer for sale. The nature of the marketplace and competitive forces will influence and determine these policies. Customer characteristics will also guide these merchandising policies. At two polar extremes are specialized merchandising and scrambled merchandising. The conventional home centers offered lumber for sale, which was the traditional offering. The merchandise assortment was narrow but deep. Lowe's follows a scrambled merchandising policy where the traditional merchandise lines are offered but also sells a broader assortment of related merchandise for the home such as television sets, VCRs, stoves, refrigerators, and washers and dryers. Frequently, these nontraditional merchandise lines carry higher margins and profits. For the customer, scrambled merchandising provides the benefit of one-stop shopping convenience.

Many of the independent home improvement centers often cannot compete with competitors like Home Depot using price as a differential advantage due to lack of buying power and financial resources. Therefore, the growth of these independents may come from an expanded assortment of product lines or the implementation of scrambled merchandising. This merchandising policy not only may increase customer traffic but also provides increased revenues and profits. In the future, expansion will probably include carrying such items as tile, carpeting, yard and patio furniture, and everything for the home. Already Lowe's plans to expand into the lucrative home-office market by selling computers, fax machines, and cellular telephones.

The decision for a home improvement center to implement the concept of scrambled merchandising depends on a broad customer base and a large retail trading area. The frequency of customer patronage and their preference for one-stop shopping is another factor in the decision process. The nature and extent of competition in the retail trade area constitute an important determinant. Financial resources and stock turnover rates become critical, and effective investment in inventories becomes crucial.

The merchandising policies of home improvement centers have been unpredictable. Lowe's has made effective use of scrambled merchandising, but some other home improvement centers have not made effective use of this policy, perhaps believing that their situation and conditions do not warrant it. Scrambled merchandising dilutes the home improvement centers' resources in all areas: budget, manpower, shelf space, and inventory management procedures. The decision for home improvement centers to implement scrambled merchandising depends on target market requirements, nature of the business and competition, and customer expectations.

THE WAREHOUSE STORE CONCEPT

Home Depot has revolutionized home improvement center retailing by effectively implementing the warehouse store concept. The warehouse store concept was first used in food retailing but has been applied by Home Depot successfully in its operation. Home Depot is a discounter, pricing items way below competitors in a no-frills setting. Frequently, the warehouse store is located in a secondary site and emphasis is placed on the sale of national brands sold at discounts. Decor is inexpensive, and promotion is done primarily through direct-mail catalogs and newspaper advertising. High ceilings are used to stack the lumber and other products. While some warehouse stores in other retail areas may not provide service, Home Depot is known for effective and efficient customer service. Because of this service policy, Home Depot has built a very loyal customer base, and word-of-mouth referrals are conducive to a well-run operation.

Home Depot is a new type of specialty store known as the category-killer store, an especially large specialty store. For example, Home Depot 100,000-square-foot stores carry 30,000 different items of lumber, tools, lighting, and plumbing supplies with prices 30 percent below those of traditional hardware stores.

The limitations of implementation of the specialty warehouse concept in home improvement centers is that they can be adversely affected by a recession in the housing market. There can be a decline in store patronage due to a decline in the popularity of its product category because its offering is so concentrated. The category-killer store may not appeal to customers interested in a small-store setting. Home Depot maintains wide, uncrowded aisles to offset customer feelings that are present in other types of warehouse stores of crowded, cramped space. Home Depot is really a superwarehouse store that is a combination of the superstore and warehouse store. This operation carries a full line of high-volume, low-price merchandise.

VERTICAL RELATIONSHIPS

Competitive advantage can be improved by the effective management of relationships with suppliers. Ineffective management of these same vertical arrangements can lead to detrimental operating results. The vertical corporate system combines successive levels of production and/or distribution within a single firm. The firm has made the decision to perform the marketing functions in the distribution system through the ownership of facilities by integrating forward or backward. All of the production and marketing functions are performed by the completely integrated firm. The firm utilizing partial or complete integration may be a producer, wholesaler, or retailer. For example, many large supermarket chains are fully integrated backward and own dairy plants and bakeries. The decision on whether to integrate the business functions and form a corporate vertical marketing system is primarily dependent on the amount of control the firm desires over distribution strategy, activities, policies, and the return on investment from integration. Vertical integration is most likely found whenever there is the opportunity to increase profitability and to reduce uncertainty and risk.

The advantages and disadvantages associated with the corporate vertical marketing system are numerous. Decreased marketing expenses are possible due to close coordination and stability of operations between manufacturing, wholesaling, or retail units. There is an element of certainty of materials and supplies on hand since units are closely monitored. Better inventory control and the quality control of products are frequent outcomes of vertical integration. Greater concentration of resources should also result in greater purchasing power. All of these factors should hopefully make possible additional profit margins.

The possible disadvantages of the vertical marketing system include the inability of some marginal firms to operate profitably in a vertically integrated setup. Although savings can be exacted, greater financial resources need to be committed to cover the higher fixed costs. Managerial limitations are sometimes a manifestation such as not monitoring closely increased inventory holdings and placing restrictions on variety merchandise assortment. All of this might lead to an inflexibility of operations, which could be detrimental.

Some retailers engage in operations at the wholesale and production levels. Sears, Roebuck purchases a large amount of its merchandise from manufacturers in which it has part ownership. Moreover, individual store units obtain most of their merchandise from Sears' wholesale distribution facilities. On the other hand, many manufacturers sell their products directly through their own stores located in factory outlet malls, such as Bass Shoes and Calvin Klein Sportswear. Manufacturers like Lenox and Wedgewood sell their merchandise direct to the consumer through their own specialty stores.

The home improvement industry is made up of a large number of small competitors with a few large competitors such as Home Depot and Lowe's. The aggressiveness and effectiveness of competitors are important determinants of the level of competition for a market area. Generally, the home improvement centers combine warehouse and showroom facilities. Warehousing fundamentals are used to reduce operating expenses and thereby offer discount prices as an important customer appeal. Evans Products is a manufacturer that used vertical integration to compete in the home improvement sector.

EVANS PRODUCTS: A VERTICAL MARKETING SYSTEM

In the 1970s, Evans Products maintained a chain of over 150 building materials stores and was the second-largest home center chain in the United States. The stores were operated under the names of Grossman's and Moore's and were located for the most part in the Middle Atlantic states and a few midwestern and southern states. These retail stores had all the aspects of a building materials supermarket. The target market was the do-it-yourself type of consumer. The company established schools that provided instruction for potential customers. Approximately 100,000 people annually received instruction in these schools.

Evans Products Company was an integrated manufacturer, wholesaler, and retailer of building products. Operations included manufacturing building materials such as lumber, plywood, hardboard, and particle board and the production of specialized building products such as interior paneling, cedar exterior siding, wood and plastic moldings, metal bifold closet doors, and mobile home air conditioners. These products were distributed through the company's wholesale and retail distribution networks.

Products were marketed to the residential home market, the mobile home market, and the multifamily construction market and serviced through the company's wholesale and retail operations. Evans also marketed damage-prevention equipment for railroad freight cars and trucks, truck heaters and air conditioners, materials handling racks, and steel castings to industrial markets. The company maintained 47 strategically located wholesale warehouses. Evans also maintained six manufacturing plants that produced kitchen cabinets for the home center market. While customers came from all age groups, the focus was on the young, married group. Customers were encouraged to finish many of these homes themselves, which was in accord with the company's retail store strategy.

Evans was the fifth-largest lessor of railcars. Lessees included not only Evans operating groups but major shippers and railroads. This operation provided savings in loading and unloading time and reduction in loss and damage while in transit. During times of railroad car shortages, the company's control of these cars ensured a steady flow of materials from Evans' manufacturing plants to its wholesale and retail facilities.

Many large retailers, such as Sears, J. C. Penney, Safeway, and A & P, have frequently integrated backward in the distribution system and now own many manufacturing or processing companies. Firms such as Firestone and Sherwin-Williams have integrated forward and own or franchise many retail outlets. Consequently, vertical integration is a structure commonly found in the retail sector. However, vertical integration is not a panacea, and Evans Products was to experience difficulties in later years.

The vertical marketing system has a number of characteristics that are different. First, vertical marketing systems consist of interconnected units through coordinated efforts or ownership by developing strategies and programs by determining the best combination of functions to be performed by specific units of the system. Second, the vertical system is designed to benefit from economies generated from systems analysis. Third, the vertical system has greater control and member loyalty that may be forced through contracts and, thus, more stability. Fourth, there is more staff and operating support to ensure coordination and implementation of strategies. Fifth, there is emphasis on total volume, costs, profits, and investment relationships for the total distribution system. Sixth, the vertical marketing system relies more on scientific decision making by specialists.

Evans Products Company, a manufacturer of plywood, integrated forward when it decided to control its own retail outlets under the names of Moore's and Grossman's. Grossman's, situated predominantly in New England, is about the sixth-largest home improvement center in sales volume and about the fourth-largest in number of retail stores. Evans purchased wholesale lumber distributors in order to market its products more aggressively. However, overextension is an important cause of financial difficulties, and Evans unfortunately had overextended itself. On the other hand, successful vertical marketing systems have been developed by Edison Stores, the Singer Company, and Radio Shack, who are among the many manufacturers actually owning part, if not all, of their vertical system components.

GROSSMAN'S: THE DRIVE-THROUGH CONCEPT

Grossman's reemerged after 17 years as a division of Evans Products as an independent, publicly held organization in 1986. By 1995, Grossman's consisted of 90 stores throughout the Northeast and 10 in southern California. It is a far cry from the first store established in Quincy, Massachusetts, in 1890. The founder, Louis Grossman, began as a peddler and added roofing materials to his product line. Lumber and used furniture were featured in the first store. Later, Louis Grossman was joined in the business by his four sons, and Grossman's was incorporated in 1928.

A new management team developed a new strategic plan to modernize the stores in 1990. Grossman's used the concept advanced in drive-through banking and drive-through restaurants and applied it to its lumberyard. The drive-through concept is fairly simple. A covered lumberyard with an extrawide aisle accommodates lumber on each side. The different types of wood are well marked, permitting the customer to select materials and quickly load a vehicle. The bill is added at the end of the yard by a cashier who can accept cash or charge for payment. The time saved by the drive-through was invaluable, especially for the contractors, who are a major segment of Grossman's business. Additionally, the lumber was covered at all times to protect the wood from adverse weather conditions and to preserve its quality, a particularly important characteristic in New England. Grossman's business is centered around the sale of lumber, power tools, and contracting.

Early and late hours were established for greater customer convenience. Services such as trained specialists to estimate, plan, and expedite orders were made available. Contractors and remodelers were provided with free computer estimates and special discount prices.

The drive-through concept in the lumberyard has been extended to many more stores, and it has proven to be successful. Grossman's is considering implementation of the drive-through concept to the entire chain. Since all of the types and sizes of lumber are clearly marked, with the price per foot clearly indicated on each group, a great time savings for customers is involved. Grossman's has successfully focused on customer service and satisfaction. Grossman's is concentrating on the professional remodeler under its slogan "Shop with the Pros." Separate sales rooms and general contractor sales offices have been established to achieve this objective.

MOORE'S: A FULL-SERVICE LUMBERYARD

Once a division of Evans Products, Moore's, like Grossman's, reemerged as an independent organization. Moore's has more than 50 stores situated primarily in Virginia, Ohio, North Carolina, Pennsylvania, New York, and Maryland. Moore's operation is much like the traditional home center. Moore's does not try to compete with home improvement centers like Lowe's. Since its financial resources are limited, efforts are not made to compete on a price basis with competitors like Home Depot. Moore's does compete favorably with traditional hardware stores; however, the primary product sold is lumber. Newspaper advertising is used, and Moore's promotes itself as a full-service lumberyard selling building supplies.

HECHINGER: A PICTURE OF UNCERTAIN STRATEGIES

Hechinger, based in Landover, Maryland, initially developed an opposite strategy from Home Depot by operating gleaming stores that attract female shoppers. However, by acquiring the Home Quarters Warehouse chain in the Southeast, Hechinger decided to diversify. The Home Quarters chain is much like Home Depot but is second in price and service. Triangle Building Centers were also acquired in Pennsylvania. When pitted against Lowe's, they were a poor second.

Hechinger is about the seventh-largest home improvement chain and has benefited immensely from the building boom in the Washington, D.C.–Baltimore area. Hechinger has established superstores that carry about 40,000 items, compared with the 25,000 to 30,000 items of its rivals. Its stores look more attractive than conventional home improvement center stores. Hechinger stores have vinyl-covered floors in contrast to the concrete usually found in no-frills warehouse outlets.

Hechinger's expansion has been ambitious, but results have been troublesome since sales have been declining in the older stores. Geographic expansion is also filled with pitfalls because of the declining economy in New England and the competition of Home Depot and Grossman's. Hechinger has tried to develop a middle ground in its strategies, presenting an image that is between a Hechinger, known for ambience, and a Builders Square, a conventional warehouse store. Hechinger lacks the financial strength of Home Depot, and sales personnel lack Home Depot expertise with customers. It would seem that Hechinger offers good prices and good service but is a poor clone of Home Depot and would find it difficult to compete with Lowe's.

WICKES: INDIGESTION FROM GROWTH

Wickes is now about the fifth-largest home improvement center in sales volume. But life was not always so serene, as a whirlwind hit Wickes caused by poor acquisitions and go-go expansion. An important reason for its failure was that Wickes did not take advantage of the population growth in the suburbs and did not target its product lines to the needs of customers in different geographic locations. Furthermore, Wickes continued to serve its traditional base of contractor customers whose purchases were directly tied to housing cycles. Wickes did not cultivate the do-it-yourselfer market as well as Lowe's and Home Depot. These new changes in the home improvement market might have been missed because managers were constantly shifted from one business format to another, and stores were not situated in good locations.

Wickes acquired more than 30 wholesale building materials distribution centers in 20 states from Evans Products in 1975 and branched out from its basic lumber wholesaling and retailing formats into such operations as food processing, farm machinery, and furniture stores. But as Wickes grew, its profits failed to keep pace. Essentially, it was the retail furniture business that proved to be Wickes' Achilles' heel. In 1975, Wickes had more than 230 building supply stores in 36 states. Battles in many markets with Levitz Furniture, a pioneer warehouse retailer, and other established merchants were too much for Wickes. Although Wickes was strong in urban store outlets, losses were incurred in suburban markets. Eventually, this situation led to a management shakeup, but problems were still to plague Wickes.

Wickes announced in 1980 that it would discontinue its money-losing buildings division, which constructed pole-frame farm buildings and commercial and industrial structures. The recession was blamed for a sharp drop in sales and subsequent losses. Finally, in 1982, Wickes filed for Chapter 11 protection. This was the second-largest retail reorganization proceeding since W. T. Grant went into Chapter 11 in 1975.

Wickes also owned the Gamble-Skogmo department store chain, plus supermarkets, drugstores, and various manufacturing operations. The immediate closings included 9 of Wickes' 24 furniture warehouse showrooms and all three of the company's Attitude stores in Chicago, which specialized in more contemporary furniture for apartments and condominiums. Wickes was the largest stockholder in such stores as Garfinckel's, Brooks Brothers, and Miller and Rhoads before these outlets were taken over by Allied Stores. The Red Owl supermarkets and Snyder's Drug Stores were also sold.

Wickes, in 1982, was about the fourth-largest retailer in the world, but its size did not guarantee its success. Untimely acquisition in 1980 of Gamble-Skogmo, a Minneapolis chain of supermarkets, drugstores, department stores, and mail-order houses, was a contributing factor to Wickes' difficulties. Wickes had 18 different divisions or subsidiaries, 375 stores in the United States, and 65 in Europe. There was a strong link to the housing industry, which was saddled with high interest rates. Even the do-it-yourself home improvement business had faltered from the impact of the recession, and competition intensified. In summary, although untimely diversification constituted a challenge, Wickes was unable to cope with the offsetting cyclical swings in the building materials business.

Eventually, Wickes reestablished itself. The furniture division was the worst problem. Customers were now offered a five-year warranty against defects and workmanship, a full refund if the customer was dissatisfied for any reason, and a promise to match any lower price by a competitor by refunding the difference within 30 days. Wickes also needed to turn around a negative shopping experience. Shelves were now fully stocked, employees were added to ensure quality service, and the more profitable stores were renovated. The new chief executive officer went on television, informing customers of the changes in Wickes and promising that customers would receive full value and entirely what they had a right to expect.

Wickes, in 1990, controlled the Builders Emporium chain of approximately 120 stores originally purchased in 1978. Builders Emporium owns only about 10 percent of its stores and leases the remainder. The stores average 40,000 square feet of selling space. Builders Emporium is one of the largest home improvement retailing chains in California. The stores' merchandise assortment includes home and lumber products, tools, hardware, garden and nursery items, and seasonal goods. Builders Emporium stores generally provide a wider selection of items and lower prices than hardware stores and greater convenience and better service than warehouse stores. Commercial customers constitute less than 5 percent of its total sales. The average customer lives within three miles of the store and makes an average purchase of under $20.

Primary competition is from warehouse store chains. Warehouse stores are generally able to offer lower prices than Builders Emporium because of higher sales volume. Home Depot—and to a lesser degree, Home Club—and Builders Square are also competitors but not as significant as the warehouse stores. Builders Emporium features brand-name merchandise, and naturally customers are able to make price comparisons that are sometimes viewed unfavorably.

PAYLESS CASHWAYS, INC.: TARGETING AN UPSCALE MARKET

The do-it-yourself segment comprises more than two thirds of the home improvement market. Sales in this market are growing at double the rate of retailing sales in general. Since the home improvement industry is fragmented, no single company has more than a 5 percent market share. The firm in a new, expanding, or fragmented industry has a strong competitive position. Payless Cashways, for example, has a strategy of developing a dominant position in existing geographic markets and selectively expanding into new areas. Future strategy was placed on developing new markets that can be served from a network of regional distribution centers providing service to its 200 stores. Positioning strategy emphasizes the concept of one-stop shopping. Payless Cashways retail stores offer a comprehensive mix of functional and fashionable goods. Lumber was made the focus of its product offerings with the thought that lumber would be purchased first for a major home improvement project. Therefore, the sale of lumber is featured in print and broadcast advertising.

Payless Cashways targets serious do-it-yourselfers and tradespeople, who together compose the most important market share of the home improvement market. The competitors of Payless Cashways include Home Depot and Lowe's and a variety of regional and local chains and independents. The target markets of these firms vary somewhat. For example, income and demographic characteristics of the 35-to 40-year-old home owner core target market served by Home Depot differ some degree from the target market targeted by Payless Cashways.

Market characteristics of a market development situation are usually favorable. Environmental factors would typically vary from geographic locations, and these may be favorable or unfavorable, depending on circumstances. Competition is more likely from existing home improvement retailers than from new entrants. Payless Cashways has achieved the third-highest sales volume figure in the home improvement center industry and hopes to challenge Home Depot and Lowe's for market dominance. Payless Cashways appears to be very strong in the midwestern states. However, Lowe's and Home Depot are much stronger in the southern states, especially where a building boom has been experienced.

Payless Cashways, currently the third-largest home improvement retailer, has varied its business format with Home and Room Designs, a 12,000-square-foot store selling home room designs, and Toolsite, a 15,000-square-foot store devoted to professional tools. Payless Cashways is pursuing a niche-store strategy in contrast to Home Depot, Lowe's, Builders Square (Kmart), and Hechinger, which offer warehouse format stores.

LOWE'S: A ONE-STOP HOME IMPROVEMENT CENTER

Home Depot is the apparent leader in the home improvement center sector but concentrates on larger population areas than are served by Lowe's. Lowe's has an orientation to small towns across the Southeast and is second only to Home Depot in the industry. Lowe's operates more than 300 stores selling building materials and consumer hard goods in small towns of approximately 20 states. Lowe's is the sixth-largest appliance retailer and is ranked 41 in sales among consumer electronics retailers.

Stores have been renovated from within, establishing vertical displays that allow selling space to be created where inventory was maintained. Larger stores have been constructed to replace older outlets. From 1988 to 1991, sales space was increased by 60 percent. Lowe's has concentrated on building stores from 40,000 to 60,000 square feet, which is above the industry average. Lowe's will lease more sites than it typically has done previously in order to accommodate its expansion strategies. The company has been able with increased selling space to expand core consumer categories that include hardware, tools, paints, plumbing, and home decor. Other categories such as exercise equipment, bicycles, and soft bath merchandise have been deleted.

Consumer durables account for only about 16 percent of Lowe's total sales, but it is still among the industry leaders. Although the home electronics offering is not comprehensive, Lowe's is among the top 50 electronics retailers in sales volume in the United States. Among appliance retailers, Lowe's is among the top 10 retailers in sales volume. In these categories, Lowe's competes with Sears, Circuit City, Silo, and Radio Shack. Since Lowe's customers are in small- and medium-size cities, value pricing is extended, usually associated with urban superstores, and this helps build a solid loyalty base.

Lowe's sales volume gains were led by product categories that received the greatest benefit from larger square footage or the advancement of the home improvement superstore concept. Home decor and illumination sales grew by 21 percent. Kitchen, bathroom, and laundry sales increased by 15 percent. Sales of tools, lawn and garden products, and heating and cooling systems also experienced double-digit percentage growth. All of these sales gains are from home improvement center superstores, in contrast to the conventional Lowe's outlets. Therefore, Lowe's is now committed to building home improvement center superstores in the future, and concentrating on larger stores is at the core of its expansion plans.

Lowe's is targeting the female consumer and developing special amenities to attract a new customer into a home improvement center. Research studies have found that women have an image of home center stores being messy, with lumber, tools, and cabinets, or plumbing fixtures stacked on the floor. Lowe's is trying hard to provide an aesthetically pleasing shopping environment. Lowe's has created complete kitchen and bath vignettes for displaying cabinets, vanities, sinks, faucets, and fittings. These products in the past had been lined up haphazardly along walls or on racks. Related products from nearby departments, including wallpaper, paint, carpeting, and small appliances, embellish these room displays. Tables and chairs are placed in some kitchen vignettes so that customers may relax while comparing cabinets and fixtures with samples brought over from nearby departments.

Since many women are taking greater interest in home improvement or are household heads, Lowe's stores schedule microwave cooking demonstrations, decorating seminars, and do-it-yourself clinics. Lowe's believes that attracting female customers lies in providing them with the same type of amenities offered in department and specialty stores. Service and total customer satisfaction are emphasized.

Lowe's has used a contiguous expansion strategy, which has been the cornerstone of its growth. A contiguous expansion strategy locates new outlets in markets close to existing ones. Once these new markets are developed, they serve as stepping stones to the next expansion stage. A contiguous expansion is necessary when stores are served from existing distribution centers and when tight, centralized control from headquarters is required. This strategy can minimize the need for major new advertising campaigns. Lowe's has expanded from its small-town base in the Carolinas eventually into Texas, Illinois, and Pennsylvania. Lowe's is also embarking on its largest expansion ever into the Midwest, where the company will find itself colliding directly with Home Depot. Lowe's so far has held its ground when competing directly with Home Depot, and this has surprised many industry analysts. This rapid expansion may place added strain on company personnel, its information systems department, and its entire infrastructure.

HOME DEPOT: A NEW CHAMPION IN HOME IMPROVEMENT CENTERS

Is Bernard Marcus, chairman and CEO of Home Depot, the Sam Walton of home improvement centers? This is the question that many ask, although some authorities have already forecasted that Home Depot will be the Wal-Mart of the 1990s. In 1995, Home Depot was ranked among the top 5 "most admired" companies in America. This is a far cry from the opening of the first two Home Depot stores, outside of Atlanta in abandoned Treasure Island Discount sites in 1980, which turned out to be a crushing disappointment. Word of mouth by customers traveled fast, and the company exploded with growth. In just ten years, Home Depot became the largest warehouse home center retailer in the United States.

Each Home Depot store stocks some 30,000 separate items of building materials, lumber, floor and wall coverings, tools, lighting, plumbing supplies, and seasonal and specialty items, frequently priced as much as 30 percent below the going rate of traditional hardware stores. Rival home improvement centers may be as well stocked but are unable to match the low prices of Home Depot.

Home Depot stores are situated in high-density shopping areas. Stores average 70,000 square feet of enclosed space and 8,000 square feet of outdoor garden area. The key to the merchandising strategy is the warehouse concept. Merchandise is displayed on the selling floor in cut cases, on floor-to-ceiling open shelving, or stacked on pallets. Forklifts and dollies are used to move merchandise directly from the receiving area to the selling floor through wide aisles. Purchases are made mostly direct from manufacturers in large quantities. Merchandise is warehouse priced typically 15 to 20 percent below conventional home improvement centers. National brands are emphasized in displays.

Although the warehouse merchandising philosophy prevails, Home Depot is a service-oriented operation. To instill the right culture in the company, Bernard Marcus participates personally in the training of every store manager and assistant manager. Management considers its employees' expertise in merchandise and home improvement techniques essential to achieving merchandising strategies. A formal employee orientation and training program provides the predominantly full-time staff with essential information and techniques. Authorities claim that Home Depot's 70,000 employees are far superior to their counterparts in rival stores for explaining information to novice repairers.

The company pays significantly higher wages than does its competition. Salespeople are not paid commissions. Management desires to make certain that if a 75-cent washer will suffice, sales personnel will not be tempted to push a more expensive part because of a commission system. Managers are constantly trying to select employees who can be promoted to operating stores. Once an employee becomes an assistant manager, he or she is eligible for lucrative stock options.

Home Depot merchandising is innovative. Bernard Marcus encourages managers to try new techniques and in return is tolerant of mistakes. Store managers have ample latitude in selecting merchandise and have direct access to top management. The overriding practice of Home Depot is to avoid the pitfalls of bureaucracy. Initial purchasing decisions are made at the corporate level by merchandise managers, and reorders are usually handled by store management personnel.

Service and customer satisfaction are more important in the 1990s than in the 1980s because in a slow-growth economy, companies survive by retaining customer patronage. Home Depot is known for customer service and among industry consultants is known as one of the best service providers in the service industry. The Home Depot culture encourages employees to build long-term relationships with customers. Employees are trained in home repair techniques and can spend as much time as necessary to educate shoppers. High-pressure sales tactics are not used. Bernard Marcus prowls the stores and often asks customers if they have found what they wanted. With such a service philosophy, is it any wonder that Home Depot has delivered to investors the second-best ten-year-return among the Service 500 firms and ranks number one in ten-year growth in earnings?

Home Depot has a strategy to be the leader in a merchandise category and was one of the largest sellers of unfinished wood furniture, developing it into an $80 million-a-year business. IKEA, the Swedish retailer with five stores in the United States, devoted the majority of its store space to selling unfinished wood furniture, offering a much larger selection. Home Depot could not match the prices of IKEA since the product occupied only from 2,000 to 7,000 square feet, and therefore volume selling was not possible. Since Home Depot could not be the power retailer in selling unfinished furniture, the item was discontinued and was replaced with an expanded selection of floor tiles and wallpaper.

The giant orange warehouses of Home Depot permeate much of California and Florida and are now sprouting up in the densely populated Northeast. Projected plans are to build 90 additional stores in the South, 128 in the Northeast, 101 in the West, and 40 in the Midwest, where there are presently none, by 1996. This would give Home Depot a total of 534 stores. Some 850 stores are planned by the year 2000.

Similar to Wal-Mart, Home Depot has upgraded its computer order and inventory system. Advanced computer systems complement and reinforce customer service. This change affords Home Depot data flexibility to satisfy changing merchandise demands of many independent customers and the need for a rapid feedback to quickly satisfy changing customer service needs. This special order system automates what had been a manual process involving thousands of special orders. The continuous adaptation to changing needs and demands is an advantage of this new special order system. Although Home Depot has followed Wal-Mart in outstanding customer service and the implementation of advanced computer systems, Home Depot has chosen to penetrate large urban markets in contrast to Wal-Mart's targeting of small urban markets.

Warehouse stores typically offer customers large discounts with minimal service and little decor. Home Depot stores have all the charm of a freight yard but provide outstanding customer service. Warehouse retailing appears simple but in reality is very complex. Home Depot must carefully monitor buying, merchandising, and inventory costs, as discounting diminishes gross profit margins. Home Depot in the home improvement center industry has been a market champion in successfully offering a union of low prices and high service.

Since the environment of the 1990s will be much more dynamic than the 1980s, retailers will need to develop and enact adaptation strategies. Home Depot has endeavored to develop what is known as a destination store, that is, a retail unit where the merchandise assortment, presentation, price, or other unique features act as a magnet for customers. Approximately 25,000 to 30,000 people walk through a Home Depot store in a week, half of whom are women. Instead of selling toys or other items, Home Depot sells only items intended for home use. Management wants the perception of the customer always to be: When considering a do-it-yourself project, think of Home Depot. Home Depot succeeds because it staffs stores with knowledgeable sales help who can advise customers with their problems. Therefore, customers perceive Home Depot as worth a special shopping trip when considering a do-it-yourself project.

MANAGING CHANGE

Lowe's has changed from a traditional home center to a modern home improvement center. Home Depot has pioneered the warehouse concept applicable to home centers and is a discounter in the home center market. Moreover, employees provide knowledgeable service and advice concerning customer building plans. Home Depot is rapidly becoming the Wal-Mart of the home center industry. In contrast to Lowe's and Home Depot, many organizations, such as Grossman's and Moore's, remain conventional home centers. The home center industry consists of many independents servicing specific geographical locations, such as Scotty's in Florida, and lacking the resources to make strategies such as scrambled merchandising or the warehouse concept work effectively. These small, independent retailers have formed cooperative groups, allowing them to realize economies of scale by making large-quantity group purchases. Independence is maintained and efficiency improved by capitalizing on quantity and time-purchasing discounts, thereby enhancing competitiveness with chains.

Environmental changes such as the do-it-yourself trend, more women interested in home repairs and remodeling, and the blurring of gender roles have caused some home center organizations to change to home improvement centers. Home centers, largely because of competitive pressures, are experimenting with new or modified formats and also with nontraditional locations. Since customers are afflicted with poverty of time and the role of women has changed, home improvement centers have placed emphasis on convenience and service. Convenience is exemplified by extended hours, short waiting times, and other factors that make shopping easier. Service includes some convenience factors and also friendly, knowledgeable sales help, easy credit, liberal return policies, and postpurchase services. Grossman's has extended service by providing a drive-through lumberyard similar to banks' or fast-food restaurants'. Lowe's has employed convenience by promoting one-stop shopping. Consumer durable goods such as washers, dryers, and television sets can be purchased in Lowe's. Payless Cashways stresses service to women, and Lowe's and Home Depot have also followed this trend. Although not new, scrambled merchandising remains a major strategy of some home improvement centers.

Home improvement centers are constantly identifying significant trends and developing marketing strategies to satisfy consumers. Changing trends either present opportunities or pose threats for home improvement centers. One trend affecting the home improvement industry is the direction of movement in interest rates. Sales in the home improvement industry usually move in tandem with home sales. From the 1980s to 1993, home improvement centers have benefited from falling interest rates, which stimulate new and existing housing sales. Rising interest rates in the 1990s or beyond could slow sales in the housing market and concomitantly in the home improvement industry. The home improvement industry might need to focus in the future on do-it-yourselfers who desire to improve or change their present homes rather than to buy a new one. Home improvement centers have continually changed and adapted to environmental trends. Therefore, the outlook for home improvement centers remains positive for continued growth in retail trade when confronted by changing environmental trends and competitive challenges.

CONTROVERSIAL RETAIL MANAGEMENT DECISIONS

The environment is dynamic. The environment can change sometimes subtly, sometimes more violently and recognizably. In response to a changing environment, the home center industry has developed strategies to become home improvement centers. At the heart of this revolution has been the warehouse concept and the strategy of scrambled merchandising.

The success of Home Depot can be traced to a cost leadership strategy that offers customers better values than competitors, better service through the personal commitment to store managers by top-echelon management, and a formula for rapid growth in a highly motivated trainer-trainee environment. Home Depot made the decision to expand store size and become a home improvement center superstore. Home Depot has designed itself to operate as a category-killer store in an effort to destroy all competition in its specific product category. Home Depot is confronted with the major challenge in carrying inventories that are large enough to satisfy customer demand but not so large as to result in excess inventories requiring significant markdowns.

Lowe's success was due to the decision to include a brand assortment of home products such as stoves, washing machines, dryers, and electronics. Since the home center industry was composed of small firms with limited resources, the strategy of scrambled merchandising was an aggressive method to satisfy customer demand. Lowe's made the controversial decision to target female consumers for home improvement center products when many women viewed the shopping environment as dusty, unkept, and a male bastion. A contiguous expansion was the cornerstone of growth limiting this stepping-stone strategy to small towns, avoiding direct conflict with Home Depot. This strategy is changing, and Lowe's is now planning to compete directly with Home Depot. This decision may backfire, and the profitability of both organizations may diminish in the future.

LESSONS LEARNED FROM PAST MISTAKES AND FAILURES

The target markets served by firms in the home improvement center industry vary. Home Depot, Lowe's, and Payless Cashways, the three largest firms in the home improvement center industry, serve different target markets. Home Depot has situated itself in either large urban or suburban communities. Lowe's has located itself in small towns. Payless Cashways follows a focused-niche strategy targeting upper-income consumers. Grossman's and Moore's maintain their home center and lumberyard images. Hechinger and Wickes have not learned the lessons of the past and need to revise strategies and make objectives crystal clear.

The home improvement center industry is in the late growth stage of the institutional life cycle or in the accelerated development stage of the retail life cycle. This is in contrast to department, discount, and warehouse retailing stores that are in the maturity stage. Retail store types, like products, proceed from one stage of growth or decline to another. A retail store type emerges, passes through a period of accelerated growth, reaches maturity, and then declines. Older retail types took many years to reach maturity, but newer retail types reached their maturity much earlier. The department store, for example, reached maturity after 80 years, whereas warehouse outlets, as more modern types, reached their maturity in approximately 10 years. Home improvement centers, a new store type, have emerged to satisfy widely different consumer preferences for service levels and specific services.

Home improvement centers such as Home Depot and Lowe's have learned the lessons of the past and have developed strategies for success:

- Make customers happy. Provide guidance in the use of products sold. Extend customers better values than the competition and present a wider merchandise assortment to select from. Maintain a high level of customer satisfaction.

- Maintain a low ratio of rent to sales because of volume selling.
- Motivate employees to have pride in the store's merchandise and to maintain in-depth product knowledge. If possible, try to save the customer money. Motivated employees should help to increase customer repeat patronage.
- Strictly enforce controlling service, cleanliness, and all other aspects of the operation.
- Take advantage of favorable word-of-mouth communication, thereby decreasing promotional costs. Satisfied customers are the best "advertisements."
- Identify and cultivate a growing market. The do-it-yourself market of both male and female consumers is growing.
- The image of the home improvement center must be clear and distinctive.

Wickes did not learn that while growth is possible, it should not exceed the capabilities of the organization to control and provide sufficient managerial and financial resources. Evans Products had not learned that the most prudent approach to growth is to keep the operation and organization as simple as possible. Both Wickes and Evans Products lost sight of the perspective that short-term growth may sometimes have to be sacrificed in order to ensure a profitable future. Home improvement centers such as Home Depot and Lowe's have learned that opportunities exist when a traditional market structure prevails and when there are gaps in satisfying customer needs by existing firms. However, Lowe's, with its recent decision to compete directly with Home Depot, may be exceeding the capabilities of its organization.

CHAPTER 8

Hamburgers: Gold in Those Hills

Environmental Changes

- Fierce competition from competitors
- Health and dietary changes
- Ethnic population changes
- Popularity of take-out food
- New upscale markets

Strategies in a Mature Market

- Maintain low price strategies
- Maintain cost-focus approach
- Broaden menu offerings
- Position image and product offerings to stand apart from competitors
- Use value approach strategies
- Offer fast, superior customer service
- Delete unprofitable product offerings

A larger and growing percentage of retail sales volume is conducted through franchise systems. Organizations such as McDonald's, Wendy's, Burger King, and Hardee's own some of their retail units but usually franchise the majority of their units to help obtain wider market coverage. Franchisors expect franchisees to conform to standardized contractual rules and regulations and to pay compensation for the privilege to use the franchise name. The franchisor provides some or all of the following services: location analysis; store development, including lease negotiations, store design, and aid in equipment purchasing; management training; promotion assistance; centralized purchasing; financial assistance in the establishment of the business; exclusive location; and the goodwill and identification of a well-known corporate name. In return, the parent organization or franchisor charges the franchisee an initial franchise fee, an operating fee based on gross sales, rental or lease fees for facilities and equipment, and management fees for rendered services and assistance.

Many firms in the hamburger industry use a type of franchise arrangement known as *business format franchising*. Business format franchising, as opposed to product/trademark franchising, emphasizes a more interactive relationship between the franchisor and the franchisee. Although variations in franchising exist in the hamburger industry, most of these firms are good examples of a business format franchise arrangement. McDonald's, for instance, provides each new franchisee with intensive training and established franchisees with updated training at its "Hamburger University" and distributes a detailed operations manual. A conventional franchisee might invest more than $600,000, about which $570,000 purchases kitchen equipment, signs, seating, decor, and preopening expenses. Royalty fees of at least 12 percent of gross sales are paid to McDonald's. It is expected that the most minute facets of the operations manual will be closely followed by the franchisee and monitored by the McDonald's organization.

Tensions do arise between franchisors and franchisees. Since the franchisee is not an employee but an independent owner, franchisor controls can be viewed as too rigid. The franchise agreement frequently contains a buy-back clause, and franchisees might fear that the franchisor would exercise this option because of higher profit potential. Another source of conflict is that restrictions on product purchases might cause franchisees to believe that they might be charged higher prices and that product assortments may be too limited.

Five key ingredients seem to be important for either success or failure in the fast-food hamburger industry: innovation, market segmentation, image, physical environmental resources, and human resources. Innovation took place when McDonald's developed the concept of the assembly-line hamburger with french fries and when Wendy's became the first hamburger chain to offer a salad bar and baked potatoes nationwide.

McDonald's earned high marks for image identification with its golden arches and for its trade character Ronald McDonald, which has become almost as well known to children as Santa Claus. Wendy's has been successful in targeting the female market. Hardee's has successfully targeted the small-town market.

Hardee's has used physical environmental resources well with vertical integration of a bakery operation, a food-processing firm, and a construction firm. McDonald's, in an effort to compete in small-town markets, emphasizes a smaller cafe-style restaurant in total square feet than units located in metropolitan and suburban areas. White Tower confines itself to primarily the New York City metropolitan area, thereby concentrating its resources while extending itself by supermarket distribution and mail order.

McDonald's has cultivated human resources well by the establishment of Hamburger University, which trains owners or franchisees. This learning center stresses the teaching of standardized procedures that are essential to a successful operation. Although both Ray Kroc of McDonald's and Dave Thomas of Wendy's have innovated in the hamburger industry, neither has approached the expertise of Sam Walton of Wal-Mart or Bernard Marcus of Home Depot as a people motivator. One reason might be that personnel in the hamburger industry are trained to follow precise rules and procedures.

Failure in the hamburger industry is represented by Burger Chef. Burger Chef did not innovate and was unable to effectively control product quality or service and therefore could not match the efficiencies of McDonald's or Burger King. Burger Chef lacked a distinctive image and was unable to successfully target a specific market segment. Mistakes were made in selection of locations, diminishing the impact of physical resources. Burger Chef had also expanded too quickly and lacked uniform franchise operational efficiencies.

THE FAST-FOOD INDUSTRY

The service franchise has become exceedingly popular in recent years. Among the larger organizations serving the fast-food market are the McDonald Corporation, Kentucky Fried Chicken, Pizza Hut, Taco Bell, and Rax Roast Beef. Fast-food franchising has greatly increased the opportunities for individuals to become independent entrepreneurs. Franchising has provided opportunities for minority group members to own their own businesses. Moreover, fast-food franchising businesses have lower failure rates than other types of businesses. Although fast-food franchising has many positive features, negative characteristics are that the franchise agreements are often drawn up to favor the interests of franchisors and thus limit the flexibility of the franchisee.

An important advantage in becoming a franchisee is the program of research and development that is designed to improve the product or the service. Wendy's and McDonald's have continuous programs of research designed to identify new menu additions that could improve profitability and satisfy customer tastes. Guidance is also available in site selection and financial record keeping.

A franchise system pools resources and coordinates product and marketing activities to make a greater market impact and to obtain operational economies of scale, which are more difficult for the unaffiliated businessperson to achieve. The capital and entrepreneurial spirit of the franchisee is combined with the strength of an established, more experienced franchisor organization. A standardized program facilitates operational economies in activities such as group purchasing and cooperative advertising. Local market entry is much easier with an established market identity.

Business format franchising, which fast-food restaurants are a part of, is forecast to expand at a rapid pace. The fast-food hamburger industry is moving toward more diversified menus including salad bars, poultry, and roast beef. A shift to ethnic foods such as tacos and burritos is increasing. Significant development of foreign markets will continue during the next decade. Canada continues to be an attractive market for hamburger organizations, but Japan and the United Kingdom also provide many market opportunities.

Hamburger organizations, which have experienced tremendous growth for the past two decades, have reached a plateau as a result of both direct and indirect competition in the United States. Convenience stores, gasoline stations, and supermarkets are just some of the places where the consumer can purchase a hamburger.

The issue of maintaining fast customer service and satisfaction in a maturing industry that has broadened its menu offerings must be considered. Additional items such as fish, roast beef, and perhaps pizza will slow customer service. A very real challenge of maintaining high customer service standards confronts not only hamburger organizations but the fast-food industry as well. Not only is the quality of the menu items an important consideration, but issues of ecology and nutrition have now pushed their way to the forefront.

Fast-food operations have been successful because their focus has been on a narrow product range, an emphasis on division of labor, standardization of tasks, and extensive short-interval measurement of performance levels.

Consumer eating habits have changed noticeably in the 1990s. Consumers have become more health conscious and concerned about the fat and sodium content of foods. Moreover, adults are monitoring their weight. Consumption of poultry products such as chicken and turkey has increased, while consumption of red meats has declined. Lean meats with lower cholesterol content are a significant consumer preference. The method of food preparation—whether it is broiled or fried—has become another concern.

As a result of consumer interest in nutritional and caloric value of foods, McDonald's has reduced the sodium content in its foods about 15 percent since 1983. Moreover, vegetable shortening is now used to fry its chicken and fish. Wendy's offers baked potatoes as an alternative to french fries, and both Burger King and Wendy's maintain extensive salad bars, while McDonald's offers prepackaged salads.

Some consumers with small children, or for other reasons, find it more convenient to eat at home. Take-out and home delivery services have rapidly emerged in the fast-food industry. Pizza restaurants have used home delivery as a competitive strategy. Chinese restaurants have stressed their take-out food services. Even supermarkets have tried to compete by offering take-out food services, deli sandwiches, and salads.

Aging baby boomers, now in their forties and more established financially, are demanding higher-quality and higher-priced entries in the fast-food industry. Many baby boomers are part of double-income families, which eat out more frequently and desire to upgrade their restaurant selection. Such chains as Mr. Steak and Red Lobster have targeted this more upscale market.

COMPETITIVE STRATEGY TECHNIQUES

Competitive strategy is marketplace driven. The objective is to develop a competitive advantage in creating value for customers. A competitive differential may stem from brand power, advertising, information systems technology, product quality, selling effectiveness, service, or some other area. This strategy may be developed through the planning process or through functional departments of the firm. Frequently, environmental forces drive competitors to develop strategies to combat varying intensities of competition. Among the forces driving the hamburger industry are the retail life cycle, market segmentation, and product differentiation strategies.

RETAIL LIFE CYCLE

The retail life cycle model maintains that over time all retail institutions pass through a series of stages known as innovation, accelerated development, maturity, and decline. The duration of each stage varies, and any given stage may last many years. During each stage, retailers must be able to adjust and adopt their strategies to meet environmental conditions such as changing consumer demands, competitive actions, and changing economic circumstances. Risks and opportunities are present at each stage of the retail life cycle.

The first stage in the retail life cycle is innovation. An innovation usually represents some marked departure from existing norms. This change from existing industry practice may be directed to cost structure and price, a unique feature, a distinctive product assortment, or a new operational strategy. The second stage, accelerated development, is characterized by geographic expansion and the market entry of new competitors. The third stage, market maturity, is marked by intense competition and therefore must be carefully managed. For example, Burger King has returned to a more functional organization, which increases central control, reduces substantial overhead, and increases opportunities for coordination. There is more attention to costs and customer service and less attention to new product introduction versus refining existing ones. The final stage in the retail life cycle is the decline stage. During this stage, industry sales and profits begin to decline, and a shakeout occurs. Burger Chef, for example, had to consolidate its resources and closed many of its retail units.

The retail life cycle model offers an explanation of how hamburger chains have evolved. Expansion by using standardized operating systems and limited menu offerings was the focus in the beginning stages. During the accelerated development stage, there is a high level of investment to sustain growth, and a preemptive market position is established. Improved productivity, efficiency planning, and control efforts become critical in maturity. Adaptation is essential toward the end of the cycle as the chains place more emphasis on nonfat and leaner products to satisfy changing consumer health preferences.

MARKET SEGMENTATION AND PRODUCT DIFFERENTIATION STRATEGIES

The mass market is large and diverse in its tastes and preferences. A marketer wishing to serve the mass market tries to be all things to all people with a single undifferentiated marketing program. In most product markets, it is likely that undifferentiated marketing will cause some consumer needs and wants to go unsatisfied. To better serve diverse customer preferences, and to potentially strengthen its competitive position through more focused efforts, a marketer can undertake a market segmentation strategy.

Market segmentation is the process of dividing the mass market into groups of consumers with similar combinations of needs, wants, demographics, life-styles, and behavior within each group segment. Each segment typically re-quires a separate marketing program. Once market segments are identified, they are evaluated for (1) strategic fit with the marketer's strengths, (2) com-petitive intensity, (3) profitability, and (4) reachability. Once the segments are screened, one or more segments are selected as target markets to be served with a tailored marketing program. McDonald's, for example, originally targeted lunch and late-night-snack customers. Following careful research and analy-sis, the store targeted other market segments such as consumers who desired a quick breakfast on the way to work. New menu items such as the Egg Mc-Muffin and pancakes were added to the menu. New promotional campaigns were developed to announce the new offering.

Unlike market segmentation, which focuses on consumer differences, a product differentiation strategy focuses on developing and promoting dif-ferences among products that compete with one another within market segments or in the mass market. For example, consumers within the market segment that likes hamburgers as part of a meal or snack can choose from McDonald's fried burgers or Burger King's flame-broiled variety. In this situation, the product is differentiated, but it is still aimed at the same market segment of consumers who like hamburgers. Thus, two or more marketers can attempt to serve the same market segment or the mass mar-ket with differentiated products.

Both market segmentation and product differentiation strategies are sub-ordinate to corporate strategic planning. Strategic planning is long range and shapes the future direction of an organization. As such, strategic plan-ning anticipates changing environments and provides for contingency plan-ning and organizational adaptation.

The changing demographic environment is especially important to mar-keters in the restaurant industry. An aging population, for example, is likely to change its patronage and product purchase behavior because of health-related concerns, higher income, and taste levels. Accordingly, firms in the hamburger industry have considered segmenting the market on demo-graphic variables such as age and gender.

Wendy's has positioned itself as an adult-oriented fast-food hamburger chain and has attracted the largest proportion of female customers. Geo-graphic segmentation is precarious in many large markets. For example, Wendy's is underrepresented in New York and California. In the late

1980s, Wendy's tried to broaden its base of targeted consumers by focusing on weekend and dinner markets and opened restaurants in Sears and even in supermarkets.

McDonald's has successfully used a differentiated market segmentation strategy by targeting the family unit and particularly children with their "Happy Meals" and prices. McDonald's has traditionally offered lower prices than other hamburger chains, thus gaining the patronage of larger-size families. The location of its outlets has been instrumental in making McDonald's so successful. It was the first hamburger chain to expand into the suburbs and into the crowded downtown areas of large urban cities. McDonald's is now opening outlets in airports and even hospitals.

Other hamburger organizations have tried to segment the market in different ways but have not been as successful as Wendy's and McDonald's with the exception of Hardee's, which has developed its strategy based on geographical market segmentation. Hardee's has focused on serving small towns, thereby avoiding fierce battles with other chains in the past.

Both McDonald's and Burger King serve multiple segments of customers. These fast-food chains serve families with young children and also serve breakfast in the morning. This service is aimed at adults who want a quick breakfast on their way to work. Since breakfast is confined to the morning hours, the two markets of adults and families are not intermingled at lunch and dinner. Both McDonald's and Burger King have thus increased sales without substantial new capital investments. Another illustration of serving multiple markets is the hamburger industry's efforts to cultivate the children's market. McDonald's, for example, has aimed promotional campaigns for its hamburgers, meal kits, and parties at children for years. Both Hardee's and Wendy's have reconsidered their objectives and strategies and are presently aiming marketing development campaigns at the children's segment of the market.

A firm must use tactics that are consistent with its strategies. For example, McDonald's provides play areas in its retail outlets and "Happy Meals" for children, since the family is the target market. Providing beer or a jukebox would be inconsistent with McDonald's strategy. Another aspect of McDonald's segmentation strategy is to provide convenient locations, clean and attractive surroundings, efficient service, and reasonable prices. Consequently, McDonald's has differentiated itself from competitors by establishing an image of consistency, efficiency, and trustworthiness.

THE HAMBURGER WARS

The fastest-growing form of competition in the retail fast-food hamburger industry is intertype competition—direct confrontation in a specific food category between different types of restaurants. Competition between hamburger chains, referred to as *intratype competition*, is intense but is not growing as fast as intertype competition. Intertype competition occurs when hamburger chains sell chicken and roast beef sandwiches and, conversely, when roast beef organizations sell burgers. Although fast-food restaurants have specialized in different foods, broadened menu offerings have pitted different types of fast-food restaurants against each other.

Scrambled merchandising by retailers has contributed to intertype competition. Scrambled merchandising is a situation where merchandise unrelated to the primary mission of the retailer is sold. Several factors may encourage a retailer to add merchandise normally sold by other types of retailers. The more important reasons include (1) the desire to increase patronage and (2) the low costs of adding items because of the overhead and labor cost already being covered. Another related reason for scrambled marketing is the perceived growth potential of certain markets. The latter has prompted McDonald's to experiment with the sale of pizza, and Hardee's to add roast beef, fried chicken, and submarine sandwiches to their product assortment.

The increased frequency of intertype competition has made it more difficult for retailers to identify and monitor their competition. Competition is indirect because all retailers compete against each other for their share of the consumer's dollar.

Intratype competition, however, is greatest when retailers offer similar products. For example, competition between a Burger King and a Wendy's located at the same intersection would be very intense since both offer similar product assortments.

MCDONALD'S: A PIONEER

McDonald's was founded by Ray Kroc, one of the pioneers of the modern franchise organization format, in 1955. Ray Kroc was a salesman of malted milk machines who observed that one of his customers, a hamburger restaurant operated by Maurice and Richard McDonald, had developed the concept of the assembly-line hamburger with french fries. There was also a large sign in front of the restaurant displaying two golden arches. Kroc became enchanted with this fast-food concept and talked the McDonald brothers into allowing him to sell the franchise rights nationwide. By 1961, there were some 228 franchise units, and Ray Kroc completely bought out the McDonald brothers' interests.

Ray Kroc strongly believed in the concept of systems. Quality, service, and cleanliness served as the basic goals for the system. The system also stressed physical standardization. While the hamburger industry in the 1950s had a reputation for slovenly conditions, Kroc emphasized clean surroundings, including personnel, equipment, and scrupulously clean restrooms.

McDonald's situated itself in suburban locations, cultivating the vast population movement of the late 1950s and 1960s. In contrast, many fast-food firms chose to remain in the central cities and ignored suburban growth. In the 1970s, McDonald's expanded into the cities and into some small towns.

In 1968, McDonald's established Hamburger University, which was to serve as a teaching and training model for the hamburger industry. The success of this learning center is attributed to the teaching of standardized procedures that are vital to a successful operation. All franchisees must attend and also receive retraining at specified time intervals.

The trade character Ronald McDonald, first played by Willard Scott, a well-known weatherman, has become almost as well known to children as Santa Claus. The work of Ronald McDonald houses adjacent to hospitals for the purpose of serving both ill children and their families has earned international respect and praise.

BURGER KING: A ME-TOO OUTLOOK

Burger King was founded in 1954 by entrepreneurs who believed that there was consumer demand for hamburger restaurants that would serve reasonably priced quality food, served quickly, in attractive clean environments. In 1967, the Pillsbury Company acquired Burger King but sold it to Grand Metropolitan in 1988, a British firm considered to be a world leader in the food, retailing, and beverage businesses. Currently, Burger King is the second-largest fast-food hamburger restaurant in the United States with more than 6,200 retail units.

Burger King has been beset with problems since the late 1970s. These problems were partially caused by management changes, strategy modifications, and ineffective advertising campaigns. An attempt to broaden menu offerings with pizza and veal parmigiana sandwiches was also unsuccessful. But Burger King has had some success with its salad bars.

Burger King, like McDonald's, targets the family market and, like McDonald's, has also segmented the adult market by serving breakfast. Burger King is considered a clone of McDonald's with only slight differences to set them apart. Consequently, Burger King is vulnerable to competitive attacks by Hardee's, which has acquired Roy Rogers and is aggressively leaving its small-town base. Like McDonald's, Hardee's also caters to the breakfast segment of the fast-food market.

WENDY'S: AN INNOVATOR

Wendy's was founded in 1969 by R. David Thomas, who was previously a regional operations director for Kentucky Fried Chicken and a vice president of operations at Arthur Treacher's Fish and Chips. Thomas's marketing strategy development was greatly influenced by Colonel Harlan Sanders, the founder of Kentucky Fried Chicken. By 1975, Wendy's had opened its one-hundredth restaurant, and by 1979, ten years after its initial opening, Wendy's had more than 1,700 units operating in the United States, Puerto Rico, Canada, and Europe.

Thomas had modest plans in the beginning. The first restaurant included carpeting, tiffany-style lamps, and Bentwood chairs. Emphasis was on providing a homey environment. The first menu included fresh, made-to-order hamburgers, chili, french fries, Frosty Dairy Dessert, and soft drinks. The restaurant chain was named after his daughter Melinda Lou, nicknamed "Wendy" by her brother and sisters.

Wendy's differentiates its offerings on product quality. Wendy's hamburgers are 100 percent ground beef, and its chicken sandwich is made from a skinless breast of chicken pressured-fried in vegetable shortening. Wendy's hamburgers, unlike McDonald's, are broiled on a grill, while McDonald's are fried. Wendy's was the first hamburger chain to offer a salad bar nationwide and the first to offer baked potatoes nationally. Wendy's offers the most diverse menu, compared with McDonald's and Burger King, and has the largest proportion of female customers.

When Thomas first opened his restaurants, Wendy's depended on word-of-mouth communication to spread the word about high-quality food, friendly service, and the pleasant dining atmosphere. But as the chain developed, Wendy's in 1973 turned to local television and radio advertising. In 1977, Wendy's turned to nationally televised commercials, winning a Clio Award for creativity. In 1981, R. David Thomas was featured in the company's national advertising campaigns, which characterized a personalized appeal to customers. In 1984, Wendy's achieved sales success with its "Where's the beef?" television ad campaign that rocked the ad world and became a household phrase.

HARDEE'S: SMALL-TOWN ROOTS

Wilbur Hardee opened the first unit of his restaurant chain in 1961 in Rocky Mount, North Carolina. This first restaurant served as a prototype for many others with a uniform design that would include ceramic tile, aluminum, glass, and approximately $25,000 in equipment. An outstanding feature was a water-purifying system that floated away grease and kept the charcoal free from impurities. This was one of the few broilers of this type operating in the United States at that time.

In 1962, Hardee's formed its own manufacturing and distribution group, now known as Fast Food Merchandisers, which services nearly all of its retail outlets. The hexagonal pagoda-style building was introduced in 1963. Hardee's first international unit was opened in Heidelberg, Germany, in 1965. Vertical integration became an important characteristic of the Hardee system as a bakery operation, a food-processing firm, and a construction company were acquired in 1967. Five years later, a 200-unit fast-food chain in the Midwest, Sandy's, merged with Hardee's. In 1981, Imasco Ltd., a Canadian conglomerate, purchased Hardee's and was able to better finance future expansion. Consequently, in 1982, more than 700 restaurants of the Burger Chef organization were acquired from General Foods. The Burger Chef acquisition gave Hardee's a Midwest orientation, but Hardee's has still focused on developing retail units in small towns. The objective was to serve markets not dominated by such chains as McDonald's and Burger King. This policy had worked well in the past, and in 1983, Hardee's size soared to 2,000 units. In the 1990s Hardee's acquired Roy Rogers and comprised approximately 4,000 store units.

BURGER CHEF: MARKETING MISTAKES

Burger Chef's approximately 700 retail units were acquired by General Foods Corporation in 1967. The chain was substantially expanded to some 1,200 outlets by 1970. Two years later, Burger Chef was in financial difficulties. Key personnel had left Burger Chef for a variety of reasons, and new management was not effective. Consequently, the chain incurred heavy losses. Expansion had been launched too quickly, and mistakes were made in selecting locations and controlling quality of product and service.

The demise of Burger Chef can be attributed to a combination of factors. Burger Chef lacked a distinctive sign such as McDonald's golden arches, the outlets themselves were cheaply constructed, and there was little uniformity in design among the franchised operations. Another factor was that its 700 outlets at the time of the Hardee acquisition in 1982 were thinly dispersed and spread over 39 states. A better strategy would have been a slower geographical expansion based on market-by-market development.

WHITE CASTLE: A PICTURE OF LOYAL PATRONS

White Castle was established in 1921 and is generally considered the original fast-food hamburger chain. Its loyal patrons are sometimes referred to as part of a fanatic cult. White Castle has preferred not to franchise and retains complete control and ownership of its own units. White Castle is a small chain with only about 200 units situated in nine states. Wider market coverage is achieved through mail-order and telemarketing operations and by selling packages of its hamburgers and cheeseburgers in the frozen-food sections of supermarkets.

THE HAMBURGER WARS INTENSIFY

McDonald's has been the leading fast-food restaurant chain in the hamburger industry. Burger King, Wendy's, and Hardee's hold second, third, and fourth positions, respectively, in the industry. McDonald's has successfully targeted the family market with an emphasis on children. Wendy's has successfully targeted the adult market, while Hardee's has successfully used geographic segmentation in small towns. In 1990, however, Hardee's acquired the 650 Roy Rogers restaurants, giving Hardee's not only a strong presence in the Northeast but also locations in larger cities. Burger King has tried to appeal to the same market segments as McDonald's but, like Montgomery Ward, appears to be a poor second. Thus, Burger King is presently the most vulnerable to both direct and indirect competition.

McDonald's marketing strategy has focused on menu diversification, site location extension, improving public relations, and price discounts in a recessionary period. In the 1980s and early 1990s, McDonald's introduced the Chicken Biscuit Sandwich, McNuggets, bran muffins, frozen yogurt, prepackaged salads, McRib, and Breakfast Burritos. The McChicken Sandwich was a failure. New retail outlets have been opened in airports and hospitals. By the end of 1994, more than 5,400 units have been established outside of the United States, in 79 countries, giving McDonald's more than 14,650 restaurants worldwide. The promotional message has advanced goodwill with the annual Charity Christmas Parade in Chicago and its Ronald McDonald House exposure. McDonald's has worked with school administrators to promote reading programs among children. During the recessionary period of 1991–1992, McDonald's has emphasized value meals in order to maintain its market share in the hamburger industry.

Through the years, McDonald's has developed a favorable image, consisting of value in its product, fast service, and a diversified product line. New McDonald's are opening in such novel locations as zoos, office buildings, hospitals, and schools. The breakfast menu is cultivating customers over the age of 35, which have not previously been an important market segment.

Burger King's marketing strategy concentrated on product differentiation in the 1980s by offering a more diversified menu. Chicken Fingers, Chicken Tenders, Fish Tenders, and a salad bar were introduced. Burger King was the first hamburger chain to cater to nutritional trends by publishing a guide that included information on calories, fat, salt, and protein content of menu items. Efforts were made to attract new market segments by including broiled chicken on the menu and by offering Haagen-Daz ice cream bars. Promotional efforts were weak, and Burger King's advertising campaigns appeared to have missed their mark.

Wendy's marketing strategy has focused on market segmentation. Wendy's in the late 1980s experimented with appealing to the family, weekend, and dinner markets. Moreover, drive-through restaurants and take-out menus have been added. Wendy's has broadened its location base by opening restaurants in Sears and supermarkets. Wendy's has positioned itself as a hamburger chain at the higher end of the fast-food spectrum. Because of the recession in the early 1990s and Wendy's desire to broaden its customer base, low-priced value-oriented menu items were launched. New and expanded training programs were also introduced to improve customer service.

In an effort to further segment the market, a breakfast menu has been offered in selected locations. Wendy's has offered, in a few hundred retail outlets, omelettes, breakfast sandwiches, and french toast. A breaded fillet chicken breast sandwich was added in 1980. Wendy's also added a Wendy's Kids' Meal, which consisted of a smaller hamburger, smaller order of french fries, and a small Frosty (much like a milkshake) or a small soft drink. Another new item was the taco salad, which capitalized on consumer interest in ethnic food, which is a growing, viable market that other hamburger chains have largely ignored.

Hardee's marketing strategy has focused on expansion through acquisition. In 1982, Hardee's acquired Burger Chef's 650 units from General Foods Corporation, giving the firm market coverage in the Midwest. In 1990, Hardee's added to its 3,110-unit chain some 650 stores of the Roy Rogers chain in key markets such as Washington, D.C., Baltimore, Philadelphia, and New York City, making Hardee's the number-three hamburger chain just ahead of Wendy's. Hardee's strength in the breakfast market, which represents about 30 percent of sales, complemented Roy Rogers' success with dinner items such as fried chicken, thus broadening the chain's customer base.

Although the Roy Rogers' acquisition was synergistically sound, Hardee's encountered difficulty in convincing Roy Rogers' 287 franchisees to convert into Hardee's outlets. Market research conducted after the acquisition confirmed that consumers in the Northeast—where Hardee's had no brand recognition—preferred the Roy Rogers name and wanted it back. Consequently, in 1992, Roy Rogers was relaunched as its own chain, and those 363 company-owned Roy Rogers' outlets that had been converted to Hardee's were switched back.

The Roy Rogers' conversion failure and plunging profits from $118 million in 1989 to $40 million in 1991 contributed to Hardee's decision to scale back plans to turn the regional chain into a nationwide fast-food company.

White Castle's marketing strategy is unique among the hamburger chains in that direct mail is used to reach a broader customer base. Some market segments are intensely loyal and place orders by mail since White Castle does not have retail outlets situated nationally. White Castle uses a product preparation method of steaming the hamburgers, which is unique in the hamburger industry. This preparation method produces a much easier-to-eat, moist product that is especially preferred by children. By the 1980s, White Castle had fewer than 300 retail outlets situated in only nine states, but their average sales per unit are the highest in the industry, exceeding even McDonald's. Supermarket distribution has been another marketing strategy employed by this chain. White Castle has established itself as a small but innovative leader in the hamburger industry that has survived in an industry populated by financially stronger hamburger chains.

The focus of the hamburger industry has been primarily on market segmentation. There is, however, a cost leadership thrust that has been developed by McDonald's. McDonald's has maintained this cost leadership advantage through rigid standardization of operating procedures and is currently adopting a different strategy in small-town penetration of the market. This strategy emphasizes a smaller cafe-style restaurant in total square feet than units located in metropolitan and suburban areas. Hardee's has used a focus strategy aimed at a target market situated in small towns. Costs were controlled by a specialized reputation but is now challenged by the emergence of McDonald's and Burger King in similar locations. Wendy's has appealed to an adult market with a differentiation strategy. Wendy's has offered a product assortment and services that were viewed by an adult market as distinctive. White Castle has also used a focused strategy in its product offering and has cultivated a very small and distinct market with unique services. Burger King has not developed a clear strategy and, as a result, has experienced below-average performance in the industry. Burger King appears to have followed the earlier lackluster pattern of Montgomery Ward as a close market follower of McDonald's.

INDIRECT COMPETITION

The shift of consumer preferences for various types of nonhamburger fast food has presented the hamburger chains with strong indirect competition. Sales of nonhamburger fast food have grown, while sales for the hamburger industry have remained constant. Chains such as Pizza Hut, Kentucky Fried Chicken, and Taco Bell hold dominant positions in the fast-food categories of pizza, chicken, and Mexican food.

Pizza Hut

Pizza Hut has changed from primarily an eat-in restaurant to an organization that concentrates on distribution and home delivery. Pizza Hut is situated in 54 countries and is a leader in 46 of these markets. Approximately 25 percent of revenue is derived from distribution. Pizza Hut, in 1977, was acquired by PepsiCo, which is also the parent company of Kentucky Fried Chicken and Taco Bell.

Pizza Hut is experimenting with a drive-thru-only kiosk and kiosks in 7-Eleven stores. Pizza Hut has also developed a franchise agreement with Washington, D.C.–based Marriott Corporation in which Marriott has placed 900 kiosks in its own contract food locations, including airports, colleges, and hospitals. Hand-tossed traditional pizza was added to the product line in 1988, which now accounts for about 20 percent of total sales. In the 1980s the five-minute personal pan pizza was introduced and positioned against the traditional fast-food hamburger industry by offering a similarly quick preparation and serving time.

Taco Bell

The fastest-growing fast-food category is Mexican. Taco Bell is the foremost fast-food restaurant chain in the Mexican food category with more than 3,200 units. Approximately 40 percent of these 3,200 outlets are franchised. Ninety percent of Taco Bell's restaurants are freestanding, but the company is investigating alternative formats.

Taco Bell has broadened its menu base by introducing Steak Fajitas, Chicken Fajitas, and Meximelt, a tortilla with melted cheese. Wendy's and McDonald's have partially entered this market, but Burger King and Hardee's have not joined in as yet. Taco Bell is noted for its value menu and most recently its "lite" menu items.

Kentucky Fried Chicken

Kentucky Fried Chicken has experienced a host of managerial problems in the past. Its original founder, Colonel Harlan Sanders, was noted by the press to have exclaimed that his original recipe had not been followed by all retail units and that the changed recipe tasted "like sandpaper."

New product offerings such as Chicken Little sandwiches and grilled chicken were introduced in the late 1980s. In addition to the freestanding stores, new outlets have been opened in shopping malls, and the chain has experimented with home delivery.

PepsiCo is experimenting with the concept of combining Pizza Hut, Taco Bell, and Kentucky Fried Chicken into one store. The objective is to provide customers with a greater selection. These combination stores have been established in at least ten locations.

MANAGING CHANGE

Several environmental trends confront managers in the hamburger industry as they endeavor to manage change. Americans have more fast-food options. Americans today are more concerned with healthy diets. Americans eat at fast-food restaurants when in a hurry but eat in family restaurants for a more diversified menu and better food. Americans are more concerned with value during economic downturns. The hamburger industry is experiencing slow growth after nearly three decades of double-digit gains.

The hamburger industry, confronted with slow growth and the competition from family restaurants, has diversified its menu. Some hamburger chains have added salad bars, and nearly all offer some varieties of chicken, roast beef, and fish. Wendy's and McDonald's are offering some Mexican foods. McDonald's is test marketing pizza, which, as an industry, is experiencing greater growth than hamburgers.

The hamburger industry has switched from cooking with beef tallow to 100 percent vegetable oil for preparing fries and hash browns. Ice cream has been replaced with low-fat yogurt, and cereal and bran muffins have been introduced for breakfast. As the industry begins to target dinner customers, spaghetti, fettucini, and fish and chips offerings will help to focus on this untapped market segment.

As Americans became more health conscious, the hamburger industry responded. Wendy's introduced the salad bar, which appealed to the more mature, health-conscious adult. In 1983, Wendy's introduced the baked potato with various toppings. Although Wendy's had traditionally appealed to the adult market, this new product introduction of baked potatoes especially targeted adult women who were not considered heavy users of fast food. Moreover, in 1991, Wendy's aimed their Supervalue Menu, which consisted of nine items priced at 99 cents each, at working mothers with children at dinnertime. Wendy's also copied McDonald's in 1983 and introduced a breakfast menu to capitalize on using restaurant space that had previously been unused.

McDonald's strengthened its existing market with the addition of about 1,000 McDonaldland Parks in 1981. However, it was not until 1987 that freshly made salads were introduced, which was belatedly seven years after Wendy's had cultivated this part of the health-conscious market. Throughout the 1980s, McDonald's made a commitment to penetrating the Hispanic market. The breakfast burrito and the chicken fajitas were both introduced for this market. However, during this period, Wendy's introduced the Mexican Fiesta and Pasta Bar to attract ethnic groups and those who like ethnic food.

In contrast, to both Wendy's and McDonald's, Burger King has not made a special effort to target the fast-growing Hispanic market. Many Americans have cultivated a taste for Mexican food, but Burger King has not done very much to attract this viable, growing market. Both Wendy's and McDonald's have featured advertisements in foreign-language newspapers and radio stations to promote their restaurants to this market segment.

McDonald's has realized that the larger metropolitan and suburban markets are oversaturated with fast-food establishments. Consequently, the decision was made to penetrate small towns, which meant that McDonald's and Hardee's would be competing fiercely in the same markets. To compete more effectively, McDonald's developed a cafe concept that has been named the Golden Arch Cafe. The cafes are approximately half the size of standard McDonald's restaurants and are able to seat 50 people.

The challenge of the toxic waste movement has presented ominous problems to the fast-food industry. As the largest user of styrofoam packaging, McDonald's image became tarnished. Polystyrene is bulky, takes up space in landfills, and does not readily decompose. By 1991, the decision was made to replace the polystyrene with polycoated paper. Although this change in packaging solved one problem, it created another. With the introduction of paper packaging, customers are more apt to receive a cold and dry sandwich. The challenge of social responsibility has been temporarily met, but other alternatives still need investigation.

The hamburger industry has made effective use of market segmentation strategies and is studying consumer behavior to learn about the factors that consumers consider in searching for, purchasing, and evaluating the goods and services they seek. Lifestyle-based market segmentation strategies have been useful as cultural changes have had a profound impact on the buying behavior of the American family. In tracing changing cultural values and lifestyles, decision makers in the hamburger industry must recognize the combined influences of subcultures based on social class, ethnic origin, race, age, and geographic location. Subcultural values are assimilated by society, frequently providing market opportunities. An example of this process is the current interest in ethnic and health foods. Although there are few certainties for the hamburger industry, one is that business and environmental conditions will change at an accelerated rate. Managers in the hamburger industry will be confronted with uncertain forecasts of environmental change, and they must therefore be flexible in their adaptation strategies.

MANAGERIAL VISION

Managerial vision should focus on decisions that have long-term implications rather than on objectives focused on a one-to two-year period. This would allow for a proactive leadership style. However, management in the hamburger industry seems to utilize a reactive perspective with a maturity and control orientation. Moreover, there appears to be less emphasis on environmental analysis and contingency planning. Management reacts to developing lifestyle trends such as changes in diet and health concerns. Management does not provide for change in menu, store decor, or store location based on long-range planning.

Management should consider the marketing environment as dynamic and constantly changing. Instead, management often concentrates on maintaining a clearly delineated business operation. However, the focus should be on broadening the corporate mission and reducing strategic gaps. Support of basketball teams and bands are effective programs for stimulating demand for existing products in the short run, but long-range planning to decrease cholesterol content of meals has been lacking. Only after effective media and consumer group pressure did the hamburger chains decide to alter their food preparation and cooking methods.

The hamburger industry suffers from oversaturation in various geographic locations. Therefore, the sales and profits of each unit within these areas have been adversely affected. Managerial vision is needed to locate in uncultivated markets, such as hospitals, schools, and industrial organizations. Firms in the hamburger industry have operated alone in the past. Perhaps cooperative agreements need to be made with other types of food retailers, such as ice cream and yogurt shops, in order to offer customers more depth and breadth of product offerings.

McDonald's would appear to be more successful than Burger King. One reason might be that Burger King overstepped the limits of product differentiation in attempting to offer a more customized service than McDonald's. As product offerings are broadened, the elements for a successful fast-food operation are compromised, resulting in slower service and higher operating costs. A return to the basics including a more limited menu and the relative standardization of both product line and operating tasks may become more necessary in the future.

LESSONS LEARNED FROM SUCCESS AND FAILURE

Many of the lessons learned from success and failure in the hamburger industry stem from the indigenous nature of franchising. There must be a high degree of brand identity and adherence to rigorous operational and quality standards. McDonald's has met these two criteria, and this basically accounts for its phenomenal success. In contrast, Burger Chef failed because it did not exercise tight operational controls and had a weak brand identity.

Since the hamburger industry is in the maturity stage of the retail life cycle, business organizations will become even more vulnerable to competitive and environmental threats. Factors such as oversaturation of the market, which has plagued the supermarket industry, will also beset the hamburger industry. Even a moderately poor site selection will prove disastrous. The loss of experienced and well-qualified executives hastened the downfall of Burger Chef. Consequently, each hamburger organization will find itself in a bidding war to retain the best managerial talent.

The lessons learned from success and failure in the hamburger industry include the following:

- *Organizational concentration is vital for success.* Hardee's concentrated its operation in small towns in regional locations. Burger Chef units were thinly spread over 39 states. A strong market identity can be promoted and rigid operational controls implemented if the organization can group its forces in smaller geographical areas.

- *Product quality and diversification are essential in a mature market.* Product quality cannot be enforced unless rigid standardization is present. McDonald's has the most rigid operating controls and owes its success largely to this factor. Menu assortment becomes necessary in a mature market in order to cultivate the preferences of diverse market segments. Burger Chef made the mistake of standing pat in a mature market, and this decision was an important factor in its demise.

- *Service is tied to customer satisfaction.* Services such as order filling, preparation, and speed of generating a final product must be standardized and controlled from unit to unit. In this way, services maintain high standards in all locations, and a quality image can be maintained.

- *Social movements dictate strategies.* The social trend toward better nutrition has had a profound impact on menu changes such as salads and potatoes. This social movement has also had an impact on cooking methods.

- *Continuous experimentation and long-term planning are necessary to maintain success.* New product offerings such as ethnic food and pizza are needed in a mature market confronted with new competitive and environmental threats. Store size and locational convenience in schools, corporate restaurants, and other sites will need continuous monitoring.

- *Competitive structure in the industry must be understood.* McDonald's and Wendy's have achieved success with a differentiated cost leadership strategy. McDonald's has distinguished itself with superior customer service and product consistency while offering low prices and high value to consumers. It has also chosen to target families and children. Wendy's has built a reputation as an inexpensive fast-food restaurant for adults. Burger King, in contrast, has not developed a clear strategy and has tried, with very limited success, to be a follower of McDonald's.

CONTROVERSIAL DECISIONS

The initial decision by Ray Kroc, David Thomas, and other pioneers in the hamburger industry that a large consumer segment would be very receptive to eating hamburgers in a clean and wholesome environment was at that time controversial. The hamburger industry—McDonald's, Burger King, Wendy's, and Hardee's—has become an American institution. But the hamburger industry no longer innovates the way it did some years ago. A small chain, known as the White Tower, has made some exciting inroads by shipping its hamburgers by mail around the country and by selling to some supermarket chains.

As consumers mature, they tend to frequent family-type restaurants rather than fast-food establishments. It might make sense to house under one umbrella a restaurant that offers only hamburgers, a return to the original format; a restaurant that offers hamburgers, pizza, fish and chips, roast beef, and other types of fast food; and a family type of restaurant such as Shoney's. Hamburger industry executives need to develop more creative strategies to satisfy future consumer needs.

The controversial decision made by Domino's Pizza involving home delivery has made significant inroads into the hamburger industry market. The hamburger industry could counter this competitive strategy by making deliveries to business organizations. This might have the significant impact of employees remaining for lunch at their employee premises and this would prove very desirable for a number of business organizations.

CHAPTER 9

Hotels: Adventures in Lifestyle Market Segmentation

Consumer's Social Profile

- Culture
- Social class
- Social performance
- Time expenditures
- Family life cycle
- Reference groups
- Opinion leaders

The Decision Process

- Stimulus → problem awareness →
- demographics → information search →
- evaluation of alternatives → social and psychological factors → purchase →
- postpurchase behavior

Service Strategies

- Get closer to the hotel guest
- Maximize electronic and technological capability
- Improve and differentiate service offerings
- Enhance value of services
- Improve cash flow, occupancy rates, and financial returns
- Identify service opportunities and position service in accordance with hotel brand identity

T

he hotel industry for years was relatively complacent. The demand for hotel rooms generally exceeded the supply. During the 1980s the hotel industry experienced a building boom, and soon there was a decline in room occupancy. Management was confronted with the problem that hotels cannot be easily remodeled to satisfy customers' changing needs and that a product differentiation strategy was needed to make an individual hotel distinctive from the others. Many hotels had similar facilities and offered comparable services.

To meet these challenges, a strategy of lifestyle market segmentation was employed. For example, when Holiday Corporation learned that its mid-priced Holiday Inn hotels were confronted with competition from budget hotels and luxury chains, Holiday Inn responded by expanding into the high- and low-priced ends of the market. Embassy Suites, a chain of multiple-room suites, targeted mainly upscale business travelers and Hampton Inn hotels, a limited-service chain, targeted value-conscious business or pleasure travelers. Holiday Corporation also developed Homewood Suites, a chain of hotels designed for guests usually staying five or more nights. Other chains such as Days Inn and Motel 6 have targeted the budget end of the market and compete with Hampton Inn, which accounts for a sizable 20 percent of all hotel rooms in the United States. The Radisson Hotel in Wilmington, Delaware, has hosted many family reunions and has decided to actively pursue that market segment by advertising a reunion package for weekends. Residence Inn, a division of Marriott, specializes in providing accommodation on a long-term basis—stays up to six months or longer. All suites have full-service kitchens, and the hotel even offers a grocery-shopping service.

Hotels carefully try to match the service offering with the desired target market. Service tangibility can be increased by emphasizing service-provider reliability. Efforts must be made to offer similar services to market segments with different demand patterns. Although hotels endeavor to standardize services, there is the danger that while these services may have more consistent quality and convenience, the personal touch may be lacking. For instance, creative pricing has been used effectively. Several chains offer lower rates for weekend night stays and charge nothing for children under 18 accompanying their parents. Other chains offer bonuses for "frequent stayers," a promotion patterned after the airlines' frequent-flyer programs. However, Omni and Radisson have dropped their frequent-stay plans, due to lack of customer participation.

Each market segment requires different services. The business traveler desires efficient service, a desk in the room, and convenient conference rooms. A regular tourist desires a comfortable room, recreational facilities, and connections for sightseeing. Transient tourists desire a convenient location, low prices, and fast-food service. An extended-stay resident desires a home-away-from-home with kitchen facilities and apartment amenities. Convention participants desire large meeting rooms, exhibit space, preplanned sightseeing, and hospitality suites. To accommodate female business executives, some hotels offer rooms on security-closed floors with special keys that must be inserted in the elevator in order to stop, for added protection. First-run movies can be seen in the room, and hotel spas provide the latest exercise equipment and indoor swimming pools.

SERVICE CHARACTERISTICS

Many of the problems encountered in the retailing and marketing of services are due to their intangibility. For example, hotels that promise a good night's sleep to their customers cannot actually demonstrate this service in a tangible way. The hotel must somehow communicate to the consumer how a stay at the hotel will leave the customer feeling well rested and ready for the activities desired for the new day. This situation makes promotion difficult as well as creating problems in offering service quality. Therefore, image becomes an important factor in differentiating the service from its competition as consumers try to reduce risk and uncertainty. In efforts to associate security with their hotels, the Hilton, Hyatt, and Radisson provide rooms on "club" floors for both women and men that require a key to enter the floor from the passenger elevator. Rooms on these floors are priced at 20 percent above those on traditional floors.

Services are perishable, and therefore many hotels try to offset this limitation with visual images and tangible reminders of their services. Hotels provide packaged shampoos and soaps, shoe-polishing cloths, sewing kits, and other amenities with their name and logo imprinted. The Waterford Hotel in Oklahoma City, Oklahoma, stocks its bathrooms with fresh fruit and Perrier. Other hotels provide bathrooms with bathrobes, heated towel racks, dual-line telephones, and remote controls for the television.

Services are inseparable from their providers. Inseparability implies that public-contact personnel and the facilities should be pleasing to consumers and that multisite locations may be vital to make the service conveniently available. For example, even though desks and other equipment are available in its hotel rooms, the Marriott has "solo" dining tables in its restaurants, consisting of a table for one or two people with a reading lamp, notebook, writing instruments, and magazines.

Services are variable. Some units in hotel chains have reputations for providing better services than other units in the same chain. The Sheraton has encountered this problem as it tries to remodel and serve different consumer markets. More than two thirds of Sheraton hotels are franchised, and the quality of service can vary. For instance, some owners did not desire to invest in such capital improvements as sprinkler systems. Others had their own ideas about hotel designs that were incongruous with the ITT Sheraton desired image. Variations also existed in franchisees' perspectives about the amenities provided, and this resulted in significant differences in services offered. The situation became so critical that ITT Sheraton found it necessary to defranchise about 250 hotels. ITT Sheraton hopes to achieve a service level of consistency that will position its hotels at the upscale end of the hotel industry.

TOTAL CUSTOMER SATISFACTION

The philosophy that marketing strategies must be based upon consumer needs and wants has come to be known as the *marketing concept*. Pillsbury Company marketing executive Robert Keith can be given substantial credit for popularization of the marketing concept in 1960. The marketing concept is a basic philosophy that maintains that an organization should endeavor to satisfy the needs and wants of customers through a coordinated set of activities that also allows the organization to achieve its goals at a profit. Some hotels have failed in this task since they did not position themselves to target specific markets and to satisfy these specific markets. The hotel industry had not realized that it is insufficient to just provide a room without attention to services and amenities desired by specific market segments.

One of the first companies to pioneer the development of the marketing concept was General Electric. John B. McKitterick, then president of General Electric in 1957, expressed the marketing concept as a customer-oriented, integrated, profit-oriented philosophy of business. This statement has a very important point: It recognized that sales is just one element of marketing—that marketing includes a much broader range of activities and that a customer focus is paramount. Hotel organizations focused on building more units from 1900 to 1930, and for the most part, hotel organizations owned rather than franchised these additional units. From 1930 to 1950, hotel organizations focused on a price orientation. Collective customer needs at a certain price were targeted—but not individual desires. From 1950 to the present, specific markets have been targeted, and in the 1980s, the belief was held that hotel management could help customers solve selected problems. The 1990s finds hotel management concentrating on total customer satisfaction within their target markets. In luxury hotels, concierges serve all guests. In less-expensive hotels, concierge floors are a way of providing similar room amenities and personal services to fewer guests. Concierges at the more than 30 Hilton Towers Hotels supply guests with wine baskets and arrange for last-minute business lunch conferences. Guests now find green plants in their rooms and freshly cut flowers in the bathrooms. Charges at the Sheraton Boston Towers are $190 for standard service as opposed to $235 for concierge service. The difference in service is like between flying coach or first-class, and the aim is total customer satisfaction. In addition to providing an office away from home, hotels are using technology to speed up the check-in and checkout process. Hyatt Hotels is testing an automated check-in machine where guests with reservations can insert their credit cards and confirm room preferences. The Touch and Go Instant Check-In machine then dispenses room keys. Furthermore, it is expected that the in-room office now in place at many upscale hotels will spread to the midprice segment.

The development of the marketing concept as a business philosophy changed the nature of activities of hotels by focusing on a customer orientation. Customers with similar needs, for example, business travelers or tourists, were identified, and strategies were directed to satisfy these market segments. This process of dividing a diverse market into groups of consumers with relatively similar characteristics is called market segmentation and has served as a key strategy for hotels in the 1980s and the 1990s. Accordingly, hotels have made alliances with Pizza Hut for hotel delivery and with the airlines to credit frequent-flyer mileage and to offer discounts to frequent flyers. More strategic alliances with other business organizations will probably be made in the future.

MARKET STRUCTURE OF THE HOTEL INDUSTRY

The largest hotel chains based on number of rooms are Holiday Inn Worldwide, Choice Hotels International, Best Western International, Marriott, Hospitality Franchise Systems, Days Inn of America, Hilton Hotels, ITT Sheraton, Motel 6, and Promus. The largest hotel chains based on number of units are Best Western, Choice Hotels International, Holiday Inn Worldwide, and Days Inns of America. The fastest-growing hotel/motel chains are Motel 6, Howard Johnson Inns, Comfort Inns, and Hampton Inns. Holiday Inn Worldwide and Best Western International dominate market share among hotel and motel franchise companies.

Choice Hotels International administers Comfort Inns, Quality Inns, Clarion Hotels, House Inns, Sleep Inns, Rodeway Inns, Econo Lodges, and Friendship Inns. Marriott controls Residence Inn, Fairfield Inn, and Courtyard. Hospitality Franchise Systems consists of Howard Johnson and Ramada. The Promus Group comprises Embassy Suites, Hampton Inn and Suites, Homewood Suites, and Harrah's.

Franchising in the hotel/motel industry has been used extensively. Hotels have used franchising to satisfy the retailing of services to meet the challenges of intangibility, perishability, inseparability, and variability. Labor intensity and quality control are other challenges that franchising has successfully addressed.

Fluctuating demand caused by seasonal variations is another facet of the market structure of the hotel industry. To meet this challenge, several ski resorts in appropriate locations have opened their facilities to tour groups during the summer months. Moreover, hotels have offered weekend rates and discounts to special groups during the off-season.

In general, hotel and motel organizations tend to be small, with more than half accounting for no more than three units. Nonetheless, like the rest of the retail industry, large organizations are steadily increasing their market share. This concentration of large organizations has developed partly because of interorganizational communication systems, franchised networks, and corporate vertical systems. A comprehensive network of travel agents, airlines, and centralized reservation and sales operations work as information clearinghouses.

Intermediaries such as tour groups hold blocks of rooms. American Express Space Bank maintains, for a fee in its computers, an inventory of available hotel rooms so that travel agents can make arrangements for their customers. Contacts with organizations that sponsor conventions and need large blocks of rooms is another source of revenue for larger hotels.

The Marriott Corporation is an example of a vertical marketing system in the hotel industry. Marriott manages the hotels under the Marriott name but does not own them. Typically, Marriott builds the hotel and sells it to a group of investors. These investors might be an insurance company, a limited partnership, or a real estate investment trust. Marriott manages the property in return for about 5 percent of the hotel's revenues and 20 percent of its operating profits and, in a minority of situations, may franchise some hotel units or may own other units outright. Marriott was one of the most successful hotel operations in the 1980s and continues to outperform the industry in the mid-1990s due to its good locations, upgraded properties, and strong occupancy.

HOTEL MARKET SEGMENTATION

A strong and clear hotel image can increase consumer confidence in its lodging and service accommodations. Because the way in which consumers perceive a hotel can influence their reaction to its offerings, management is very concerned with the development of hotel image. Perception of a hotel image is derived not only from functional attributes of price and convenience but also from the influence of architecture, interior design, colors, and advertising.

Luxury hotels include Fairmont, Four Seasons, and Westin. Upscale hotels include Hyatt, Lowes Anatle, Marriott, Omni, and Stouffer. In precarious economic times, luxury and upscale hotels can reduce rates to maintain occupancy. Budget hotels cannot readily counter this strategy. Moreover, should a geographic area become overbuilt with hotels, high-price hotels may lower their rates in an effort to limit their losses and keep occupancy from falling below 60 percent. Again, midscale and budget operations would find it difficult to counter this move.

Middle upscale hotels include Courtyard by Marriott, Doubletree, Harvey, Hilton, Radisson, Sheraton, and Wyndham. These middle upscale hotels are also able to lower rates in adverse economic environments. Many of these hotels find it profitable to cooperate with such organizations as the American Association of Retired Persons and the Automobile Association of America in offering discounts during off-season periods or during adverse economic periods. All-suite middle upscale hotels include Ameri-Suites (Howard Johnson), Embassy, Guest Quarters, Hawthorne, Homewood, Lexington, and Residence Inn by Marriott. Both Howard Johnson and Marriott have diversified by serving different target markets that desire longer stays and more residential facilities and services than ordinary travelers.

Full-service midscale hotels include Best Western, Howard Johnson, Holiday Inns, Quality Inns, and Ramada. Full-service midscale hotels, especially Best Western and Howard Johnson, are among the fastest-growing segments of the hotel industry. However, it is not always feasible to operate a restaurant physically inside a midprice hotel for long-term profit. Therefore, it might be better to separate the operations, thereby permitting specialization efficiencies. There is a real danger that losing restaurant operations might not allow necessary hotel renovations. Holiday Inn tried and abandoned its "Piper's," a restaurant concept, in the early 1980s and in 1989 sold the Holiday Inn brand to Bass PLC. Instead, Holiday Inn pursued the strategy of segmenting other target markets with the development of Hampton Inns and Embassy Suites.

Limited-service midscale hotels include Drury, Hampton, and LaQuinta Motor Inns. Both Holiday Express and Ramada Limited have been expanding quickly, but this is a market that can become oversaturated rapidly. Limited-service midscale hotels will probably increase total market share since the potential is present, but individual hotel shakeouts may occur along the way. Advertising clout and market visibility—and, in this instance, "big is better"—will probably determine the winners.

Budget hotels include Allstar Inns (Motel 6), Comfort Inns (Choice International), Days Inns, Econo Lodges (Choice International), Motel 6, Red Roof Inns, Rodeway Inns (Choice International), Super 8 Motel, and Travelodge (Forte Hotels). Days Inns and Motel 6 have dominated this market. However, market share has remained stable for this market segment, and therefore casualties will probably result in the future.

Limited-service, all-suite, and courtyard-style hotels will probably increase market share in the future. Generally, these hotels are affiliated with a chain and do not include an in-house restaurant. Hotel investments in the 1980s were not always sound, and many geographic areas were overbuilt. Financing for refurbishing is needed, so this situation presents opportunities to purchase hotels. Consumer demand has changed from the 1980s to the 1990s, and this factor also may cause disruption in the hotel industry.

Market segmentation and a focus on lifestyle can be surmised by ascertaining how the bathrooms in hotels are furnished. Although those baskets of toiletries are appealing, the cost has diminished profits at luxury hotels such as the Westin. Luxury hotels may include in their bathrooms: fresh flowers; potpourri; designer soaps; baskets or trays with bath gel, talcum powder, shampoo, hair conditioner, cotton balls, Q-tips, emery boards, nail-polish remover, mouthwash, and shaving, manicure, and sewing kits; shoehorns and shoeshine mitts; lighted makeup mirrors; shower cap; terry robes; portable hair dryer; bathscale; retractable clothesline; telephone; often separate tubs; showers; and toilets. Upscale hotels may include in their bathrooms: baskets or trays with shampoo, bath gel, body cream, cotton balls, mouthwash, emery board, shoe sponge, mitt, and shoehorn, and sewing and manicure kits; shower caps; oversize towels; and double sinks. Full-service midscale hotels would include two medium-size bars of soap, shampoo, glass cups, and two plush bath-size towels, and some may have double sinks. Limited-service hotels would include two medium-size bars of soap, shampoo, plastic cups, and two bath-size towels. Budget hotels would include two small bars of soap, plastic or paper cups, and two bath-size towels.

IMPACT OF MODERN LIFESTYLE ON HOTELS

Changing lifestyles have had a profound impact on hotel management. The traditional roles of housewife and mother have changed considerably as women have smaller families and re-enter the workforce as soon as possible. Double-income families spend substantially more on vacations and traveling than single-earner families. This may take the form of short getaway vacations at full-service, limited-service, or budget hotels. For those families where both spouses are college graduates, earning capacity may mean that vacations could include stays at luxury or middle upscale hotels. Another facet of women in the workforce is the career female executive who is a frequent traveler and desires many of the luxury bathroom amenities and also hotel security.

Many of the baby boomers who are executives and other travelers desire the use of health spas and indoor swimming pools. Physical fitness has become paramount. Hotels include treadmills, punching bags, and other physical equipment in their health spas and also provide whirlpool baths and steam rooms.

An increasing amount of attention has been given to the elderly market. The growth rate of this group is expected to be twice that of the general population. Addressing the elderly market is the Marriott with a retirement-community business that incorporates the features of a nursing home and a scaled-down model of its regular, full-service hotel aimed at smaller markets and known as Brighton Gardens. Seniors account for 80 percent of all commercial vacation travel, especially first-class air travel and luxury sea cruises. Seniors also spend 30 percent more than younger tourists while traveling. One year after Quality Inns started a 10 percent discount program, there was an increase of 60 to 80 percent in senior travelers. Quality Inns reports that senior stays remain 50 percent above the prediscount level.

Social class status influences consumers' complex purchase decision-making processes and extends to many aspects of life such as travel and vacations, as well as activities, interests, and opinions. Because social class affects so many dimensions of a person's life, it has an impact on consumer buyer behavior. Marketers have been able to segment markets by social class. For example, San Francisco's Four Seasons Clift Hotel appeals to upper-class guests with luxurious accommodations. Hampton Inn Hotels appeals to middle-class and lower-middle-class target markets with reasonable rates and limited services. Sheraton Hotels in Hawaii has added extensive day-camp activities to attract families with children aged 4 to 12.

Surrogate groups are ones with key individuals or firms performing all or part of a consumer's information-gathering, decision-making, and transactional tasks. Examples include doctors, interior decorators, and travel agents. Many authorities believe that the selection of consumer goods and services by surrogates will be increasingly significant in the future. Doctors prescribe drugs for their patients; interior decorators order furniture and accessories for their clients; and travel agents suggest appropriate tours for their clients. Travel agents are in a position to recommend specific hotels, restaurants, and means of transportation. Thus, hotels, airlines, and resort areas appropriate large sums to influence the thinking of travel agents, hoping in turn that travel agents will influence their clients.

Consumers perceive these surrogates as experts and frequently accede to their suggestions. Travel agents need to understand and discuss their clients' lifestyle patterns. Hotel management needs to focus on appealing to lifestyle characteristics in order to maximize satisfaction. Surrogate experts, such as travel agents, tend to diminish the role of the consumer, and therefore hotel promotional campaigns should be more sophisticated since these are directed to professionals.

MARRIOTT HOTELS: A SUCCESS STORY

Marriott is an upscale hotel that competes with Hyatt and Stouffer hotels. Although Marriott may have overextended itself in the 1980s, its performance continues to improve more rapidly than that of its direct competition. An important factor in the success of Marriott has been the effective management of its financial assets. Occupancy rates were identified that were needed to cover construction costs and established as goals. A second important factor in Marriott's success is the ability to provide total customer satisfaction. Concierge service, video checkout, frequent-flier points, weekend rates, and the administration of customer surveys to identify customer needs and wants were all elements of a successful service approach. A third reason for success has been effective leadership and the ability to know when to change. Finally, the development of a successful strategy of market segmentation has focused resources and promoted a loyal customer base.

Marriott was a fast-growing organization until it was derailed by a declining real estate market, an oversupply of hotel rooms, and a lingering recession. Profits tumbled by half between 1989 and 1992, and Marriott was devastated by $3.6 billion in debt. A controversial plan to split the company into two parts—one a profitable hotel and food-service business, and the other a debt-laden owner of depressed real estate—proved successful. Another strategy that proved successful was to accelerate franchising hotels. In 1989, 21 percent of hotels were franchised, and by 1993, 27 percent were franchised and plans were formulated to franchise 50 percent by 1997. Marriott avoided the risk of a loss of quality by selecting franchisees with the same philosophy about quality and by quickly withdrawing a franchise if standards are lowered in any way. Marriott also has a product in every price category: the high-end J. W. Marriott, business-class Marriott, moderate Courtyard by Marriott, budget-priced Fairfield Inns, and suite hotels. Moreover, Marriott has invested heavily in the burgeoning retirement accommodation business.

Marriott, like Wal-Mart, Mary Kay, and Home Depot, is heavily dependent on a single individual for leadership. Bill Marriott inherited the business from his father and has made many important changes. Bill Marriott, like Sam Walton of Wal-Mart did, closely monitors expenses. One of Marriott's most admired financial strategies is to design, build, and manage its hotels but not to own them. Although each manager has a fair degree of autonomy over operating costs and pricing, there are literally a dozen encyclopedia volumes concerning task performance. For example, maids follow a 66-point guide to making up bedrooms, and guidelines cannot be changed without headquarter's approval.

Another aspect of the Marriott success story is its corporate cultural guidelines. These cultural guidelines are not necessarily similar to Mary Kay, but, nonetheless, they are clear and distinct and evolved from the Marriott ethic. The Marriotts are a Mormon family, workaholic and devout. The Book of Mormon is placed in Marriott hotel rooms along with the Gideon Bible and a biography of the founder. The cultural guidelines range from the development of team spirit to the management of time and to personal habits relating to physical fitness and spiritual commitment. After financial or strategic plans have been specified, Marriott has shifted to building commitment among people in the organization.

The major change, and the most difficult, has been the development of new operating cultures that are required to succeed in new markets. None of Marriott's traditions appear sacred at the Courtyard division. Even the all-cotton towels, a tradition of Marriott's hotel chain, have been replaced with cheaper fabric. The biography of the company founder, offered for free at Marriott hotels, is sold at Courtyard vending machines. These cultural changes were also implemented at other hotel divisions aimed at serving different target markets. The company is attempting to operate the smaller, less complicated hotels with managers who have less experience than its traditional managers. Another deviation from tradition is to hire managers from competing chains rather than from within the Marriott organization.

Marriott competed on the strong organizational capability to change. Marriott hotels competed directly with such firms as Hilton, Hyatt, Four Seasons, and Sheraton. Although many strategies were similar, Marriott tried to serve its clientele better. Marriott focused on becoming an employer of choice, and this meant competing with indirect competitors such as McDonald's, Burger King, Sears, and other organizations that hire large numbers of employees from the traditional applicant pool. To compete, Marriott has tried to become a more attractive employer.

Marriott began by focusing its resources on food with its Hot Shoppe restaurants and by serving airlines with food. Institutional food service to airlines, hospitals, airports, schools, and business organizations became an integral part of its business. Marriott also offers a product portfolio ranging from luxurious accommodations (Marriott Suites) to traditional rooms (Marriott) to lodging for family vacationers (Residence Inn), business travelers (Courtyard), and those desiring economy (Fairfield Inn). This product portfolio has contributed to the Marriott success story.

Although during the 1980s the number of hotel rooms grew more than 40 percent, leading to overcapacity and weak profits adversely affecting the Marriott and the hotel industry, the Marriott has bounced back in the 1990s. Like many other retail service organizations, close cost control procedures, the innovation of new customer service approaches, and the capability of knowing when and how to change have been responsible for a success story. In addition, Marriott is future oriented and is pulling out all the stops in one market, senior life-care communities, which combine deluxe retirement housing with medical and nursing facilities.

THE SHERATON: TROUBLE ALONG THE WAY

The Sheraton is classified as a middle upscale hotel competing with the Hilton, Radisson, and Wyndham. The Sheraton Corporation, a wholly owned subsidiary of ITT, currently controls approximately 500 hotels, inns, resorts, and all-suites situated in over 60 countries. The Sheraton has a swanky image abroad, but a "ho-hum" image in the United States.

Sheraton hotels are located in major cities and accommodate the needs of business and leisure travelers. Although such competitors as the Hilton in Chicago, the Hyatt Regency in Reston, Virginia, and the Westin in downtown New Orleans have diversified their marketing strategies to target families with young children, especially aimed at weekend stays, the Sheraton lags far behind the competition. The Four Seasons Hotel offers flameproof bathrobes for kids, children's menus, cribs, bed rails, and video games. Sheraton Inns offer moderate prices to satisfy more modest budgets. Most of the inns are located in suburban areas near major highways, airports, and business districts. Sheraton Resorts offer unique accommodations for leisure and business travelers around the world. Sheraton Resorts offer special recreation facilities and services to make family vacations, business conferences, or holiday fun. Oceanfront locations provide golf and tennis as well as water sports. A new addition to the Sheraton product portfolio is the Sheraton Suites, established in 1990. The two-room suites offer travelers many special features such as wet bars, microwave ovens, and sofa beds.

The Sheraton Corporation was formed in 1946. In 1962, a franchise division was established, and this division has been a constant problem. In 1968, International Telephone and Telegraph (ITT) Corporation acquired Sheraton. The corporate client is the largest market segment that Sheraton endeavors to cultivate. Leisure travelers constitute mostly a weekend market. Lodgers are mainly in professional or management positions in the 30- to 50-years-old age range.

Sheraton has had difficulties with franchises that offered substandard service quality. Approximately 300 franchises were either bought out, sold, or closed. Sheraton has placed a greater emphasis on its services than on amenities. These services include meeting rooms of all sizes to accommodate 10 to 1,000 people, A/V teleconferencing, and video equipment. Rooms provide an ample amount of space for the business traveler to work.

Sheraton is expanding its presence in the all-suites market. Business travelers are provided with facsimile equipment, copier machines, personal computers, and typewriters. Sheraton made a conscious decision not to enter the all-suite market first but to wait until it could be determined how to satisfy this target market. Thus, the Sheraton was not an innovator but again a follower.

Michael Porter has introduced the theory of competitive advantage and value. The creation of value is dependent on a firm's ability to achieve and sustain a competitive advantage over its rivals. The Marriott was able to control costs and to serve its target markets better than its competitors by differentiating its services, amenities, and strategies. An organization cannot create value without achieving a competitive edge over present and potential rivals.

The Sheraton in the United States has not achieved a uniform image of quality. The Sheraton has appropriated about $1 billion to improve its product in New York, Chicago, San Francisco, Hartford, and elsewhere. Coffeemakers have been placed in every room in its hotels, but this is also true of Howard Johnson hotels, for example, which is really not a direct competitor. The strength of the Sheraton continues to be in the corporate or business-to-business market segment. Amenities in the Sheraton would probably not please family travelers as well as in the Hilton. The Sheraton is not an innovator in entering new markets or providing new types of services. Hotels at the upper-luxury extreme such as the Four Seasons, Marriott, Hyatt, and Stouffer present a clear-cut product differentiation strategy that the Sheraton has not achieved, perhaps because of a tarnished image of uneven quality. Full-service Best Western, Howard Johnson, and Holiday Inn have had a wide appeal to many business travelers and family travelers. Business travelers vacationing with families may prefer the amenities provided by hotels like the Hilton or efficiencies and prices at Best Western, Howard Johnson, or Holiday Inn. The middle market personified by the Sheraton appears to illustrate Porter's theory of competition as an organization "stuck in the middle" and lacking a precise strategy to maintain a competitive advantage in the United States. Current strategies may promote stability in market share, but it is doubtful that market share will increase.

HOLIDAY INN: ADVENTURES IN MARKET SEGMENTATION

Holiday Inn developed several different brand names appealing to varying lifestyles and needs. Traditionally, lodging was classified as budget, midscale, and upscale, but Holiday Inn was able to extend this categorized system. Holiday Inn expanded into four types of lodging: Hampton Inn, budget; Embassy Suites, all-suite; Residence Inn, apartments; and Crowne Plaza, upscale. In addition, Harrah's Casino Hotels was also acquired. Emphasis was placed on diversification by engaging in differentiation by developing and purchasing niche or segmented brands such as Embassy Suites and Hampton Inn. However, in 1987, Residence Inn was sold to Marriott (apartments for the elderly), and in 1989, Harrah's, Hampton Inn, Embassy Suites, and Homewood Suites were sold to Bass PLC, and a new company named Promus assumed control of the hotels. Thus, Holiday Inn at one time had a portfolio of strategic business units much like General Motors (Cadillac, Buick, and Chevrolet).

These properties—Hampton Inn, Residence Inn, Harrah's, and Embassy Suites—were divested for a combination of reasons. First, Holiday Inn was concentrating too much on the rapidly growing Hampton Inn and Embassy Suite segments to the detriment of the original midscale segment. Second, Holiday Inn had the pressures of transforming itself from a hotel owner to a hotel manager. Third, many Holiday Inn franchise owners viewed other market segments as competition, and this was especially true since present franchise owners were not given the first right of refusal when Hampton Inns were constructed nearby. All of these pressures were aggravated by the overbuilding of hotels and declining occupancy rates.

While Holiday Inn is positioned in the midprice market segment, the Crowne Plaza Hotels opened in 1983 and were positioned at the upper end of the midpriced range. Crowne Plaza targets the business traveler who desires extra services and amenities and, for example, offers two restaurants per facility. Crowne Plaza hotels are situated in major metropolitan areas, as opposed to Holiday Inns, which are located in more secondary sites.

In the United States, over 80 percent of Holiday Inns are operated by franchisees, in contrast to overseas establishments that are either owned or managed by the parent company of Holiday Inn, Bass PLC. Although Holiday Inn continues to add new or converted properties, the overall size of the organization is actually decreasing. Holiday Inn, in an effort to maintain high standards, has suspended franchises of hotels until remodeling or other changes have been completed and has also withdrawn franchises for violations. Insistence on high standards is an important reason why Holiday Inns are highly regarded in the hotel industry. However, Holiday Inn competes against Best Western, Howard Johnson, Quality Inns, and Ramada directly, and both Best Western and Howard Johnson are growing faster than Holiday Inn, which is a much larger chain on a worldwide basis. Demand patterns will vary over time, and Holiday Inn's all-suite and budget hotels have experienced greater growth than full-service midscale hotels.

Holiday Inn targets mainly business and vacation travelers. A moderate price position is maintained. Business travelers tend to be mostly men between the ages of 29 and 49 who are managerial or professional and have a large amount of discretionary income. Vacation travelers tend to be between ages 35 and 44. In order to satisfy business travelers, new facilities included one king- or queen-size bed with leisure and work areas with lounge chairs, small tables, and desks. Amenities included larger soap bars, thicker towels, shower massagers, toiletries, and AM/FM clock radios.

Holiday Inn has a reputation as an innovator since it was the first in the hotel industry to provide swimming pools at every location, children-stay-free programs, guaranteed all-night reservations, and accommodations for the handicapped. Additional services offered to travelers are a wide range of cable stations and the installation of satellite dishes. These satellite dishes are used for teleconferencing and in-room services. A bimonthly magazine is provided in all rooms with current articles on a gamut of subjects. The magazine informs guests about new and current services or special offers at Holiday Inns.

The Holiday Inn Crowne Plaza Hotels are designed to serve the more discriminating business traveler. Special features include specialty restaurants, health facilities, executive floors, and larger conference rooms. Hotels provide two-line, direct-dial telephones, a central duplicating facility, facsimile machines, and computer equipment.

Holiday Inn Express Hotels target the cost-conscious business and vacation traveler. A buffet breakfast is offered as well as facsimile services. Holiday Inn Express Hotels compete with Drury, Hampton, and LaQuinta Motor Inns. Thus, Holiday Inn tries to segment varying markets and has been both successful and unsuccessful in accomplishing market segmentation objectives.

HAMPTON INN: STRATEGY INNOVATION

Once owned by Holiday Inn, Hampton Inn is a subsidiary of The Promus Companies of Memphis, Tennessee, and one of the fastest-growing hotels in the industry. Hampton Inn is a limited-service midscale hotel that competes with Drury, LaQuinta Motor Inns, Marriott's Fairfield Inns, and Choice Hotels' Sleep Inns. Hampton Inn has grown rapidly and has expanded into more than 40 states.

Originally, Hampton Inn was developed by Holiday Inn because it believed that Holiday Inn had saturated the midrange market. During Holiday Inn ownership, about half of the Hampton Inn franchisees were operated by owners of Holiday Inns. Hampton Inn's new strategy has been to build scaled-down motels in towns smaller than 75,000 population. The Hampton Inn prototype was modified for locations that can support 50 to 90 rooms from typically 125 rooms. Costs are about $23,600 per room, compared with $31,000 for a larger Hampton Inn hotel. Hampton Inn charges about $45 per night, depending on location, compared with the smaller hotels that charge between $35 and $39 for a room. Hampton Inns and Suites are very profitable and are targeted for expansion in the future.

Hampton Inn has differentiated itself from competitors by developing a strategy to guarantee customer satisfaction. Realizing that service personnel turnover is high in the hotel industry, Hampton Inn permits every regular employee who deals with customers to fulfill the inn's pledge that if a guest is dissatisfied for any reason, one night's free lodging will be offered. In this way, Hampton endeavors to maintain high, uniform standards. The belief is maintained that a single customer complaint will alert management to possible weaknesses throughout the chain and contribute to improved service nationwide. The secret to making the guarantee operational is to give employees the authority to implement it. Employees vested with such authority include not just managers but even housekeepers. According to research, guests have not taken advantage of this unconditional guarantee. This policy not only fosters the loyalty of guests but also increases the retention rate of employees, who take pride in their work.

The typical Hampton Inn is situated along an interstate highway or other well-traveled area and nearby to a full-service restaurant. The lobby, with sofas and chairs, doubles as the breakfast area where guests can obtain a complimentary continental breakfast. The rooms do not offer extra frills but do offer such extras as free in-room movies and local telephone usage.

Hampton's growth evolves in part from construction in secondary markets that are less overbuilt than large urban centers. Although more than half the hotels in the nation are losing money, Hampton is experiencing growth by cultivating a price-sensitive market. The future bodes well for Hampton.

DAYS INN: GROWING PAINS

Days Inn competes against Motel 6, Comfort Inns, Econo Lodges, Rodeway Inns, and Sleep Inns. These hotels appeal particularly to young families and the elderly market. Many of these chains allow children under 18 years of age to stay free with parents or grandparents. Seniors can obtain a 10 to 30 percent discount off the regular rate. Guests get new rooms with amenities such as an oversize shower and telephone with data ports. Days Inn of America has approximately 1,400 hotels in the United States. The elderly constitute about 40 percent of its business; families, 20 percent; and couples, groups, and business travelers, 40 percent.

Days Inn is confronted with two major problems. One problem is the lack of uniform quality from franchise to franchise. Stained walls, worn furniture, broken air conditioners, and sleazy characters are among the conditions found. At one time, Days Inn of America prohibited the sale of alcohol on its properties and established a security department that was a model throughout the industry. But the situation changed as a result of a leveraged buyout in 1984. Days Inn franchises almost 20 new properties a month, receives royalties from 6 to 10 percent of revenue, and is one of the hotel industry's least selective franchisers. The operation has been profitable.

Security is lax, and crime is a problem for many Days Inn units. However, crime is a problem for many budget hotels, not just Days Inns. Motel 6 has also had security problems but seems to have made greater efforts to control crime by hiring security guards in some locations and by requiring identification from cash-paying customers. Lax security is not a problem in a great many Days Inn units, but the lack of uniform standards is disconcerting. In a survey commissioned by Promus, travelers ranked Days Inn last among 11 chains in guest satisfaction. Days Inn occupancy rates have declined from about 70 percent in 1984 to about 60 percent in the early 1990s, almost 10 percentage points below the Hampton and Red Roof motels.

Days Inn does publish its hotel rating performance, conducted by its own inspectors in an effort to increase quality. However, its ratings would seem to be in disagreement with American Automobile Association (AAA) ratings. More rigorous standards need to be specified, and inspectors should be encouraged to enforce standards.

Days Inn has improved the quality of its workforce by hiring older workers. Despite entrenched beliefs, older workers seem to be less expensive to train and more productive than younger workers. Older workers consist of about 25 percent of Days Inn reservation staff. Hiring older workers has been an innovative policy and a very successful one. Retention rates are higher, labor costs are similar, older workers are more successful in booking reservations, and absenteeism is less.

CONTROVERSIAL DECISIONS

The strategies of market segmentation and positioning have been successfully used in other industries long before the hotel industry became marketing oriented. The service industry has lagged behind manufacturing and retailing in the development of effective consumer-oriented marketing strategies. Therefore, the use of market segmentation and positioning strategies are not really controversial. The main challenge has been how to use these strategies effectively.

There is some controversy about the value of hotel strategies specifically aimed at women. The issue has arisen whether or not hotels should separate the business traveler market into two segments—men and women—or direct strategies to each one individually. Female business travelers account for about 40 percent of all U.S. business travel. The Econo Lodge has replaced dim incandescent lamps in its parking lots with high-intensity sodium lamps in an effort to attract women business travelers. The Hilton, Hyatt, and Radisson hotels innovated, by offering rooms on special floors for both women and men priced 20 percent above rooms on traditional floors, with increased security features. The Radisson Plaza in Minneapolis has reported success with its special emphasis on female business travelers since special accommodation rooms are booked up faster than regular rooms. The Marriott has announced that all its new hotels will feature special or club floors with added security features.

Initial attempts by hotel organizations to cultivate female business travelers encountered limited success. Overt approaches tended to ostracize and were perceived as patronizing. Some hotels have found that female executives prefer suites so that they can have conferences in their rooms without the bed being visible; other hotels have found that female executives rarely hold business conferences in their rooms. Many hotel executives believe that they should be doing similar things for all business executives, regardless of gender. Travelers of both sexes do not like walking down long, dark hallways, and all prefer security features.

Another controversial issue is that of competition between hotel organizations. Until the 1990s, hotel organizations were content to develop institutional prestige and service advertising campaigns and relied on price competition. Suddenly, Ramada, with about 600 hotels in the United States, blasted Holiday Inn in scathing advertisements. The Ramada advertisements suggested that it gives more value for travelers than Holiday Inn. Ramada has even offered a $5 rebate to Holiday Inn customers who switch hotels. This campaign may be the start of future hotel wars where few winners will emerge but does take a leaf from the history of retail store organizations.

MANAGING CHANGE

The role of managerial vision is to manage present and particularly future changes that will affect hotel organizations. Essentially, hotel management must determine what they can do either differently or better than the competition. Four key ingredients in the hotel industry seem to be important for either success or failure: innovation, target market segmentation and image, physical environmental resources, and human resources.

Innovation in the hotel industry would include architecture, guest amenities, and promotional programs. Conrad N. Hilton in 1920 made an investment of $5,000 in the Mobley Hotel in a small oil town in Texas that began his career to eventually form his world-famous hotel empire. Hilton has traditionally operated some of the largest hotels in cities all over the United States. While Hilton Hotels stand out, larger-size hotels contribute to occupancy problems. The importance of architecture is vital in attracting the convention trade to Hilton, which accounts for a very high percentage of Hilton's profits. Therefore, facilities for conferences, banquets, and large gatherings are necessary. Promotional programs have appreciably increased the occupancy rates on weekends, which challenged not only Hilton but other hotels as well, especially those situated in downtown areas of metropolitan cities.

Hilton Hotels have maintained a worldwide image for spectacular accommodations. Name recognition is such that the theme "Hilton, it's all in the name" can be used. The growth of global tourism has provided Hilton with increased opportunities in the 1990s.

The Holiday Inn, although positioned in the midprice market, has targeted its Crowne Plaza Hotels to the upper-scale market, and its Holiday Inn Express motels are positioned against the limited-service Hampton. The Marriott has also targeted several different markets from luxury (Marriott Suites) to traditional (Marriott) to family lodging (Residence Inn) to business travelers (Courtyard) to economy (Fairfield Inn). Thus, future market resources would include large conference and banquet rooms, which the Hilton has constructed, and indoor swimming pools or all-weather pools, spas, and steam rooms. Facilities for business travelers especially designed by the Marriott are desks, computers, and fax machines. The Hilton and Hyatt hotels are especially noted for maintaining several different types of restaurants that feature various food specialties.

It is in the area of human resources that leadership by the Marriott has excelled. Bill Marriott has built an esprit de corps equal to that established by the late Sam Walton in the discount sector. Every employee has been made aware of the vision of Bill Marriott. The Hilton has excelled at monitoring the bureaucracy so that guests can speak directly to management. The Hampton, with its guaranteed refund policy if dissatisfied, has made even housekeepers think of themselves as the customer by authorizing them to implement refund policies. The Four Seasons insists that executives stay in contact with customers. Regional vice presidents talk extensively with housekeepers and concierges about their jobs. The Four Seasons has installed a computer bank that stores information about each guest, such as their choice of brand of tea or whether they prefer a nonallergenic pillow. As a result, the Four Seasons Clift Hotel in San Francisco has repeat occupancy of almost 70 percent of their guests.

LESSONS LEARNED FROM SUCCESS AND FAILURE

In considering hotel failures, even the most successful organization has made mistakes but can and does survive as long as factors such as innovation, image, physical resources, and human resources contribute more frequently to success and only infrequently result in failure. Days Inn has had a security problem but has one of the best reservation systems in the hotel industry. The Sheraton has had problems with its franchising system but has been able to survive this pitfall by trying to reinforce its past well-earned image and by improving its physical surroundings. Holiday Inn found that diversification caused weaknesses in systems control and divested itself of some holdings and also strengthened its existing structure. Even Marriott had to split the company into two parts, one a profitable hotel and food service business, the other a debt-saddled owner of depressed real estate, in order to survive and expand the franchising part of its business.

The major lesson for the hotel industry is to closely monitor hotel occupancy rates. Days Inn has demonstrated that an improved reservation system can overcome other drawbacks. Clearly, overbuilding has plagued the hotel industry. Large hotels with many rooms such as the Hilton have a particular problem in maintaining acceptable or profitable occupancy rates. The question remains what to do with physical resources that are already present. How can these physical resources be used profitably? In uncertain economic periods, upscale hotels can reduce price rates in an effort to maintain occupancy, whereas the low-price hotels cannot counter this strategy by adding more upscale facilities or by lowering rates. The main problem of the hotel industry has been oversupply. In order to counter adverse conditions, hotels that are a part of chains with well-known, distinct images seem to profit. Upscale, limited-service, and budget hotels appeared to squeeze the midscale hotels very hard. By successfully targeting precise markets, some midscale operations have avoided failure. In an improved economic environment, there is a real danger that the budget hotels have overbuilt and that a shakeout will occur.

Retail stores have learned in the past that technology can improve shopping conditions, and hotels will need to monitor carefully how advancing technology can improve service to their clientele. For example, a magnetic card reader on the door lock of guest rooms could coordinate with the computer. When making reservations, room numbers can be assigned, and guests could proceed directly to the room without checking in and waiting in line at the hotel desk. Credit cards could be inserted through the mag card reader that would open the door, trigger billing, and message taking would commence. The credit card would serve as the room key. Technological innovation can open up new vistas for hotel marketing. Days Inn has used a reservation system to advance its organization, and other hotel organizations will need to use technology profitably in order to compete successfully.

CHAPTER 10

Credit Cards: The Plastic Wars

Lifestyle Classifications: Outer-Directed Consumers

All groups desire social approval and acceptance of others.

- *Belongers*. This subgroup was characterized as traditional, conservative, puritanical, and reluctant to experiment
- *Emulators*. Ambitious, status-conscious, desirous of climbing the proverbial ladder of success, and very competitive
- *Achievers*. Leaders in business, government, and professions in their communities

Lifestyle Classifications: Inner-Directed Consumers

- *I-am-me's*. Young, impulsive, individualistic, and narcissistic
- *Experientials*. Desires inner growth, direct experience, and involvement
- *Societally conscious individuals*. Desire simple living and supports such causes as conservation, environmentalism, and consumerism

Market Segmentation Strategies

- Demographic (age, occupation, income, sex, etc.)
- Socioeconomic (family life cycle, social class values)
- Geographic (region, county size or city, density)
- Psychological (lifestyle, personality traits)
- Consumption patterns (heavy, moderate, light users)
- Perceptual (perceptual mapping, benefit segmentation)
- Brand-loyalty patterns (none, medium, strong)
- Combination or integrating strategies (positive, indifferent, negative)

Many traditional values have been changing over the years. In the past, many people accumulated savings for a long time to buy a home, but as consumers became increasingly affluent and inflation left its impact, this value changed. Postponed gratification of wants changed to immediate gratification. Another traditional value has been to view credit as a sign of poor management of personal finances, and this has changed, as most Americans accept credit as a method of purchasing. One of the strongest values of the past was the Puritan ethic with its emphasis on hard work, economy, and thrift, which has shifted to a new ideal of self-indulgence and pleasure. Another generation would have been shocked by the prevailing attitude of "Buy now, pay later." The belief was held in the past that goods and services should not be purchased unless payment could be made immediately. Lifestyle trends are at the heart of the plastic wars.

When designing marketing programs, four service characteristics should be considered: intangibility, inseparability, variability, and perishability. Service industries include hotels, airlines, banks, and other organizations. As a result of increasing affluence, more leisure time, and increasing product complexity that requires servicing, the United States has changed from a manufacturing to a service economy.

Services are intangible. For example, credit card users have nothing but a plastic card and the promise of a reliable and accurate accounting of their purchases. Since services are intangible, consumers look for signs of service quality in order to reduce risk and uncertainty. Image becomes an important factor in differentiating the service from its competition. Marketers try to get the consumer to link a specific image with a specific brand name. For example, American Express hired Karl Malden, the actor, to convey a prestige image for American Express Travelers Cheques. An image of reliability and security was also conveyed, should the traveler's checks be lost, stolen, or misplaced.

Services are inseparable from their providers, whether the providers be people or machines. Inseparability implies that the public-contact personnel and the facilities should be pleasing to consumers and that multisite locations may be vital to make the service conveniently available. Efforts have been made to make automatic teller machines available in some restaurants and other public places that have high degrees of safety, convenience, and security.

Services are variable. To illustrate, some hotels have reputations for providing better services than others. Because services are variable, companies are in a position to offer several versions to different target markets. American Express offers its regular credit card to consumers but also targeted its more prestigious Gold and Platinum credit cards with different services to other distinct market segments.

Services are perishable, and therefore promotional campaigns are especially important. Many service marketers try to offset this limitation with visual images and tangible reminders of their services. Hotels offer packaged shampoos and soaps. Restaurants offer book matches. Prudential Insurance Company associates its product with "the rock," a symbol of permanency. Travelers Insurance associates its product with the Travelers "umbrella," demonstrating comprehensive offerings.

There are some organizations that combine the sale of goods and services with future purchases. For example, General Motors has issued a credit card that will give a rebate toward the purchase of a new automobile based on previous purchases. General Electric and Carnival Cruise Lines have also issued such credit cards.

In considering the successes and failures of the credit organizations, mistakes have been made, but these organizations have survived by making constant adjustments with such variables as innovation, target market and image, physical environmental resources, and human resources. These credit organizations did not necessarily obtain high grades using all variables, but some of the variables were used and implemented in an exceedingly capable manner.

When Discover entered the market, cardholders were offered a 1 percent credit rebate at the end of the year, and this constituted an innovation in the industry. When AT&T entered the market with its Universal card, cardholders were offered a no-fee-for-life card for those who signed up the first year, provided the card was used once a year, and this constituted an innovation in the industry. Co-branding and affinity cards when first offered were at the initiative of institutions outside the credit industry. It would appear that the firm that operates outside of the credit industry becomes an innovator and disrupts the status quo. Therefore, it is reasonable to conclude that many innovations were initiated in the credit industry by outsiders. Credit organizations have a reactive approach rather than a proactive approach to many types of innovation.

Strategies to delimit target markets and firm up images have been used well in the credit industry. The Platinum and Gold cards issued by American Express were excellent attempts to appeal to a status market. MasterCard and Visa followed the American Express strategy and would seem to have better implemented it. Retailers who have not appealed to status preferred to offer MasterCard and Visa cards. Another facet of this strategy was that retailers had to pay higher fees for the use of American Express cards. Co-branding by retailers such as Macy's and Nordstorm is another attempt to segment markets and is the shape of the future. Affinity cards by various nonprofit organizations is another effective strategy. MasterCard and Visa are obtaining a lion's share of this market. Visa is also trying to penetrate new markets by extending its card to supermarkets. Visa has more Gold cardholders than American Express. The American Express status image, while it does constitute an advantage, is also a decisive limitation.

Physical environmental resources have been well utilized by credit organization networks. Automatic teller machines are particularly good at providing convenience in using credit cards. Debit cards, which are used in supermarkets, are tied directly to the customer's checking account. Since member banks are international in location, credit can be extended to customers globally. Tourists traveling in other countries have direct access to credit and funds. Visa with Interlink and MasterCard with Cirrus have made credit convenient and given customers direct access on both a national and international basis.

The use of human resource management has not been an important factor in credit organizations. Neither Visa, MasterCard, Discover, or American Express has a key executive who has effectively mobilized human resources. One reason might be that the use of technology and gaining cooperation of retail institutions have been overriding factors, rather than the use of personnel. There is more emphasis on services of an impersonal nature than in retail institutions, and this is another important distinction in concentrating on the extension of these services rather than on motivating human resources.

MAJOR CREDIT ORGANIZATIONS: YESTERDAY

Travel Related Services (TRS), a subsidy of American Express, introduced the Amex card in 1958. TRS believed that with its other financial products such as traveler's checks that a comprehensive assortment of payment and travel products could be offered to satisfy the lifestyle and business needs of its individual and company clients.

Market segmentation strategies of credit card organization have traditionally targeted travel and entertainment markets and general-purpose segments. The business traveler and entertainment segment was now able to make a more convenient form of payment. Retail store customers were now able to use a form of revolving credit to finance purchases. The distinction between the travel and entertainment and retail store markets has over-lapped in recent years. American Express, the dominant product in the travel and entertainment market, has entered the retail market, and both Visa and MasterCard have added premium cards to compete with American Express in the travel and entertainment markets. Credit card companies have also sought to expand their international presence.

The challenge to market segmentation strategy was to distinguish the convenience-user segment from a market segment that incurred interest charges. American Express had traditionally captured the convenience-user segment by appealing to upscale and status-conscious cardholders. Almost half of the 4 million households earning more than $50,000 in 1985 possessed an American Express card. In contrast to the convenience-user segment, more than two thirds of cardholders did not pay off outstanding balances in full at the end of the month. The revolving credit market segment was to grow appreciably and become a lucrative source for finance charges. These finance charges for banks were, and still are, an attractive revenue source.

The credit card industry has been characterized by technological innovation. This innovation was motivated by the desire to decrease operating costs and by the desire of retail organizations for faster and more convenient credit card handling. Point-of-sale terminals obtained authorization for the sale and credited the retailer's account while debiting the customer's. By 1985, more than half of specialty stores used third-party processors for their credit card sales.

American Express introduced its Personal card, known as the Green card, in 1958 primarily as a defense against the Diners Club card, which threatened its lucrative Travelers Cheques market. The American Express card was positioned as a premium product over the Diners Club card. American Express charged an annual fee of $6 versus $5 for the Diners Club card. The Personal card, or Green card, was available in 16 currencies by 1976 and had become an important profit center within the company.

American Express introduced the Gold card in 1966. Originally, the Gold card was restricted to high-income households with incomes greater than $35,000 per year. Agreements were reached with local banks in each state, and because of varying agreement terms, credit terms for individual customers were not uniform. Gold cards numbered more than 3 million by 1985. The Gold card was positioned as more prestigious than the Green card and charged an annual membership fee of $65 versus $45 for the Personal card. The Gold cardholder usually held a managerial or professional job, and card usage was more than six times as often as the average Personal cardholder.

American Express introduced the Platinum card in 1984 with an annual fee of $250. Extra services were offered to cardholders that included $10,000 check-cashing privileges, $500,000 in travel insurance, 24-hour, worldwide travel service, and nonresident membership privileges at 25 private clubs in the United States and abroad. The Platinum card appealed to a market segment that desired these new services. The Platinum card was marketed solely by direct mail, and great care was exercised not to cannibalize customers from the Gold card or to damage the prestige of the Green card. American Express also offered a corporate card to business organizations that was marketed primarily through a direct-sales force.

Visa was developed from Bank of America's Bank Americard, which was established in 1958. Visa, by 1986, was the world's largest credit card issuer and is still the leading credit card. Visa is owned by member banks that number about 15,000 in 100 countries. Each member bank can issue its own credit cards and is responsible for soliciting customers and collecting payment. Each bank is free to provide service to retail organizations and charges usually from 1 to 3 percent of the face amount of the transaction.

Visa International, the umbrella organization, formed a worldwide image and operates a credit authorization service that verifies to the retailer that the customer is a valid cardholder. Visa International also provides an automated clearing service that provides settlement service between the retailer's bank and the bank that has issued the customer's Visa card.

In 1981, Visa was able to authorize low-risk transactions of under $50. In 1982, Visa issued its Premium card, aimed at affluent households. This card did not gain immediate success since it was difficult to sell the idea of another status card. Soon increased competition between member banks, especially Citicorp, began to distinguish services offered by the member banks. These distinguishing services ranged from travel insurance to varying card administration programs.

MasterCard has been traditionally viewed as Visa's primary competition. But both organizations are owned by many of the same banks. Banks in the MasterCard network are permitted to emphasize their own logos and to enhance their cards' functionality. MasterCard, in 1981, introduced its Gold card in an attempt to capture a segment of American Express's affluent customer base. The MasterCard Gold card was issued a year before Visa's and was marketed much more aggressively and became more successful at this time. Instead of appealing to status, MasterCard emphasized value and benefits.

The Sears Discover card was issued in 1986 and was the first general-purpose credit card issued since the 1960s. With over 30 million active cards outstanding, Discover is still the largest single card issuer in the mid 1990s. The Discover card offered some unique enhancements: a savings account, a 1 percent yearly rebate on purchases, and no-annual fee compared with the current average annual fee of $19 and $45 on the American

Express Green card. Sears also provided discounts on its automobile service and discounts from retail organizations that accepted the Discover card. Sears targeted a mass market with emphasis on the middle and lower end. Other retail organizations, especially competitors, feared revelation of the billing information to local Sears stores and were therefore slow to accept the Discover card.

The Citicorp organization sought to expand from its strong base in commercial banking to providing consumer credit. Citicorp, in 1986, offered the following credit cards: MasterCard and MasterCard Gold, Visa and Premium Visa, Diners' Club, Carte Blanche, and Choice. Citicorp acquired the Diners' Club card in 1981, which had been losing money since 1974, and spent more than $70 million to relaunch the card. Incentives for consumers to acquire the Diners' Club card included a credit toward the first $25 in charges, free Citicorp traveler's checks, and a round-trip ticket to any destination in the United States for $175. These incentives initially appeared successful, and more than a million cardholders were added by 1984. However, this new inroad did not successfully take away market share from American Express, which gained an equal number of cardholders during this same period.

Citicorp's Choice card had its origins to 1977 when the Baltimore-area charge card was acquired. Choice had captured 25 percent of the charge volume generated by retailers in the Baltimore-Washington area by 1983. Citicorp expanded the retailer base by offering lower discount rates and charged cardholders with no annual fee. However, the Choice card had the tendency to cannibalize Citicorp's existing Visa and MasterCard products, and consequently Choice has not been aggressively marketed.

American Express, because of the competition from Visa and Master-Card, entered the retail market segment in 1980. American Express cards were extended to such prestigious retail establishments as Tiffany's, the upscale New York–based jeweler, and Bloomingdale's. Charges were 5 percent of the ticket purchase price, as opposed to 3 percent charged by competitors. American Express believed that since its cardholders had higher average household incomes, more would be spent in the retail establishments and American Express cards would enhance the prestige of retailers—hence, extra charges were justified. This philosophy was not entirely successful, and after opposition from retailers, adjustments were made.

RETAILER CREDIT SYSTEMS

A variety of credit systems can be used by retail organizations, which include in-house credit, third-party, and affinity and co-branding credit cards. Each of these retailer credit systems provides advantages and disadvantages. The store image generated by selection is important, and since customers expect this service and competitors offer credit arrangements, selection should be carefully considered.

An in-house credit system is owned and administered by the retail organization. An in-house credit plan tends to promote customer loyalty. Credit-granting stores more easily generate repeat patronage, since credit customers tend to be more loyal than cash customers. Store credit customers generally buy more merchandise and pay higher prices than customers who do not use credit. Moreover, credit applications provide considerable demographic information about charge customers. Information is also provided as to an analysis of merchandise purchased that is helpful for future promotional purposes. The monthly credit statement is an effective vehicle for promotional literature. However, operating costs from additional personnel, equipment, and facilities are incurred to provide credit services. Fees and commissions need to be paid to outside credit agencies, and there are losses from uncollectible accounts. These additional costs are acceptable if balanced by more revenue. Sears, for example, makes substantial profits on its retail credit operations and so does J. C. Penney.

An alternative to offering in-store credit cards is for retailers to use third-party credit systems issued by banks such as MasterCard and Visa and entertainment card organizations such as American Express, Diners' Club, and Carte Blanche. This type of credit system relieves the retailer of establishing and operating a credit department and the costs of investigating credit applications, billing customers, and collecting accounts. Since financial institutions make their credit cards very attractive through a number of enhancements such as ATMs and travel insurance, retailers gain more charge customers, and some of these customers may be from out of town and are tourists or business executives. However, the costs of bank service and the depersonalization of relationships with customers might offset the advantages, depending upon circumstances.

Affinity cards and co-branding credit cards are two additional credit systems available to the retailer. Affinity cards are based on a relationship with an organization administered by a third-party credit system such as Visa or MasterCard. The relationship might be emotional, such as the Sierra Club; professional, such as the American Marketing Association; or intellectual, such as New York University. Therefore, greater card loyalty should be forthcoming.

Co-branding cards involve a relationship with a retailer and a third-party credit system. May's, Macy's, and Casual Corner cards each has a Visa or MasterCard logo on it that allows the cardholder to use it not only in the retailer's store but wherever the card is accepted. Ford, General Motors, Charles Schwab, and American Airlines also use co-branding. A co-branded card provides users with more incentive to charge purchases on the card. For example, Ford and General Motors extend a certain amount based upon purchases toward the purchase of a new car. Consumers using Citicorp's card, offered in conjunction with American Airlines, earn frequent-flier points at the rate of one mile for every dollar charged on the card. American Express has recently embraced co-branding and has made an agreement with Harrod's, a London-based department store, and has its cards linked to brokerage accounts at Smith Barney and Lehman Brothers. This type of an arrangement should further enhance and maintain store loyalty. This arrangement should also create greater convenience and total satisfaction. The retail firm realizes most of the advantages associated with in-house credit systems while avoiding many of the problems of administration. Co-branding is an attractive option for retailers who do not desire to incur the high costs of operating and maintaining their own credit system. Co-branding cards are the shape of the future. Partnered cards now constitute approximately 80 percent of MasterCard International new business and more than one third of its volume.

THE PLASTIC WARS: TODAY

MasterCard and Visa International, made up of mostly member banks, issue more than 80 percent of general-purpose credit cards in the United States. The Sears Discover card accounts for about 14 percent of all cards. Optima, issued by American Express (Amex's other cards demand immediate payment), and the AT&T Universal card constitute most of the remainder. Retailers such as J. C. Penney and Spiegel have entered the market but are not viewed as serious competitors.

Each company's strategy is different. Since MasterCard is smaller than Visa, it desires to grow and is endeavoring to bring new issuers into its organization. Visa has made it more difficult for nonbanks to join but is trying to penetrate new markets by extending its card use to the grocery field and to professionals such as doctors and dentists. American Express has tried to appeal to merchants by increased advertising and by downsizing its mail-order business, thereby avoiding direct competition with retailers. The American Express charge card operation has two important sources of income: cardholder fees and merchant discounts. Visa and MasterCard have a third source of income that is derived from interest charges on unpaid card balances. In 1987, American Express introduced Optima, a credit card that gives holders the option of making extended payments and competes directly with Visa and MasterCard. The Optima card offers a comprehensive list of benefits and has not cannibalized other American Express cards. However, it is the corporate card where American Express is dominant when confronted with competitive threats and unfortunately has not been successful.

Visa, MasterCard, American Express, and Discover are the major players in the credit card industry. The three largest banks that own Visa and MasterCard are Citibank, Chase Manhattan, and Universal Bank. Universal Bank operates the AT&T Universal card. The Discover card is owned by Sears and managed by the Greenwood Trust bank. Retailers pay an interchange fee to the cardholder's bank. The fee covers customer service, resolution of disputes, and liability for fraudulent use of credit cards. Nearly half of all cardholders pay their bill in full each month, and the other half leave unpaid balances that accumulate interest.

American Express has promoted an image of an upscale credit card for many years. This upscale image has been used to justify the substantially higher fees it charges merchants. However, Visa has more cardholders with $50,000-plus incomes, as well as with $100,000-plus incomes, than American Express. Visa also has more Gold cardholders than American Express has Gold and Platinum members combined.

Approximately one fourth of all supermarkets accept the Visa credit card. Ohio has the most credit card acceptance, with over 70 percent of supermarkets honoring plastic in Columbus and Cincinnati. Rochester, New York, Denver, Atlanta, Houston, Dallas, San Francisco, and Los Angeles are other strong markets for supermarket credit card acceptance, with more than 50 percent of stores.

The Discover card offers strong competition by giving more travel insurance coverage ($500,000) than any other competitive credit card. Discover also offers cardholders a 1 percent credit rebate at the end of the year and does not charge an annual fee. Discover offers banking services through the Greenwood Trust that are very competitive in extending interest on savings and money market accounts. Discover offers retailers the lowest interchange fee, compared with American Express, Visa, and MasterCard.

The entry of the AT&T Universal card in March 1990 was to modify the structure of the plastic wars. Visa and MasterCard charged up to $55 as an annual fee for their Gold cards. AT&T made consumers aware that they have some options in fees, interest rates, and extras. AT&T's offer of a no-fee-for-life card for those who signed up the first year and a 10 percent discount on long-distance calls was very attractive. AT&T was later to change this policy and charge a $20 fee and withdrew the long-distance telephone discount. Critics maintain that the Universal card attracted those customers who pay their bills promptly and do not pay interest charges. Banks do not value these price-sensitive customers.

In fall 1992, it seemed like everyone was getting into the credit card business. General Electric and General Motors were among the big-league entrants. With these new entrants, a flurry of special deals, discounts, and interest-rate cuts was offered. Rampant competition was accelerating the plastic wars. For example, General Motors is using its credit card as a marketing tool for promoting purchases of its automobiles. The General Motors card permits consumers to earn rebates equal to 4 percent of their total charges, up to $500 a year over a seven-year period, to be applied toward a purchase or lease of any new General Motors automobile or truck. The General Motors credit card offers no annual fee and a floating interest rate fully a point below what the competition offers as an incentive for potential customers.

THE PLASTIC WARS: RETAILER PERSPECTIVES

The rise of debit cards for point-of-purchase transactions is now aggressively pushed by both Visa and MasterCard. The question arises as to why retailers should be receptive to debit cards and accept them. First, the debit card is affiliated directly to the customer's checking account. Debit cards are essentially electronic checks and are a guaranteed form of payment. Unlike paper checks, the retailer assumes virtually no risk. Second, retailers benefit from the lower costs of debit card transactions. The use of debit cards is much faster at point of purchase than checks and a better audit trail than cash, preventing pilferage. Supermarkets, with heavy check-handling environments, significantly reduce office expenses. Third, retailers, by accepting debit cards, are able to offer customers more payment options that are desired. In California, such supermarket chains as Safeway and Lucky offer comprehensive payment plans including debit cards and credit cards. Retailers believe that by offering as many payment options as possible this helps to provide the highest level of customer service and satisfaction.

Consumer behavioral research reveals that consumers prefer to use credit cards for costly items. It is not unusual for consumers to use one credit card for costly purchases and another at restaurants. Consequently, some consumers use debit cards as a method to pay for goods and services usually purchased with cash and checks for such items as groceries and gasoline. Moreover, consumers find that a debit card transaction is faster at point of purchase than check writing and relieves them of carrying a checkbook.

MasterCard, Visa, and Discover have enormous retailer acceptance, but the impact of a company's own card or private label is minimal. According to surveys, merchants have no preference as to whose third-party cards are used just as long as customers shop and make purchases in their stores. The exception would be the General Electric MasterCard, which extends discounts at some of the largest retailers in the United States, including Macy's and Kmart.

Credit card status in different types of retail institutions varies. Home centers such as Home Depot and Lowe's have been penetrated by Visa and MasterCard with 100 percent acceptance. American Express and Discover were accepted by over 80 percent of companies, and 60 percent offer their own in-house credit cards and over 40 percent have private-label cards.

Kroger, the Cincinnati-based supermarket chain, has introduced Master-Card in its stores in Texas and its Louisiana markets. The most commonly accepted credit cards in supermarkets are MasterCard and Visa, followed by Discover. However, credit cards and debit sales currently accounted for only 2 percent of transactions. Over 10 percent of supermarkets accept debit cards, and this is a fast-growing method of payment. Some customers do not like to carry cash or find payment by check slow at point of purchase. Debit cards offer shopping convenience and is expected at all chain locations by those customers using this form of payment.

Nonapparel specialty stores accepted all types of cards, with both MasterCard and Visa gaining more than 95 percent penetration, followed by Discover with about 90 percent. Again, American Express was third, with about 75 percent penetration, followed with about one third that offer their own credit cards and take private-label cards. Debit cards were not widely used but would appear to be a promising future of potential payment.

The vast majority of discounters accept MasterCard, Visa, and Discover, with about one quarter offering private-label cards. However, only approximately 10 percent of total transactions were derived from credit cards. Again, American Express, perhaps because of its upscale status image, lagged far behind the leaders. Another reason might be that American Express charges retailers higher fees than Visa, MasterCard, and Discover and therefore has a more difficult task gaining discount retailer acceptance. Because of its status image, shoppers in discount stores might feel more comfortable charging items with cards other than American Express. Small merchants are especially concerned with what they consider excessive credit card fees.

Retailer store credit card use has declined. Customers would seem to be interested in carrying fewer and not more, credit cards. Not all corporate credit cards have been successful. General Electric, even though providing discounts at Macy's, Foot Locker, and Toys "R" Us, has not reported much growth. Consumers may be oversaturated with credit cards and consequently not that receptive to new market entries. Whereas American Express does provide retailers with more customer demographic information than any other credit card organization, inroads into retail trade are difficult due to higher retailer fees.

THE PLASTIC WARS: CHALLENGES AND PROBLEMS

The strategy of Visa and MasterCard has been to solicit membership from as many people as possible. Even college students without incomes have been targeted. American Express, in contrast, has higher standards for membership. The majority of American Express cardholders are professional/managerial, technical, and salespeople. Moreover, the majority of cardholders have college educations and incomes over $60,000 a year. Although American Express has many less members than Visa and

MasterCard, its cardholders spend much more on a yearly basis. The American Express card, with the exception of the Optima card, which has been a disaster, is essentially a charge card, and customers are expected to pay their balances in full each month.

American Express has targeted a status market and therefore charges retailers more than any other credit card organization. Visa and MasterCard have attempted and have been successful with their Gold cards in taking part of this market away from American Express. Merchants have rebelled against the high fees of American Express. American Express has maintained that because of its prestige market membership, higher charges are justified. However, Discover, the Sears credit card, has entered the market and has offered merchants lower fees and surprisingly has seized a good segment of the retail market. It had been expected that other merchants would maintain that Sears is a competitor and therefore not be receptive to the Sears Discover card. But this resistance on the part of retailers for this reason has not been an important factor. AT&T, General Motors, General Electric, and affinity cards, all backed by Visa and MasterCard, have eroded further the American Express prestige market. Consumers once thrilled with the prospect of carrying a dozen credit cards are now endeavoring to limit their affiliations with only three or four cards or less.

The largest concentration for American Express growth has been international markets that have been limited by competition. Visa International and MasterCard, the two largest global card brands, have a network of member banks such as Citibank, Barclays, First Chicago, Chase Manhattan, AT&T Universal, Bank of Montreal, National Westminster, Credit Agricole, and Lloyds Bank. These banks issue credit cards to consumers that allow them to buy on credit. American Express, which issues charge cards that must be paid off monthly, is trying to promote its Optima card, which permits balances to be carried forward each month.

In 1994, Visa held the lead in global card wars with more than 300 million cards worldwide and more than a 50 percent share of card volume. MasterCard has a little more than 200 million cards outstanding but is experiencing pronounced growth patterns. American Express has only about 35 million cards in force but has targeted a more limited and affluent market of frequent business travelers and wealthy individuals. A lot of resources have been devoted to cultivating corporate clients in the United States and abroad.

American Express, behind in the plastic wars, has made the decision to combine its name with other corporate names and to offer co-branded cards. This is a response to a loss in market share that has eroded in the past decade. Since 1983, American Express has lost more than 25 percent market share of the volume charged in credit purchases. Again, American Express has entered the co-branded market late, and many organizations such as Apple, General Motors, and Shell have already affiliated with Visa and MasterCard.

American Express has revitalized itself in the travel industry. The company's standing in the travel industry is high since American Express is able to provide customer demographic profiles of travel users. However, airlines, hotels, rental-car companies, and cruise lines do complain about American Express. Just like merchants, these organizations pay American Express a transaction fee every time a card is used for payment, and the fee is typically higher than the fee that Visa, MasterCard, and other card companies charge. Carnival Cruise Lines, in protest, stopped accepting the American Express charge card. Carnival claimed that an extra $1 million in fees were incurred a year. American Express travel agencies retaliated by dropping Carnival as a preferred customer and cut back on Carnival sales. American Express has, through acquisitions, become the United States' largest travel agency and is able to exert power pressure in the travel industry. This role in the travel industry will be expanded once the acquisition of the U.S. travel offices and the international business-travel unit of the London-based Thomas Cook Group is completed. The U.S. travel offices number close to 400 and should help American Express to bolster its charge card business.

American Express has endeavored to target affluent women by allocating significant resources to marketing joint promotions. Joint promotions have been coordinated with high-status retailers, Sanofi beauty products, and *Elle* magazine. Through such coordinated joint promotions, American Express attempts to attract new customers as well as reinforce an upscale image. American Express gears its advertising to reach educated women who do not like pressure tactics but like to be informed. To offset this strategy, both Visa and MasterCard offer Gold credit cards with all sorts of rewards such as travel insurance, automobile rental collision insurance, rebates, and theft coverage. AT&T even offers with its Gold Universal card to arbitrate disputes between customers and retailers. Citibank is beginning to eliminate its annual fee for some classifications of cardholders, and AT&T entered the market initially with the pledge not to charge an annual fee, provided the card was used once a year. The Sears Discover card does not charge an annual fee, but American Express charges an annual fee of $55 and $75 fee for its Gold card. This competition has forced American Express to also offer some rewards for membership.

The strategy of Visa is to make its card available to as many consumers as possible. Visa renamed its upscale card Visa Gold in 1988, and subsequently cardholders have more than doubled. Visa, in an effort to attract business card members, has offered such services as faster hotel check-ins, a guaranteed reservation service, and greater protection against unauthorized charges. Visa owns and operates Interlink, the nation's largest point-of-sale network that accepts credit cards at retail stores and restaurants. Visa is also trying to make more feasible the rise of automatic teller machines from which customers can obtain cash with their credit cards. Visa and MasterCard have both competed for the automatic teller machine market. Visa in 1987 paid $5 million for a one-third share of Plus System, a network of ATMs. This battle intensified when MasterCard made a similar arrangement with Cirrus, another network of ATMs. Visa accomplishes two objectives with ATM dominance: It receives 3.5 cents for each transaction and offers customers more convenience, which is a very strong consideration.

Visa and MCI Communications have joined forces in the telecommunications field and have developed a card called VisaPhone. Cardholders are allowed to charge phone calls on their Visa card, and the need for a separate calling card is eliminated. This strategy is a move that counteracts the AT&T Universal card, which also permits cardholders to charge calls and provides long-distance discounts.

Discover, like the AT&T Universal card, does not charge an annual fee. Discover continually tries to undercut the competition. When a credit card is used, retailers must pay a transaction fee. American Express charges merchants 4.5 percent of the total transaction; Visa and MasterCard charge 3.8 percent; and Discover charges 2 percent. Retailers have reacted favorably, and Discover is accepted by 150,000 more retailers than American Express. Another reason for the growth of Discover has been the strategy of providing a cash-back option to consumers. Customers are offered a 1 percent cash bonus over charges of $3,000. Since $3,000 is more than most families charge and 1 percent of $3,000 is only $30, this offer is more of a marketing tool than an actual service for many customers.

American Express, in an effort to combat competitive inroads on its upscale market, has tried to broaden its marketing efforts. Shoney's, a 675 family restaurant chain, has accepted the American Express credit card. This is a pronounced departure from the use of the American Express card at such restaurants as the Four Seasons in Manhattan, New York, which charges $40 for a sirloin steak. American Express runs the danger of blurring its image with consumers. Moreover, since retailers are charged higher transaction fees because American Express claims that its cardholders are more affluent and charge in higher volume, any tarnishing of its image may diminish a strategy used for some years. If American Express is not careful, its credit card will become less popular because of high fees charged to both cardholders and retailers and because of a blurred image.

The AT&T Universal Visa and MasterCard have changed strategies in the plastic wars. The initial offering required no annual fee and was guaranteed for life, provided the credit card was used once a year. This drift toward no annual membership fees is especially bad news for American Express and banks, which have depended on card fees for over 50 percent of their income. Banks have tried to convince consumers that the annual fee is worth it by adding incentives. This strategy seems to be unsuccessful, and banks are rapidly retreating from requiring annual fees. AT&T also offered a 10 percent discount on long-distance calls, and in order to offset this goody, banks began to offer competing incentives. AT&T has since changed its strategies and now charges a small annual fee and has eliminated the discount on long-distance calls. High costs were responsible for the changes in strategies.

American Express has an extraordinary expertise in discerning the purchasing preferences of its card members through the use of marketing surveys. A manifestation of this expertise has been enhancements such as automatic car-rental insurance and 24-hour phone lines for service. American Express segments its cardholders into market segments based on income and lifestyle characteristics and provides this information to retailers. Visa and MasterCard have been unable to match this expertise. Retailers find this information valuable, and it somewhat offsets the high fees that are charged.

New credit card arrivals are just beginning to enter the plastic wars. Nordstrom, the Seattle-based retailer, co-branded with Visa in 1994. Nissan is also considering a credit card, and so are some of the supermarket and fast-food retail chains. The entry of prestigious retailers into the plastic wars is bound to take away from the American Express upscale target market. The entry of airlines such as United and Dean Witter's Discover card will further erode the upscale market for American Express. Since General Motors, Ford, and General Electric all offer incentives based on frequent usage, there is a tendency for customers to concentrate their purchases with only one or two credit cards. This is another trend that will have a severe impact on American Express.

MANAGING CHANGE

Strategy in the plastic wars has focused on the development of competitive position. *Competitive position* refers to the degree that a firm's use of marketing strategy has allowed it to differentiate itself from competitors in the perceptions of consumers. The credit card industry has paid close attention to market opportunity, which is the amount of sales coming from a market. The industry has recognized that the market segment with the most customers is not necessarily the one that provides the optimum market opportunity. Heavy users of the credit card service can yield more profits. American Express, MasterCard, Visa, and other credit card organizations therefore place high priority on the premium card segment. Premium cards have generated more revenue in the past from annual customer fees, which tend to be higher than on regular cards. Prestige cardholders also use larger lines of credit and more services than traditional credit card customers.

In efforts to chip away at the upscale market dominated by American Express, both Visa and MasterCard have issued Gold credit cards. Moreover, affinity cards have also been used to gain this prestigious market by Visa and MasterCard. For example, college alumni associations such as Texas A & M have established the affinity relationship with their credit cards. The affinity relationship might be emotional, such as the Sierra Club. Greater loyalty should be forthcoming by cardholders of both Texas A & M and the Sierra Club credit cards. Both Visa and MasterCard have demonstrated managerial vision in entering the affinity market, allowing these organizations to segment markets once clearly dominated by American Express.

Co-branding credit cards is another strategy used by Visa and MasterCard to take away part of the upscale market held by American Express. Retailer credit cards such as Nordstrom Company branded with either Visa or MasterCard invade the status market once dominated by American Express. Co-branded cards with General Motors and Carnival Cruise Lines are still other examples of the impending future. Co-branding is another strategy that has involved managerial vision.

Patronage and increased use of credit cards have been accomplished by helping customers learn about newer services such as cash advances, automobile collision coverage, guaranteed reservations, toll-free hot lines, use of automated teller machines, faster lost-card replacement, and quick credit approvals. Another important objective has been to promote and maintain brand images based on prestige.

Mass market segmentation strategies are directed to all adults with minimum income levels. Market segmentation approaches have been directed to use situations such as travel, business, and entertainment. Both mass market and market segmentation strategies are used extensively. Demographic segmentation has been employed with mixed results. For example, the American Association of Retired Persons has issued a credit card, and consequently, the elderly who are members of a large organization can help their organization when making charges, and this approach seems successful. In contrast, the market segment for professional and managerial women has not been cultivated that well, and credit card organizations still need to close this gap in their strategies.

There are possible future changes in the credit card industry. A more widespread use of debit cards, particularly in supermarkets, drugstores, and convenience stores, is a future objective. Consumer behavior trends would seem to indicate a desire not to carry cash. Professionals such as doctors and dentists will allow credit card use and may also consider the use of debit cards. Credit card organizations may possibly pay interest to cardholders for credit balances and overpayments. There may also be a tightening of minimum requirements for issuance of new cards in efforts to reduce default expenses. Along similar lines, Citibank gives cardholders the option of having their photos printed on the front of their cards. Citibank claims that fraud expenses have been significantly reduced, enabling it to eliminate its $20 annual fee on its standard Visa and MasterCard and its $50 Gold fee. Computerized credit cards may also be possible in the future and the greater use of premium cards targeted at select market groups.

The credit card industry has a number of strengths that will probably continue in the future. The coverage of the travel market is extensive. The industry through the addition of automatic teller machines is particularly good at providing convenience in using cards and providing 30-day interest-free credit, revolving credit, and high prestige.

Both Visa and MasterCard have made inroads into the market share held by American Express, but probably this strategy has stabilized and is not expected to continue. MasterCard, with more than 25 million co-branded cards in circulation has been a leader in co-branding and has taken away market share held by Visa and American Express with this strategy. However, in the future, backing American Express will no longer be enough. Doctors, dentists, and hospitals will be encouraged to allow patients to pay medical bills with credit cards. It is conceivable that the use of debit cards in supermarkets and drugstores will grow significantly. The current market share of Visa, which is approximately 45 percent, MasterCard, 28 percent, American Express, 22 percent, and Discover, 5 percent, may not fluctuate that much. Discover still needs to be accepted by more outlets. By clever use of strategies, it will gain a few more points of market share, but more potential would seem to be limited. Future growth for credit card organizations would be in uncultivated markets, and therefore innovative strategies will be needed in exploring new frontiers.

American Express has lost significant market share to competitors. The AT&T Universal card, co-branding, and affinity cards have all taken a toll of American Express's market share. However, there are times when one suspects that American Express has been its own worst enemy. Chic restaurants such as Azalea in Atlanta and others in Boston have refused American Express's high fees. This practice may continue if these warning signals are not heeded.

Many of the credit industry's marketing strategies are sound because they satisfy the prevailing demand in market segments or because they effectively satisfy market requirements. Such strategies are credit card organization strengths. These strengths must be matched in some way by all members of the industry. For example, a card issuer must offer 30-day free credit to match similar offers by competitors in order to remain competitive. The Mellon Bank, with their Cornerstone MasterCard, rebates 10 percent of interest charges to cardholders in good standing for two years. Apple Computer is also giving rebates of 2.5 percent on annual purchases up to $3,000, and so is Shell on gasoline purchases. Credit card organizations such as American Express and Discover may need to find a way to match these rebates in the future.

LESSONS LEARNED FROM SUCCESS AND FAILURE

Success does not guarantee continued success. American Express has lost touch with its customers and now is confronted with the difficult task of wooing them back. Discover has gained ground on Visa and MasterCard. Among the reasons for Discover's popularity are that no annual fee is charged and cardholders receive a cash rebate of as much as 1 percent on transactions. The AT&T Universal card has also made significant inroads initially by offering not to charge an annual fee for life, provided the card is used once a year. Visa and MasterCard have both reacted slowly to all of these new competitive threats.

Although American Express, Visa, and MasterCard have made mistakes, they can and do survive as long as they maintain many more strengths than weaknesses. American Express had an enviable growth pattern but yet succumbed to marketing myopia. Even Visa and MasterCard found that their success actually exposed them to the vulnerability of competitors. Complacency is an affliction for a successful firm and leads to a disdain for lesser competitors. Organizations can be resistant to change because it can be threatening to the strategies that had been previously successful. Success encourages the perspective that the future will be a repetition of the past. Therefore, a changing marketing environment can go undetected for a long time. It is indeed encouraging that both Visa and MasterCard have extended their marketing strategies to make their credit cards available to the mass market.

For the most part, the credit card industry has adopted to a changing environment. Efforts have even been made to cultivate the college student market, which is currently without much in the way of financial resources but has the potential to remedy this situation in the future. The credit industry has been innovative with the establishment of Platinum and Gold cards for a premium market. The debit card, which is a convenience and allows consumers not to carry cash, will become more widespread in the future. The development of new markets such as doctors, dentists, and hospitals will also become much more attractive in the future. Thus, the plastic wars present strategies that are both adaptive to the marketing environment and innovative.

CONTROVERSIAL DECISIONS

The development of effective marketing decision making in the credit card industry is dependent on an understanding of numerous environmental factors. The realization of objectives is significantly related to management's ability to develop strategies that account for environmental forces. A comprehension of cultural and social dimensions is important to the credit card industry because of their impact on consumption behavior.

Population dynamics and income redistributions have influenced lifestyle trends and consumer buying habits. Consumers of the future will be different. The multiincome or double-income family, the increasing singles market, and the new fragmented family will cause important changes in the credit card industry. Even the rising crime rate has had an impact on the credit card industry. The goals of credit organizations need to include the careful monitoring of environmental forces and adapting to changes and trends in more sharply defined consumer market segments.

Controversial decisions in the credit card industry center around the expansion of markets, the segmentation of markets, the use of incentives as an integrated part of marketing strategy, and changing social values. Both Visa and MasterCard have extended their upscale customer base to include many more eligible customers. The gamble was taken that this effort would not diminish usage of Gold or premium cards and would not cancel out the snob appeal. Research studies have suggested that their lower-status market would use their bank credit cards for installment purchases, while members of the upscale market would pay their credit card bills in full each month. Credit card organizations have profited immensely from those consumers who do not pay their bills in full each month.

Retailers are also confronted with a controversial decision in accepting third-party credit cards such as Visa, MasterCard, American Express, and Discover. The cost of the service is a negative, and that is an important reason why, in the beginning, many retailers were so eager to embrace the Discover card, which charged a lower rate than competitors. Second, there is a depersonalization of relationships with customers. Therefore, there are many retailers that prefer either to provide their own credit cards, which is costly, or to consider co-branding as an effective strategy.

The plastic wars of offering incentives to prospective cardholders do run the danger of escalating costs but have proven to be an effective strategy in promoting a customer base. The decisions to rebate a percentage of purchases or a percentage of interest charges, or to offer no-annual-fee cards, or to provide collision insurance on car rentals all involve heavy expenditures. A decision must be made whether or not the costs justify the financial returns. The AT&T Universal card, for example, after the initial promotion, decided to charge new cardholders on their Gold Visa and MasterCards an annual fee.

The segmentation of precise customer markets with either premium cards, affinity cards, or co-branding cards has been very successful. Lifestyle usage of credit cards is an important consideration. For example, the American Express Company offers its Optima credit card to consumers in an effort to expand its customer base but has also targeted its more prestigious Gold and Platinum credit cards with different services to other distinct market segments. The original Optima card launched in 1987 was a disaster, and American Express is now offering the Optima Time Grace card.

While user conditions have been modified, it is doubtful that this card will be really successful. Even American Express executives doubt its widespread appeal.

Credit has become either an essential or an expected part of the retailer's service strategies. The problem for most retailers is not *whether* to offer credit but *what type* of credit to provide. Although credit card usage is somewhat a reflection of social class attitudes, the days of the Puritan ethic are over for all social classes. Perhaps more than anything else, the family structure has changed and become more egalitarian as women seek a broader role in family decision making. Marriage and the family are important institutions in the United States that influence values and lifestyles. These values and lifestyles are manifest in purchasing expenditures. Because the marriage age is rising, consumers have better financial resources and are more sophisticated. The double-income family will become more interested in services such as life insurance, credit cards, rental cars, and travel. Credit organizations and retailers must respond to these changing social values in formulating their credit system strategies.

CHAPTER 11

In-Home Shopping: Retailing Without Walls

Environmental Challenges
- More women in the workforce
- Blurring of gender roles
- An increase in double-income families
- The graying of America
- Smaller family size
- A larger percentage of college graduates
- Increased multiculturism
- Sharper separation of social classes
- Higher postage rates and state taxes on mail order

Strategies to Combat Environmental Challenges
- Merchandise assortments and services not available to many consumers
- Targeting consumer segments with home computers
- Product availability to and in the workforce
- Lower prices than found in retail stores
- List targeting of consumers responsive to direct retailing and direct selling
- Neighborhood segmentation

Negative Challenges
- Poor image associated with direct-mail and door-to-door selling
- Some consumers will not open their doors to salespeople or talk to telephone sales representatives
- Sales costs high due to turnover and part-timers not well supervised

Corporate Responses to Environmental Challenges
- Avon places greater emphasis on workplace sales (one third of revenue)
- Mary Kay and Tupperware use community residents and create a party atmosphere
- Fuller Brush now uses mail-order to supplement door-to-door selling
- Kirby vacuum cleaner personnel make more evening in-home presentations to accommodate working women

I n-home shopping is one of the fastest-growing areas of retail trade. Direct retailing is a form of retailing that targets the customer through a nonpersonal medium such as direct mail, telephone, or television shopping networks. Higher levels of education and income, time pressures created by dual-career households, advances in communication technology, and proliferation of credit cards have contributed to this extraordinary growth of in-home shopping. J. C. Penney, Spiegel, and Home Shopping Network are examples of general merchandise retailers using direct retailing strategies. L. L. Bean, Time-Life Books, and the Franklin Mint are marketers using direct retailing strategies to sell specialty merchandise. J. C. Penney, Bloomingdale's, and Banana Republic are heavily involved in catalog selling. Retailers also use a combination of telephone and mail order as an effective strategy. More than half of all adult consumers have ordered some merchandise by phone or mail, but there are complaints about high shipping costs and the inconvenience of returns, which can be minimized by returns directly to the store but not necessarily to such firms as Time-Life Books.

Direct selling is another strategy to accomplish nonstore retailing objectives. This method encompasses in-home and in-office personal selling or seller-originated telephone calls. Among the leaders in direct selling are Avon and Mary Kay in door-to-door selling and Tupperware in party plan selling. J. C. Penney uses decorator consultants to sell a complete furnishings merchandise line, not available in its stores, in consumers' homes. Direct selling revenues have increased relatively slowly compared with direct retailing, although direct selling firms such as Avon also utilize catalogs as a marketing strategy.

Advances in technology have had an important impact on direct retailing. Videotex is a two-way system that links the seller's data banks by cable or telephone lines with customers. The videotex service is a computerized catalog offered by manufacturers, retailers, banks, and other business organizations. Consumers perceive it as less risky. There is a relationship between product assortment and higher income, with higher-income households more likely to purchase a greater variety of products.

Convenience is the paramount reason why consumers buy from direct retailers. Direct buying eliminates the need to shop in person at a store, thus saving time and the cost of travel. Moreover, many direct retailers offer merchandise not available at stores. Specialty direct retailers typically sell a wide assortment of merchandise not always conveniently available elsewhere. Montgomery Ward has reentered direct retailing with specialty catalogs and seems to be successful. Price is another reason for purchasing direct. Frequently, a product available at a store is also available at a lower price from a direct retailer. Purchasing is convenient to the extent that the item may be described through the mail and/or on the telephone. Customers can order through the mail or on the telephone or on a computer terminal and pay with a credit card.

CHARACTERISTICS OF DIRECT RETAILING

Many of the leading firms in direct retailing are well-known retailers or manufacturers that have used direct retailing strategies to supplement their conventional strategies. These firms include Burpee, with seeds; Williams-Sonoma, with gourmet cookware; Spiegel, especially with women's apparel and home furnishings; Banana Republic, with apparel; L. L. Bean with apparel; and Victoria's Secret, with lingerie. J. C. Penney and Bloomingdale's are heavily involved with catalog sales.

Customers interested in purchasing through direct retailing frequently purchase merchandise items such as books, records, tapes, casual clothing, intimate apparel, sports equipment, small kitchen appliances, home tools, children's clothing, cosmetics, and costume jewelry. However, even such items as shoes, and expensive dresses and jewelry, are purchased through direct retailing. There is a low customer response rate of from 2 to 3 percent responding favorably when contacted. This low response rate has caused many problems for direct retailers.

Serious efforts have been made to increase the response rate, but operating costs are high and can get out of control when generated by very low response rates. Direct mail and catalogs involve high printing, paper, and mail costs. Moreover, order-processing and shipping costs can be high relative to the sales volume produced. Large-scale operations include computer systems and specialized personnel for telephone ordering. Low response rates can increase these costs significantly. Sears and Montgomery Ward have found competition intense and, even with their well-known reputations, have encountered serious problems. Furthermore, there are any number of consumers who would prefer not to purchase from a direct retailer but desire to actually see and examine the product before making a purchase.

Changing environmental variables have made direct retailing more attractive even though negatives are present. The high proportion of women in the workforce and lifestyle reflecting time poverty leave less time for shopping in conventional retail stores. Crowded shopping malls and congested traffic arteries have made shopping more arduous and inconvenient. Technology has made direct retailing more convenient with computer-to-computer ordering, computerized inventory control systems, telemarketing, and the ubiquitous use of 800 numbers in telephone ordering. The Home Shopping Network and retailers such as Saks Fifth Avenue and Macy's utilizing television communications have been another impetus for direct retailing.

CHARACTERISTICS OF DIRECT SELLING

Direct selling started centuries ago with roving peddlers in Europe. In the United States, the fast-talking image of the Yankee Peddler, coupled with devious and ethically questionable selling practices, decorates the history books. Pioneers in door-to-door selling were Fuller Brush and Electrolux. Avon helped to change the image of door-to-door selling. Mary Kay Cosmetics and Tupperware helped to popularize home-sales parties, where friends and neighbors attend a party and products are demonstrated and sold.

Some of these direct selling firms, such as Avon, have pursued a different strategy by using catalogs to supplement personal selling. Prospects have also been contacted at work rather than at home. Nontraditional target markets such as Hispanics have received increased direct seller attention.

Direct sellers have been constrained by environmental factors. With so many women in the workforce, door-to-door sales representatives have found no one at home to respond to ringing doorbells. Moreover, good salespeople are extremely hard to recruit and retain. Some states have passed "cooling off" laws that allow customers to cancel a sale for up to several days after the transaction.

On the other hand, direct selling is very convenient since merchandise can be purchased either at home or at work. Direct selling also permits customers to obtain a thorough sales presentation concerning the merits of a product and to request additional information if needed.

Both direct retailing and direct selling offer marketers the opportunity to target a large uncultivated potential market of customers from all income and social strata. Since more married women are in the labor force, these selling systems are a convenience for a large market segment. If the system is operated efficiently, lower costs are possible than maintaining a field sales force. Furthermore, an improved technological environment, especially in interactive teleshopping, has made possible regional and even national systems.

Direct retailing and direct selling systems do have limitations. Some customers have negative impressions based on either their own experiences or the experiences of friends. Many consumers would prefer to examine the actual product before purchase, and this leads to low response rates. Moreover, there are high overhead costs from computer systems that must be offset by volume purchasing. Already, Sears and Ward's have experienced difficulty in their established catalog operations due to intense competition. Sears and Ward's ceased operation but Ward's started again with specialized catalogs a few years later. This intense competition will probably accelerate in the future as more firms enter the marketplace.

Five key ingredients seem to be important for either success or failure in the in-home shopping industry: innovation, target market segmentation and image, physical environmental resources, human resources, and customer satisfaction. Customer satisfaction is a fifth variable added in this analysis because of the wait between ordering merchandise, the receipt of merchandise, and the aftermath of adjustment if necessary. In the previous chapters, customer satisfaction is viewed as a total outcome or result of the effective use of the key ingredients that determine if firms are successful. The converse is present in varying degrees if these key factors have not been well implemented.

Innovation happened when Fuller Brush decided on door-to-door selling and Montgomery Ward and Sears commenced direct-mail operations. L. L. Bean emphasized customer satisfaction with charm and grace, and this in the early 1900s constituted an innovation. Innovation associated with new product introductions or established products through new strategies frequently is the nucleus of an in-home shopping network. Innovation among in-home shopping organizations is in itself a determinant of profit or survival.

Target market segmentation and image are a reflection of the inevitability of change affecting in-home shopping firms. This process of change frequently means that firms must diversify by restructuring their target market segments and adjusting their product offerings to satisfy a changing target market. For example, Avon broadened its product offerings to target men. The hope was that women would purchase Avon products for men, but it was uncertain as to whether or not men would use Avon products that were once targeted only to women. Another illustration is Spiegel's changing its target market from mainly middle-class consumers to an upscale market. New product offerings reflected this change in target market.

Image refers to how the in-home shopping organization is perceived by customers and potential customers. A firm may be perceived as upscale, discount-oriented, specialized, or broad-based. To be successful, a retailer must create and maintain a distinctive, clear, and consistent image. Once the image or positioning is established, the in-home shopping firm is placed in a niche relative to competitors, and it becomes very difficult to change consumer perceptions of the firm. Montgomery Ward had an image as a broad-based cataloger and found that customer demand was diminishing. As a result, Ward's left the mail-order establishment. A change of image was successful, but Ward's had to leave mail-order retailing for a few years to effect this successful change in image.

Physical environmental resources are vital to the success of the in-home shopping industry. Electronic retailing would include videotex, videodisc, videologs, and access to interactive cable television. Telemarketing provides a desirable alternative for consumers who wish to avoid traffic congestion and parking problems and those consumers afflicted with poverty-of-time problems. An updated mailing list is necessary for mail-order retailers.

The management of human resources with direct selling firms such as Fuller Brush or Electrolux is much more apparent than in the operation of mail-order firms. Mary Kay with its organizational structure and motivating incentives has used leadership, rather than coercive power, to influence its sales personnel. Mary Kay knows the desires and ambitions of those it leads and uses this knowledge to guide its in-home sales representatives into the necessary activities—whether they be learning or performing. Mary Kay, by using group dynamics, is able to "sell" sales personnel on strategies, policy changes, and anything else that affects them. Sales personnel turnover is an expense and a challenge confronting direct selling firms. A solid knowledge of group dynamics and its implementation may offset and reduce employee turnover.

Customer satisfaction is the fifth element that challenges direct retailers and direct selling firms. One of the most successful mail-order houses is L. L. Bean. All of L. L. Bean's products are guaranteed to 100 percent satisfaction in every way. Customers can return products at any time, even years later, if the product proves unsatisfactory. L. L. Bean either will replace the merchandise or refund the purchase price. Such a policy could easily prove expensive, and some in-home shopping organizations would not emulate this strategy. However, L. L. Bean has won the hearts and minds of its customers. This has not always been true in a field where many consumers have mistrusted mail-order establishments.

If used wisely, all five of these elements—innovation, image and target market segmentation, physical environmental resources, relationships with employees, and customer satisfaction—can help firms to succeed and develop sustainable, value-adding relationships with customers.

COMPETITIVE STRUCTURE OF DIRECT RETAILING: YESTERDAY

The heart of the market for the two mail-order giants before the turn of the century, Montgomery Ward and Sears, Roebuck, was rural America.

The arrival of the catalog was eagerly awaited by farm families throughout the country. A money-back guarantee was offered if the customer was not satisfied, and these mail-order giants became the most trusted names in the nation. The Sears' catalog was to surpass Ward's, and the Sears name dominated and even dominated manufacturers' brands advertised in the catalog.

After the turn of the century, the economy changed and urban cities developed, and the importance of the rural target market diminished. Although the catalog could reach the target market in all parts of the country, operating a mail-order business was especially difficult in periods of rising or declining prices. Reading the catalog was exciting and sales volume was substantial, but following World War I, there was a drop in prices and the department store was far more nimble in adjusting prices than either Sears or Ward's. Rural customers could now make purchases from a variety of nearby stores. Another factor working against mail order was the growth of chain store retailers, some of which pursued a cost leadership strategy. These retailers achieved economies of scale through volume purchases, and customers were also able to see and inspect merchandise before buying. Finally, mail-order firms were unable to maintain lower operating expenses, and with the growth of the automobile, rural America was no longer geographically isolated. Sears is no longer in the catalog business.

L. L. BEAN: A FIRM OF QUALITY

Freeport, Maine, is the home of L. L. Bean, a firm specializing in the sale of sporting goods to hunting and fishing enthusiasts. The backbone of the L. L. Bean business was the sale of its own boots and shoes. Originally, Bean designed a hunting shoe in 1913, and by the early 1920s, sales passed the $100,000-a-year mark. By 1937, sales reached $1 million.

The charm and low-pressure selling of L. L. Bean gained the patronage of notables such as Calvin Coolidge and Babe Ruth. Customer satisfaction is fundamental to the operation. L. L. Bean would refund the purchase price on merchandise sold if the customer was not totally satisfied. The L. L. Bean organization valued word-of-mouth referrals. Often not only was the price of the merchandise refunded, but a small gift was also enclosed. L. L. Bean personally tried out every merchandise item sold either in the retail store or catalog. Such was the success of L. L. Bean that over 2 million people a year would make a visit to Freeport, Maine, a small village of only 6,000 people, to make purchases at the store.

L. L. Bean's target market was divided into two large market segments: the outdoor enthusiasts and the highly educated "preppie" type. During the 1960s, the recreation boom focused on family camping and backpacking. Many young adults sought to return to nature and indulge in outdoor activities. Soon these people were to wear their outdoor apparel and footwear for everyday purposes.

The lifestyle trend of voluntary simplicity contributed, in part, to L. L. Bean's growth. This lifestyle developed in the 1960s and 1970s became more widely accepted in the 1980s. Consumers who adopt this lifestyle seek material simplicity, strive for self-actualization, and adopt an ecological ethic.

Voluntary simplicity is marked by a new balance between inner and outer development and growth. It is a throwback to frugality and puritanical self-reliance. Those consumers who subscribe to this lifestyle desire a more simple life. Outdoor activities such as camping, rafting, and fishing reflect a part of this lifestyle. Ecological awareness becomes paramount, and so does the interconnection between people and natural resources. This new consciousness notes the need for the reduction of environmental pollution and is receptive to new products, such as bottled water, which preserve and maintain the natural environment. Thus, L. L. Bean was to profit from the lifestyle trend of family camping and backpacking.

Consumers desired value in their purchases. Customers wanted lighter weight, longer wear, extra comfort, more safety, and higher product performance. L. L. Bean responded to these new consumer demand patterns. The organization offered free clinics in hunter safety, fly tying, game cooking, winter camping, whitewater canoeing, and other outdoor activities. L. L. Bean placed a particular emphasis on environmental efforts in Maine and played a significant role in preserving the St. John River in northern Maine.

SPIEGEL: AN UPSCALE MAIL-ORDER RETAILER

Spiegel was founded by Joseph Spiegel in 1865 as a quality retail furniture store in downtown Chicago. Spiegel by the early 1900s began issuing catalogs to appeal to the large number of lower-income immigrants who settled in Chicago. Spiegel pioneered the concept of no-money-down credit plans and became almost exclusively a direct marketer. Sales were strong until the 1970s, but Spiegel began to lose market share to Sears and Ward's, both of whom were better known and customers could return the merchandise to the store. At that time, Spiegel targeted low-income consumers in small rural communities in the South and Midwest. In catalog marketing, Spiegel basically copied the approach used by Sears and Ward's. This me-too response contributed to Spiegel's shrinking market share.

As a result of declining sales and market share, Spiegel adopted a focused strategy: The new target market was the upscale consumer, particularly the female, engaged in the workforce or in activities outside the home, who is fashion, quality, and brand conscious. Spiegel aimed to target a younger, better-educated customer employed in a managerial or professional position, with a higher income than most other catalog users. Competition was primarily from L. L. Bean and Neiman-Marcus. Spiegel's repositioning meant replacing the previous merchandise assortment with high-fashion home furnishings and apparel. Spiegel has also targeted precise segments of a fragmented target market. For example, Spiegel received a 1991 Gold Award from the American Catalog Awards for placing an oversized woman on the catalog cover. The plus-sized woman is a part of an upscale fragmented market for Spiegel. Spiegel specializes in satisfying the apparel needs of working women. Women are targeted according to lifestyle analysis: Starting Out, Career Growth, Family Growth, Starting Out II, Mid-Life Crisis, Aging Well, and Mature. Promotion materials are directed to women in specific stages of the life cycle.

Spiegel offers a wide variety of services to its catalog customers. These include a toll-free 800 telephone number; order takers available 24-hours a day, even Saturdays and Sundays; acceptance of American Express, MasterCard, and Visa; and very liberal return goods privileges. Spiegel pays all shipping costs for returned goods regardless of the reason.

There is intense competition among department stores such as Saks Fifth Avenue, Lord & Taylor, and off-price chains to target the upscale customer. A number of upscale department stores such as Marshall Field use fashion consultants to assemble apparel assortments for managerial and professional women with limited time for shopping. Since many potential customers are reluctant to order by catalog, mail-order firms are beset with many problems and threats.

COMPETITIVE STRUCTURE OF DIRECT SELLING: YESTERDAY

Although itinerant merchants such as Richard Sears and Montgomery Ward traveled the countryside, and the colorful yet nefarious Yankee Peddler was to earn a place in the history books, it was not until Alfred C. Fuller began an enterprise known as the Fuller Brush Company in 1906 that house-to-house selling was to become known worldwide. In the 1990s, a variety of firms such as Avon, Mary Kay, Electrolux, Kirby, World Book, Herbalife, and Amway dominate house-to-house selling. Tupperware innovated successfully the home party plan, which has been emulated by other firms. Cosmetics, household goods, vacuum cleaners, and encyclopedias are among the items sold by direct selling. Avon is the largest firm in this field, with annual sales over $3 billion and a sales staff of more than a million.

AVON CALLING: KNOCK, KNOCK

A door-to-door book salesman named David McConnell in 1886 had an idea to motivate women to purchase books. A gift of perfume was included with each book purchase. Soon the perfume was more popular than the books, and that marked the beginning of Avon Products.

Avon was in its heyday in the 1960s and early 1970s. Avon paid its representatives a 40 percent commission on each sale but no base salary. Wholesalers and retailers were circumvented. Avon had profit margins that were the envy of the industry. Suddenly, the knock, knock of the Avon representative at the door was not answered. As the proportion of working women increased, fewer women were at home to make purchases, and fewer women were available to sell Avon products. Avon's door-to-door distribution system began to disintegrate as more women moved from home to the workplace.

In the early 1980s, Avon revised its strategy. Sales personnel were trained to sell at the workplace without alienating employers. Younger women were targeted since they were more likely to spend more on their appearance than Avon's traditional core market of women older than age 50. Avon linked the sales representatives to catalog and phone sales. Under a program called Avon Select, each representative is paid for each customer name submitted. Avon then sends these customers catalogs with the representative's name on it. The customer can either call Avon or the representatives; either way, a commission is still paid to the representative. Avon has also diversified by offering products for men and children.

Avon manufactures many of its own products and has constructed distribution centers in strategic locations. Avon has ceased experimentation with animal research in response to environmental pressures. Avon has also developed new target markets by acquiring Giorgio, Inc., and Parfums Stern. These firms manufacture perfume and have permitted Avon to sell perfume to department stores. Avon sales representatives are now allowed to sell products to drugstores. Avon has also diversified by offering apparel, jewelry, and collectibles.

MARY KAY: LESSONS IN LEADERSHIP

Founded in 1963 by Mary Kay Ash, much of the firm's competitive advantage has been based upon motivating and supporting its sales force. Initial strategies included heavy emphasis on personal relationships, with no geographical restrictions on sales territories, and a beauty consultation presentation in the home for no more than five or six women. Mary Kay Ash has mastered the power of employee recognition. The firm's color is pink, and a "pink Cadillac" and other automobiles and prizes offer encouragement to sales representatives.

Mary Kay revolves its strategies around the beauty consultants scheduling "make-over parties" with five or six potential clients. These clients are then contacted for reorders and follow-ups. Promotional mailings are sent to clients of the sales representatives, thus offering support to its field sales force and helping to reduce turnover.

Most of Mary Kay's competitors sell entirely through department or fashion specialty stores. Major competitors are Erno Lazlo, Elizabeth Arden, Estēe Lauder, Clinique, and Merle Norman. Only Avon competes in direct selling markets. Mary Kay Cosmetics concentrates its primary efforts on marketing skin-care products in contrast to other firms that produce and market a much broader product line.

Mary Kay sales have grown from approximately $200,000 in 1963 to over $600 million today. The firm has a sales force of over 300,000, of whom more than 6,500 are driving complimentary Cadillacs and other cars worth over $90 million. More than 70 sales representatives have earned commissions of $1 million or more over the course of their careers.

Employee recognition is the nerve center of this organization. The use of national and regional seminars, career conferences, and management conferences provide inspiration, training, and general professional upgrading. At the national level, an elaborately produced three-day session, called Seminar, attracts some 300,000 sales participants at the Dallas Convention Center.

This highly motivational event has a tradition of recognition, education, and entertainment. Color-coded suits, sashes, badges, crowns, bees, and other emblems show the advancement stages of each woman. Women wear metal lapel bars giving the amount. These symbols are like military ribbons or decorations. Typically, participants claim such expensive prizes as mink coats, gold and diamond jewelry, trips to places like Rome or Paris, and the use of new pale-pink Cadillacs, Buicks, and Oldsmobiles. The prizes are claimed on a stage, and traditionally Mary Kay Ash herself arrives in a carriage drawn by white horses and surrounded by footmen. Indeed, Mary Kay Ash has achieved her objective: "To establish a company that would give unlimited opportunity to women."

AMWAY: A MASS MOVEMENT

Amway manufactures and sells soap, floor and furniture care products, room fresheners, kitchen care products, water filters, clothing, and thousands of other items through its catalog and distributors. Amway maintains an army of sales representatives—approximately a half million in the United States and Japan and several hundred thousand more in places like Germany, Mexico, Korea, and Malaysia. Although the average distributor sells only about $1,700 worth of goods a year, when this amount is multiplied by an army of sales representatives, the total sales are considerable. Nearly half of Amway's distributors drop out each year, only to be replaced by others. Many Amway distributors, themselves, buy a considerable amount of Amway products. Amway would seem to operate a legal pyramid scheme.

Amway sells their distributors a dream. A dream out of poverty. A dream to educate children. A dream to develop a business and work independently. Whatever the dream, it is both an inspirational and motivational source.

Moral values such as clean living and traditional family values are stressed at conventions. Salespeople who are role models are cheered at conventions. Amway is one of the fastest-growing companies in Japan, Mexico, and Korea.

TUPPERWARE: THE PARTY CONTINUES

The Tupperware strategy is directed to an in-home shopping group, which typically consists of a group of women who meet in the home of a friend to attend a "party" devoted to selling a line of Tupperware products. Early purchasers tend to initiate a bandwagon effect, which stimulates undecided women to buy when they see others buying the product. Moreover, some of the guests may feel obligated to buy since they have accepted the hospitality of the sponsoring hostess. The Tupperware party plan demonstrates the phenomena of peer pressure and group influence on buyer behavior. The more than 100,000-member Tupperware sales force sets up housewares parties for 22 million consumers each year. Since many female consumers are in the workforce, the firm is now hosting lunchtime parties in office buildings. Tupperware, after Avon and Amway, is the third-largest direct sales company in the United States.

Sales declined from 1982 to 1986 until the firm introduced a new merchandise line. Tupperware technicians recognized that about 85 percent of all American homes had microwaves, but Tupperware had not responded to this change. Soon Tupperware developed a complete system that featured a "stack cooker." Parties are now referred to as *classes*, and salespeople are no longer called dealers but *consultants*. It is easier for women to leave their husbands as babysitters to attend a class, and the term *dealer* conveys an aggressive posture. Although well known for its home parties, Tupperware, in a new aggressive strategy, derives about 25 percent of its revenues from demonstrations during coffee breaks at work sites and other convenient places near work.

In the 1990s, Tupperware has become "yupperware." Tupperware is colorful, and it is a well-known brand name. The product is not available in stores. The customer has to be invited to a "class" or a "party" to buy the product, which gives it a certain selectivity. Tupperware with its colors is stylish.

Rubbermaid is Tupperware's closest competitor. The secret of Tupperware's success is making products that Rubbermaid does not offer. In addition, Tupperware will replace, free of charge, indefinitely, tupperware that breaks or fails to do its job such as lid seals that leak. Group dynamics influence consumer behavior in many ways and in particular by the patterns of interaction among its members. Those who attend Tupperware parties share a set of norms, values, or beliefs that have even been extended to men in this society of blurred gender roles.

THE PROMISE OF TECHNOLOGY

Television home shopping has become more than a billion-dollar business with a loyal, almost cultlike following. Moreover, home shopping television allows a form of instant test marketing as merchandise items are moved on and off the viewing screen based on tabulated sales. Retailers such as Nordstrom and Macy's have entered this market, joining the successful entry of Saks Fifth Avenue.

Interactive home video ordering systems permit consumers greater control over viewing than is possible with television home shopping. Electronic shopping via personal computer, primarily CompuServe from H & R Block and Prodigy offered by IBM/Sears, has grown appreciably. Experimentation with interactive electronic systems as a consumer information source also appears promising.

Prodigy, a joint venture of IBM and Sears, is the largest of the videotex services, with more than 1,750,000 subscribers, an increase of more than 1 million in a two-year period. Prodigy users with a personal computer and a modem can shop, trade securities, bank, make travel arrangements, and exchange information with other subscribers. Major merchants on Prodigy include Sears, J. C. Penney, Musicland, Computer Express, and Lands' End. On the other hand, Kmart and Lionel Kiddie City are examples of retailers who have withdrawn from electronic cataloging.

Television home shopping features a price appeal. In addition, as long as firms do not have a physical presence in the buyers' state, exemption from state sales taxes is possible. Further consideration of this situation may be forthcoming, but for now, buyers, depending on their state taxes, may save from 6 percent in Connecticut to varying percentages in other states.

Electronic shopping provides a convenience because shoppers can make purchases when they desire without leaving their homes. In contrast, the convenience of shopping at home may be more than offset by the lack of social involvement that some consumer segments gain from in-store shopping. Shopping malls may have taken the place of the bygone "corner drug or candy store." On the other hand, time pressures may be such than some consumer segments may increasingly favor this type of shopping in the future. Quality time spent with family may assume greater importance as more women opt for careers instead of just jobs.

Television shoppers are younger than average shoppers and tend to be better educated and reasonably affluent. Television shoppers are more open to new styles and trends, compared with store shoppers. Surprisingly, television shopping is increasingly attracting more men. Barriers do remain to gaining more affluent shoppers. Shopping channels are still long on inexpensive jewelry and short on major brands. Moreover, TV shoppers may endure long periods of watching before they find what is wanted.

Consumer acceptance of electronic shopping seems to be affected by a host of factors. Environmental factors, including legislation, economic trends, and consumer lifestyles, are likely to have an impact on electronic shopping. Consumers learning how to use new technology such as computers will also affect the magnitude of acceptance.

THE WORST AND BEST OF TIMES

There were a number of reasons for the stagnation of mail order. The most significant reason was the decline of the rural market as new urban areas developed as a result of the growth of a mass transportation system and the growth of manufacturing centers. Moreover, as the American consumer became more urban, the consumer was to fall in love with the romance of the automobile. Consumers were now in a position to see and feel the merchandise before purchasing. Chain store retailers were another factor in the stagnation of mail order, as these retailers satisfied consumer needs very well. By the 1960s, mail-order payroll expenses were comparable to their store counterparts and in some cases even exceeded their retail competitors.

The Sears catalog suffered its worst year in 1992, losing approximately $4 billion. Through its 97 years, the Sears catalog was perhaps only second to the Bible as the most read book. What was once a pillar of retail trade was pummeled by competition from emerging specialty catalogs and discount department stores. Some 2,000 catalog stores are scheduled to close, although some, mostly in small towns, may be converted to regular merchandise stores.

Strategies of market segmentation had caused the downfall of the Sears catalog. The Big Book, as the Sears catalog was called, had become a dinosaur. There are few retail stores that could match the merchandise assortment of the Big Book. But times had changed. Specialty catalogs now better served the needs of consumers.

While it was the worst of times for general merchandise mail-order leaders such as Sears and Montgomery Ward, it was the best of times for market segments such as apparel-oriented sporting goods and full-line business suppliers. L. L. Bean, Lands' End, and Quill and Reliable profited from focused strategies developed in response to changing consumer-purchasing patterns. The forces that had been responsible for mail-order growth in the 1970s, and that succeeded in revitalizing the growth of general merchandisers, were now operating in favor of specialty mail-order organizations. These forces were the influx of women into the workforce, the increase in double-income households, and the fragmentation of media and markets.

Mail-order specialty merchants continued to fragment the market and offered more depth and breadth in specialty lines than general merchandisers. However, consumers using mail order do complain about high shipping costs, the inconvenience of returns, and the inability to see the goods at purchase time.

A number of mail-order organizations achieved a 15 to 20 percent growth rate in the early 1990s. J. Crew was a leader in the traditional sportswear category. International Masters Publishers assumed leadership in the recipe continuity field. The American Association of Retired Persons health insurance services increased to more than $2.5 billion in 1990 from only about $200 million in 1989. Frederick's of Hollywood assumed leadership by targeting the young female market. Viking Office Products assumed leadership in the business field by selling office products at 30 to 50 percent below manufacturers' list prices, delivered free and, in many instances, overnight. Other leaders in specialty fields were USAA, Hamilton Collection, Cosmetique, Horchow, and Royal Silk.

MANAGING CHANGE

Many authorities believe that direct marketing will grow in the future. The reasons most frequently cited include less time for working women to shop and the increased emphasis on the standardization and branding of products, thereby reducing the purchasing risk of customers. Moreover, technological innovations, including in-home computer ordering systems and computerized inventory systems, should broaden the opportunities for direct marketers. However, one of the most fundamental reasons for the success of direct marketing will be the ability to offer the consumer convenient purchasing.

Television marketing and electronic interactive shopping are relatively new dimensions of direct marketing, while door-to-door retailing is centuries old. An important form of electronic shopping is videotex. Videotex is a two-way system that links the sellers' data banks by cable or telephone lines with customers. The videotex service is a computerized video catalog offered by manufacturers, retailers, banks, and other business organizations.

Consumers are more likely to use electronic shopping for information services rather than for shopping. Potential consumers tend to be younger, better educated, and relatively affluent. Researchers have speculated that because in-home shopping had become more widespread in the 1980s, today's consumers perceive it as less risky. There is a relationship between product assortment and income, with higher-income households more likely to purchase a greater variety of merchandise.

Middle-aged households will experience a pronounced gain in affluence in the future. These households are oriented to their families, homes, and communities and are very concerned about the symbolic meaning of their purchase. Another significant segment of the affluent market will be in the 55- to 64-year-old married couple household. The majority of this segment will be in the empty-nest stage of the family life cycle and largely free of the financial burden of child rearing. For the first time in their lives, this group will have spending on themselves as their highest priority. In-home shopper personality characteristics reveal that they tend to be more self-assured, venturesome, and cosmopolitan in outlook and in shopping behavior.

Avon, Amway, Tupperware, and other direct marketing organizations are relying less and less on knocking on doors and have adapted to new lifestyles of consumers. Relationships with coworkers are exploited. Tupperware, well known for its home parties, derives about 25 percent of its revenues from demonstrations during coffee breaks at work sites and other convenient places near work. Direct marketers have had to modify their approaches because more of their customers, still predominantly female, are employed in the workforce.

The affluent consumer has been the traditional target market of direct marketers. The evidence, while not conclusive, suggests that this trend will continue. Therefore, the increase in the affluent market segment—particularly among double-income, married couples—will most likely mean a continued increase in direct marketing sales volume. Because the affluent market will be more familiar with international tastes and products, these consumers will probably travel more than past generations. The rise in affluence will probably decrease price sensitivity for consumers who are willing to make purchases from direct marketers. Spiegel has upgraded its product assortment and service offerings, and more direct marketers will probably follow this policy. As affluent consumers feel more time constraints, the more likely they are to desire better-quality leisure goods and services. Direct marketers need to position themselves as offering a time-saving value-laden service.

There are several ominous signs on the horizon for some direct marketers. Direct mailings in the future may decline because of increased postage rate costs and rising paper prices. Consequently, direct marketers are researching the use of improved customer databases and better lifestyle segmentation techniques. It would obviously be more cost-effective to use customer lists that generate a better-than-2-percent response rate, which is the industry norm. The possibility of more states enacting legislation that would tax direct-mail goods and services is of great concern for direct marketers. It is uncertain how consumer purchasing behavior might change if the legislation becomes widespread.

Still, there are a number of conditions favoring direct marketers:

- Consumers are more concerned with self-identity through the purchase of goods and services and therefore desire a broader product assortment than most retail stores can display.

- A higher proportion of double-income families have less time to shop.

- There is a greater demand for specialty products and services that are not available to many consumers.

- More consumers have the education to make use of home computers and other technology that facilitate in-home shopping.

- Shopping convenience and the increase of upscale households are factors that will continue to influence direct marketing purchases in the future.

Direct retailers or marketers such as Spiegel and direct sellers such as Avon will continue to broaden their strategies by combining direct marketing and direct selling techniques. For example, telemarketing will be used in conjunction with mail order, and direct sellers will use catalogs and mail order. Some of these direct marketers and sellers will try to sell their products to and through various types of retail outlets.

Door-to-door sellers are confronted with more difficult challenges than direct retailers. Since many women are in the workforce, evening selling and more selling away from the home will be necessary. Some consumers will not open their doors to salespeople because of a rising crime rate. To overcome this obstacle, selling appointments may be necessary. In addition, some potential customers are inundated with telephone calls from salespeople and are reacting negatively to this privacy-invading strategy.

LESSONS LEARNED FROM SUCCESS AND FAILURE

General merchandise retailers such as Sears and Montgomery Ward have learned that consumer demand for comprehensive mail-order catalogs has diminished. Specialty mail-order catalogs offered by L. L. Bean and others in specialty fields such as J. Crew and USAA have been astonishingly successful. Strategies to fragmented markets with products and services tailored to the market would seem to be very successful in affluent segments. Markets in the future will be narrowly defined. Marketers will be able to say that an in-home shopping firm is the best at marketing to real estate brokers or to retired schoolteachers or to left-handed professional people. Surviving in-home shopping organizations will not be able to say that everyone constitutes their market. Mass marketing strategies have not proved successful. Another conclusion is that direct retailing and direct selling strategies may be combined in order to offer the lowest prices and best services to the target market. Avon and Mary Kay are illustrations of direct selling firms already using this strategy. L. L. Bean is an example of a direct mail-order firm with a retail outlet that attracts millions of shoppers each year.

The process of identifying customer preferences and determining their accessibility necessitates focusing on customer needs. Thus, through database refinement the in-home shopping firm moves toward accomplishing the marketing concept. Firms concentrate on the customer first and then design and refine the product and service strategies through an integrated organizational effort to satisfy the needs of a precise consumer market segment. The strategy of market segmentation keeps the organization alert to changes in market conditions, changes in competitor actions, and changes in environmental opportunities and threats.

An analysis of consumer behavior will determine those customer market segments that can best be served by the firm. These segments are the target market. Information is then accumulated to determine how best to satisfy the promising market segments. Market research is also useful in developing new markets and in avoiding potential threats in serving present markets. Market research provides a systematic approach for controlled market coverage as opposed to the indefiniteness of mass marketing strategies.

Successful in-home shopping firms in the future, in order to better target market needs, will need to study the way consumers live and spend their money as well as how they make purchase decisions. Purchase decisions emanating from lifestyles are learned from many sources including culture, subcultures, social class, reference groups, and family. Activities, interests, and opinions reflect how consumers spend their time and their beliefs on various social, economic, and political issues. For example, there are some consumers who are computer buffs, cooking buffs, and outdoor buffs, and some successful catalog marketers have targeted these groups and have won their hearts and minds.

Group dynamics have been used successfully by direct selling firms such as Tupperware and Mary Kay. The more the group is interdependent by sharing a set of norms, values, or beliefs, the better the possibility of accomplishing objectives. Tupperware helped popularize the home party method of selling. In addition, firms specializing in selling sportswear, toys, jewelry, and other merchandise lines have successfully emulated Tupperware's strategies. The party method used by these organizations is a process whereby one consumer acts as host and invites friends and acquaintances to a sales demonstration in his or her home.

Groups frequently include individuals known as group leaders or opinion leaders. These leaders might be the vice president of the local school PTA or the secretary-treasurer of the local garden club. If someone is planning to purchase stereo components, that consumer may consult someone who has acknowledged expertise in that area. The same individual may consult a different "expert" when purchasing an art picture or investment plans. Recent developments in shopping groups include calling on prospects at work rather than at home. More attention is now given to nontraditional customers such as Hispanics and to such supplements as catalogs. Home demonstrations meet consumers' new lifestyle needs for convenience and personal service. However, the growth of interactive telephone-computer home shopping may diminish the impact of party plan sales.

Mary Kay has strongly motivated its salespeople. It would seem that salespeople who work independently in their own territories need the satisfaction of constant reinforcement. Some in-home sales representatives will give their best effort without any special coaching from management. Selling, to them, is a way of life. They are ambitious and self-starters. However, the majority of sales representatives need encouragement and special incentives to motivate their best efforts. Recognition, liking and respect, and a sense of achievement seem to be valued highly by in-home sales representatives. Naturally, financial rewards and other symbols of success are also highly valued. The in-home sales organization is a social organization with values, norms, roles, and statuses. The in-home organization for many salespeople is an occupational group that represents their aspirations. Thus, the Mary Kay organization with its seminars and conventions demonstrates how the aspirations of some fellow counterparts have been achieved. The motivation is present that others can also achieve the desired status. Since norms, goals, and values of the group are shared, the motivational techniques stand a good chance of success.

CONTROVERSIAL MANAGEMENT DECISIONS

Since nonstore retailing includes a wide variety of formats, controversial management decisions are present in several sectors. The party plan method of at-home retailing was a controversial decision when first implemented by Tupperware. This plan involves the use of presentations in the home and might have been perceived as an invasion of privacy; in addition, there might have been a reluctance to invite friends for the purpose of purchasing merchandise. Instead, the party plan caught the fancy of consumers, and many items such as toys, home decorating products, household goods, and jewelry are just a few of the products sold in this manner.

Another at-home method of selling opened up horizons for Avon. When first implemented, it was not known whether cosmetics could be sold door-to-door. Household items sold by Fuller Brush had been successful, but cosmetics had been traditionally sold to and through department stores and other types of retail institutions. Avon has in more recent times entered the workplace to sell its products, and the reception from many employers has been positive. Employers find that presentations during lunch hours are especially worthwhile since employees remain on the premises and are ready for work at the conclusion of the presentation.

Spiegel, in the mail-order retailing sector, made the controversial management decision to sell its catalog to consumers. Initially, the catalog was offered at newsstands in Chicago for a $1 price. The issue remained whether consumers would pay to receive a mail-order catalog. Some retailers like J. C. Penney sell their catalog but will refund the price with a purchase order. Many other retailers also follow this practice. As a result of Spiegel's management decision, it has been proven that consumers will pay for mail-order catalogs, and these customers would seem to believe that for them it constitutes a convenience.

The decision to enter the field of television home shopping was indeed a controversial area for retailers. J. C. Penney encountered many obstacles and withdrew. Meanwhile, Saks Fifth Avenue was very successful. Sears entered the electronic retailing sector with IBM with a system known as Prodigy. Consumers with a personal computer and a modem can shop in this manner. Sears and Lands' End have been successful with this method of operation, but Kmart's venture was proven unsuccessful. Therefore, the advisability of retailers using this method is still controversial. In-home shopping is a sector that is constantly changing, and controversial decisions will probably continue to permeate this area in the future.

Selected Bibliography

BOOKS

Albrecht, Karl, and Ron Zemke. *Service America*. Homewood, IL: Dow-Jones-Irwin, 1985.

Applebaum, William. *Supermarketing: The Past, the Present, a Projection*. Chicago: Super Market Institute, 1969.

Beasley, Norman. *Main Street Merchant: The Story of the J. C. Penney Company*. New York: McGraw-Hill, 1948.

Bucklin, Louis P. *Competition and Evolution in the Distributive Trades*. Englewood Cliffs, NJ: Prentice-Hill, 1972.

Buzzell, Robert D., ed. *Marketing in an Electronic Age*. Boston: Harvard Business School Press, 1985.

Fox, Richard Wightman, and T. J. Jackson Lears, eds. *The Culture of Consumption: Critical Essays in American History, 1880–1980*. New York: Pantheon Books, 1983.

Ghosh, Avijit, and Charles A. Ingene, eds. *Spatial Analysis in Marketing: Theory, Methods, and Applications*. Greenwich, CT: JAI Press, 1991.

Hower, Ralph M. *History of Macy's of New York, 1858–1919: Chapters in the Evolution of the Department Store*. Cambridge, MA: Harvard University Press, 1943.

Hoyt, Edwin P. *That Wonderful A & P!* New York: Hawthorne, 1969.

Katz, Donald R. *The Big Store: Inside the Crisis and Revolution at Sears*. New York: Viking, 1987.

Kotler, Philip. *Marketing Management: Analysis, Planning, Implementation, and Control*. 8th ed. Englewood Cliffs, NJ: Prentice-Hall, 1994.

Levitt, Theodore. *The Marketing Imagination*. New York: Free Press, 1983.

Mason, J. Barry, and Morris L. Mayer. *Modern Retailing: Theory and Practice*. 5th ed. Homewood, IL: BPI/Irwin, 1990.

McCracken, Grant. *Culture and Consumption: New Approaches to the Symbolic Character of Consumer Goods and Activities*. Bloomington: Indiana University Press, 1988.

McNair, Malcolm P., and Eleanor G. May. *The Evolution of Retail Institutions in the United States*. Cambridge, MA: Marketing Science Institute, 1976.

Michman, Ronald D. *Lifestyle Market Segmentation*. New York: Praeger, 1991.
———. *Marketing Channels*. Columbus, OH: Grid, 1974.
Michman, Ronald D., and Stanley D. Sibley. *Marketing Channels and Strategies*. 2d ed. Columbus, OH: Grid, 1980.
———. *Marketing to Changing Consumer Markets: Environmental Scanning*. New York: Praeger, 1983.
Palamountain, Joseph C. *The Politics of Distribution*. Cambridge, MA: Harvard University Press, 1955.
Penney, James Cash. *J. C. Penney: The Man with a Thousand Partners*. New York: Harper, 1931.
Porter, Michael E. *Competitive Advantage: Creating and Sustaining Superior Performance*. New York: Free Press, 1985.
———. *Competitive Strategy: Techniques for Analyzing Industries and Competitors*. New York: Free Press, 1980.
Stern, Louis W., and Adel I. El-Ansary. *Marketing Channels*. 4th ed. Englewood Cliffs, NJ: Prentice-Hall, 1992.
Trimble, Vance H. *Sam Walton: The Inside Story of America's Richest Man*. New York: Dutton, 1990.
Wood, Robert E. *Mail Order Retailing: Pioneered in Chicago*. New York: Newcomen Society, 1948.
Zeithaml, Valerie A., A. Parasuraman, and Leonard L. Berry. *Delivering Quality Service: Balancing Customer Perceptions and Expectations*. New York: Free Press, 1990.

ARTICLES

Appel, David L. "Market Segmentation—a Response to Retail Innovation." *Journal of Marketing*, April 1970, 64–67.
———. "The Supermarket: Early Development of an Institutional Innovation." *Journal of Retailing*, spring 1972, 39–53.
Bates, Albert D. "The Expanded Specialty Store: A Strategic Opportunity for the 1990s." *Journal of Retailing*, fall 1989, 379–388.
Bruner II, Gordon C. "Music, Mood, and Marketing." *Journal of Marketing*, October 1990, 94–104.
"Electronic Marketing Enters Supermarket Isle." *Marketing News*, April 1, 1991, 14–15.
"Extend Your Reach with Catalog Sales." *Nation's Business*, March 1992, 33–37.
Fram, Eugene H. "Application of the Marketing Concept to Retailing." *Journal of Retailing*, summer 1965, 19–26.
Gaski, John. "The Theory of Power and Conflict in Channels of Distribution." *Journal of Marketing*, summer 1984, 9–29.
Greco, Alan J., and D. Michael Fields. "Home Video Ordering for Groceries: Insights on the Elderly." *Journal of Food Products Marketing*, no. 2 (1993): 23–42.
———. "Profiling Early Triers of Service Innovations: A Look at Interactive Home Video Ordering Services." *Journal of Services Marketing*, summer 1991, 19–26.

Greenland, Steven J., and Peter L. McGoldrick. "From Mail Order to Home Shopping—Revitalizing the Non-Store Channel." *Journal of Marketing Channels*, no. 1 (1991): 59–85.

Hollander, Stanley C. "Notes on the Retail Accordian." *Journal of Retailing*, summer 1966, 29.

———. "The Wheel of Retailing." *Journal of Marketing*, July 1960, 37–42.

"How Kresge Became the Top Discounter." *Business Week*, October 24, 1970, 62–63.

"Information on Demographics and Psychographics Serves as Guidepost to Help Retailers Prepare for Turn of the Century." *Chain Store Age Executive*, May 1987, 19–25.

Jacob, Rahul. "Corporate Reputations." *Fortune*, March 6, 1995, 54–57, 60, 64.

Jan-Benedict, E. M., and Michael Wedel. "Segmenting Retail Markets on Store Image Using a Consumer-Based Methodology." *Journal of Retailing*, fall 1991, 300–320.

Johnson, Jay L. "The Future of Retailing." *Discount Merchandiser*, January 1990, 70.

Kumar, V., Roger Kerin, and Arun Pereira. "An Empirical Assessment of Merger and Acquisition Activity in Retailing." *Journal of Retailing*, fall 1991, 321–38.

Lieberman, Marvin B., and David B. Montgomery. "First-Mover Advantages." *Strategic Management Journal* 9 (1988): 41–58.

Lodish, Leonard. "A Marketing Decision Support System for Retailers." *Marketing Science*. winter 1982, 31–56.

Loomis, Carol. "The Leaning Tower of Sears." *Fortune*, July 2, 1979, 78–85.

"Master Plan to Revitalize Sears Still Under Scrutiny." *Chain Store Age Executive*, January 1989, 38–40.

Maursky, David, and Jacob Jacoby. "Exploring the Development of Store Images." *Journal of Retailing*, summer 1986, 145–165.

McNair, Malcolm P. "Trends in Large-Scale Retailing." *Harvard Business Review*, October 1931, 30–39.

McVey, Phillip P. "Are Marketing Channels What the Textbooks Say?" *Journal of Marketing*, January 1960, 61–65.

Michman, Ronald D. "Business Theories and Alternate Strategies of Product Differentiation and Market Segmentation." *Business Perspectives*, winter 1970, 24–27.

———. "Channel Development and Innovation." *Marquette Business Review*, spring 1971, 45–49.

———. "Foundations for a Theory of Marketing Channels." *Southern Journal of Business*, November 1971, 17–26.

Moyer, M. S. "The Roots of Large Scale Retailing." *Journal of Marketing*, October 1962, 55–59.

"The New Stars of Retailing." *Business Week*, December 16, 1991, 120–122.

Ozment, John, and Greg Martin. "Change in the Competitive Environments of Retail Trade Areas: Effects of Discount Retail Chains." *Journal of Business Research*, November 1990, 277–288.

Phillips, Charles F. "The Supermarket." *Harvard Business Review*, winter 1938, 188–200.

Rausch, Richard A. "Retailing's Dinosaurs: Department Stores and Supermarkets." *Business Horizons*, September-October 1991, 21–25.

"Retailing in the '90s: How It Got Here from There." *Marketing News*, June 25, 1990, 14.

"Retailing: Who Will Survive?" *Business Week*, November 26, 1990, 134–144.

"Retailing's Winners & Losers." *Fortune*, December 18, 1989, 69–78.

Rosenberg, Larry J., and Elizabeth C. Hirschman. "Retailing Without Stores." *Harvard Business Review*, July-August 1980, 103–112.

Schwartz, Joe. "The Evolution of Retailing." *American Demographics*, December 1986, 30–37.

———. "Will Baby Boomers Dump Department Stores?" *American Demographics*, December 1990, 42.

"Sears' Big Book: Dinosaur or Phoenix?" *Direct Marketing*, July 1986, 71–74.

"Sears' New 5-Year Plan: To Serve Middle America." *Advertising Age*, December 4, 1978, 3.

Sternlieb, George, and James W. Hughs. "The Demise of the Department Store." *American Demographics*, August 1987, 31–33, 59.

"A Supercenter Comes to Town." *Chain Store Age Executive*, December 1989, 23–30.

Tracy, Eleanor Johnson. "How A & P Got Creamed." *Fortune*, January 1973, 104–106.

"Wal-Mart Rolls Out Its Supercenters." *Chain Store Age Executive*, December 1988, 18–19.

"What Selling Will Be Like in the '90s." *Fortune*, January 13, 1992, 63–65.

"What Woolworth Didn't Know Apparently Kresge Did." *Financial World*, May 22, 1974, 18–19.

Zimmerman, Robert. "Technology in the Year 2000." *Discount Merchandiser*, May 1991, 76–80.

Index

About the Authors

RONALD D. MICHMAN is Professor Emeritus of Marketing from Shippensburg University, Shippensburg, Pennsylvania. He previously taught at the Utica Campus of Syracuse University and the University of New Hampshire. He is a member of the editorial boards of *The Journal of Consumer Marketing*, *The Journal of Business and Industrial Marketing*, and *The Akron Business and Economic Review* and has served as Associate Editor of the *Journal of Marketing Abstracts Section*. He received his doctoral degree from New York University. Dr. Michman is the author of *Lifestyle Market Segmentation* (Praeger, 1991) and *Marketing to Changing Consumer Markets* (Praeger, 1983), which was published in a Japanese-language edition, *Marketing Channels and Strategies*, Second Edition (1980), and *Strategic Advertising Decisions*. He is editor of two bibliographies, *Market Segmentation* and *Marketing Channel Strategy*, and has contributed articles to numerous professional journals, including *Business*, *Business Horizons*, *Industrial Marketing Management*, *Journal of Business Communication*, *Journal of Retailing*, and *The Journal of Business Strategy*. He has served as chairman and discussant at the conferences of the American Marketing Association, The Southern Marketing Association, The American Collegiate Retailing Association, and the Mid-Western Business Association.

ALAN J. GRECO is Associate Professor of Marketing at The School of Business and Economics at North Carolina A&T State University in Greensboro, North Carolina. He has taught in entrepreneurship workshops and in traditional and executive M.B.A. programs. He has held faculty positions at Winthrop University, The University of North Carolina at Charlotte, and The University of Alabama in Birmingham. Dr. Greco earned his Doctor of Business Administration degree at Mississippi State University. Dr. Greco is the author of numerous articles in academic and professional journals, including the *Journal of Advertising*, *Journal of Advertising Research*, *The Journal of Consumer Marketing*, and *The Journal of Managerial Issues*. He has presented papers at the meetings of various professional associations including the World Marketing Congress, The Academy of Marketing Science, The Southern Marketing Association, and the Southeast Decision Sciences Institute. Dr. Greco serves on the editorial review boards of *The Journal of Consumer Marketing*, *The Journal of Marketing Theory and Practice*, the *Journal of Business Strategies*, and *Business Journal*. He is an ad hoc reviewer for *The Journal of Managerial Issues*.